The Hiker's Guide
to **FLORIDA**

by
M. Timothy O'Keefe

ꭼALCON
ꭼRESS ®

Helena, Montana

To my son Pat and all the
trails we have yet to trod.

ACKNOWLEDGMENTS

A guidebook to Florida hiking is possible only because of the untiring efforts of the Florida Trail Association, the volunteer organization responsible for creating and maintaining many of the state's best wilderness hiking trails.

Also responsible for opening up and conserving hundreds of miles of forest pathways are the staffs and volunteer helpers of Florida's state park system; the state and national forests; and the state and national wildlife refuges.

They have made it so easy for the rest of us.

Cover photo by M. Timothy O'Keefe
Book photos by M. Timothy O'Keefe
Maps by Marita Martiniak
Edited by Will Harmon

Library of Congress Cataloging-in-Publication Data
O'Keefe, M. Timothy
 The hiker's guide to Florida/M. Timothy O'Keefe
  p.   cm.
 "A Falcon guide"
 ISBN 1-56044-168-2
 1. Hiking—Florida—Guidebooks. 2. Florida–Guidebooks.
I. Title.
 GV199.42.F6054   1993   93-43608
 796.5'1'09759—dc20   CIP

 Text pages printed on recycled paper.

TABLE OF CONTENTS

CAUTION

Outdoor recreation activities are by their very nature potentially hazardous. All participants in such activities must assume the responsibility for their own actions and safety. The information contained in this guidebook cannot replace sound judgment and good decision-making skills, which help reduce risk exposure, nor does the scope of this book allow for disclosure of all the potential hazards and risks involved in such activities.

Learn as much as possible about the outdoor recreation activities you participate in, prepare for the unexpected, and be safe and cautious. The reward will be a safer and more enjoyable experience.

PREFACE

NO MOUNTAIN HIGH ENOUGH, NO VALLEY LOW ENOUGH...WHAT FLORIDA HIKING IS LIKE.

Florida hiking may be the easiest in all of North America. Florida, essentially a spit of sand between the Gulf of Mexico and the Atlantic Ocean, is an incredibly flat place. You'll find no mountains to climb, no deep valleys to descend, no dangerous precipices to teeter on.

Rolling hills do occasionally break up the flat landscape in a few places, but these mounds are hardly formidable. The highest elevation in the state is a stunted 345 feet above sea level. That puts almost all Florida hiking within the means of anyone, from the youngest walker to the oldest.

And during the driest months—from January to May—when the ground is hard, many of these trails are barrier free. Boardwalk nature trails at many of the state parks are well suited for wheelchairs year-round.

You may be surprised at the number of Florida hiking and walking trails. As this is written, Florida has more than 1,600 miles of designated hiking trails, 500 miles of nature trails, and 400 miles of multi-use trails (for bicycling, jogging, and hiking). Most of these trails are found on state or federally operated preserves. New hiking trails are added every year, so the statistics are out-of-date even as they're written. As people-packed as Florida may be (it is the fourth largest state in terms of population), the Sunshine State is in the enviable position of gaining—not losing—hiking areas.

In addition to wilderness paths, you'll find mile after mile of beautiful beaches, the best in the nation. That's not Florida tourist bureau hyperbole but the conclusion of a scientific study conducted by Stephen Leatherman, director of the University of Maryland's Laboratory for Coastal Research. Leatherman found that Florida has seven of America's ten finest beaches and fifteen of the top twenty. Highest ranked beaches are not in South Florida, as you might expect, but in the most northerly region, the Panhandle.

You'll notice this book contains a considerable number of city walks, an unusual feature in a conventional hiking guide. However, Florida is not a conventional state. As the nation's most popular playground, the peninsula receives millions of vacationers annually. A number of cities have become Florida attractions, likely to be visited by many who will want to explore them on foot; hence the city tours.

One point about Florida wilderness hiking that might trouble out-of-state visitors: be aware that your dog will not be welcome on most Florida wilderness trails. Some parks and recreation areas require that pets be kept on a leash and confined to a picnic or camping area, and even at these areas pets are not allowed to stay overnight. Many recreation areas are off limits to pets of any kind, under any condition, with the sole exception of seeing-eye dogs.

Walks in Florida can be as brief, or as long, as you wish. Many nature walks are quite short, taking only an hour or two. If that seems too tame, try the Florida Trail, which will keep you occupied for weeks at a stretch, as it winds through miles of thick forest and wetland nature reserves. The Florida Trail, which runs from Northwest to South Florida, is still a piecemeal route, interrupted in many places by private land. It's not yet possible to walk from one end of the state to the other, but one day...maybe!

"Walking is virtue, tourism deadly sin."
Werner Herzog, Film Director

LOCATION OF HIKES

INTRODUCTION

WHAT YOU'LL SEE

Florida doesn't have the eye-popping panoramas of a Colorado or Utah, but its landscape is still quite striking, in a subtler way. The terrain varies from wet cypress swamps to dry pinewood forests. Despite continued development, about half the state is still forested.

Florida is only a subtropical region, though the humidity may make you dismiss the mere 100 miles or so to the true tropics. The state receives between fifty-three and sixty-five inches of rain a year; yet it shares the latitudinal belt with some of the earth's great deserts: the Arabian and the Sahara.

The Florida peninsula is believed to be the last part of the continental United States to rise from the ocean, making it the youngest region geologically. Only Alaska can claim a longer shoreline.

Florida topography is usually classified according to its dominant biological communities. These are typically broken down as follows:

Cypress Swamp: The tall, gnarly bald cypress tree festooned with huge strands of gray Spanish moss—that is the classic image of Florida. Bald cypress swamps are usually found near rivers. The pond cypress, a second species, creates the cypress domes that occur on the prairies and in pine flatwood forests.

Only aquatic animals such as snakes, otters, and lizards can survive in the cypress swamps that are flooded most of the year. Deer and wild hogs live in swamps that are inundated only seasonally. Wet or dry, cypress swamps also house a limited variety of other plants, such as ferns, bromeliads (air plants), saw grass, and pickerel weed.

Scrub Cypress: Common to South Florida, these are much smaller cypress swamps than the above. Scrub cypress swamps consist of the few small pond cypress that face the challenge of growing in marl, the poor marshland soil. Because vegetation is scant, animal life is correspondingly sparse. Alligators, deer, and wood storks are among the residents.

Forest Swamp: Also known as floodplain forest, these swamps are wet only part of the year. They are dominated by hardwoods such as water oak, black gum, sweet gum, and water hickory. Bald cypress and cabbage palm are usually mixed in, as well. Floodplain animals are bobcat, turkey, deer, squirrels, otter, snakes, ducks, and songbirds.

Hammocks: In Florida, the term hammock applies to any significant grouping of broad-leafed trees. A prime example is the live oak-cabbage palm hammocks of Central Florida. The name comes from the Indian word meaning "shady place." All hammocks generally enjoy fertile soil, and the trees remain green year-round. Common animals are toads, flying squirrels, wood rats, and birds such as the flycatcher.

Cypress swamp with Spanish moss hanging from the trees at Wakulla Springs State Park.

Tropical Hammock: Limited primarily to South Florida and the Everglades, tropical hammocks have a huge diversity of trees and plants. They may contain more than thirty-five tree species (gumbo-limbo, ironwood, mastic, and poisonwood) and sixty-five plant species (ferns, vines, and air plants). The wood rat, cotton mouse, and marsh rabbit are common residents.

Salt Marshes: Most commonly found along the coasts, either mixed in with mangroves or existing as a separate community. Black rush and cordgrass are the dominant plants. When salt marshes extend into tidal rivers, they often merge with freshwater marshes to form a fertile transition zone. Saltwater marshes are typically rich in bird and animal life—including otter, raccoon, turtles, and snakes.

Freshwater Marshes: A blend of sedge, grass, and rush, freshwater marshes have standing water for two or more months out of the year. Land with a shorter period of standing water is classified as wet prairie. Freshwater marshes often house many endangered species. Look for the wood stork, sandhill crane, and Everglades kite. Gators, wading birds, frogs, turtles, otter, and waterfowl also thrive here.

Dry Prairies: These treeless plains contain grasses and saw palmetto, with live oak-cabbage palm hammocks and dome cypress occasionally punctuating the flat spaces. A dry prairie may seem a lifeless, barren place, but closer inspection may reveal a considerable number of animals. Look for burrowing owls, sandhill cranes, raccoons, and bobcats.

Pine Flatwoods: Pine flatwoods are the most common type of biological community in Florida. The trees grow in sandy soil deposited thousands of years ago, when the state was covered by the sea. There are three types of pine forests: pond pines grow in wet conditions, longleaf pines in the higher and drier regions, and slash pines in the transition zone between the two. Although each forest type is dominated by its particular pine species, animal life is far more diverse. Black bear, deer, bobcats, raccoons, gray foxes, squirrels, birds, and black snakes live among the pine forests.

Sandhill Areas: These are dry and sparsely populated regions. Fire is common due to the arid conditions; it sometimes eliminates the longleaf pines, which are supplanted by turkey oak and red oak. Animals who burrow to avoid heat and to escape the frequent fires are common here: gopher tortoises, Indigo snakes, and pocket gophers are characteristic. In old-growth forest communities, you may be fortunate enough to spot the rare red-cockaded woodpecker.

THORNS OF THE TRAIL

Flat, easy terrain is the big plus of Florida hiking. Regrettably, there are also a few seasonal factors that make walking not as enjoyable as it might be.

Heat & Humidity: By far these are the two biggest drawbacks of Florida hiking. From June until as late as mid-November the temperatures routinely soar into the ninety-degree range, and it's often too hot to hike comfortably except during early morning. It's not just the heat that tends to make summer hiking unbearable: it's the humidity.

Ninety degrees in Florida feels hotter than ninety degrees almost anywhere else, thanks to the humidity. It creates a soaking wet—as opposed to dry—heat that can rapidly exhaust you.

How comfortable you are depends on the combined effects of humidity and air temperature. The National Oceanic and Atmospheric Association offers this chart as a guideline.

Air Temperature   **Percent Humidity**

	10%	20%	30%	40%	50%	60%	70%	80%	90%	100%
125F	123	141								
120F	116	130	148							
115F	111	120	135	151						
110F	105	112	123	137	150			*Feels Like*		
105F	100	105	113	123	135	149				
100F	95	99	104	110	120	132	144			
95F	90	93	96	101	107	114	124	136		
90F	85	87	90	93	96	100	106	113	122	
85F	80	82	84	86	88	90	93	97	102	108
80F	75	77	78	79	81	82	85	86	88	91
75F	70	72	73	74	75	76	77	78	79	80
70F	65	66	67	68	69	70	70	71	71	72

Summer humidity often falls into the sixty to eighty percent range, which is why Floridians usually limit their daytime summer activity to moving from one air-conditioned spot to the next. Locals like to label anyone over the age of twenty-five with a summer tan as a tourist or a recent transplant.

Mosquitoes: Another thing that makes the summertime wilderness uncomfortable—some would say hellish. You may be interested (or disturbed) to learn Florida has sixty-seven species of mosquitoes. They are divided into two categories, saltwater and freshwater mosquitoes.

Saltwater mosquitoes are active year-round in coastal areas because they have continual access to the water they need for breeding. Freshwater mosquitoes are most active during the rainy season; of course, Florida's summer weather means a regular, daily afternoon shower. Any time of year after heavy rains, expect to encounter mosquitoes wherever you hike. Swampy areas also have a good crop of mosquitoes most of the time.

You can wear long-sleeved shirts and pants and bathe in insect repellent, but that's more of an endurance contest than fun. If it's any consolation, mosquitoes usually hide out until twilight. At that time, you may want to be off the trail, hiding in a tent or standing around a smoky fire. Smoke is an excellent mosquito deterrent; the first white Everglades settlers relied on it extensively to make their life bearable. Others used a mixture of garlic and olive oil to exude a disagreeable scent.

While most mosquito bites are only annoying, occasionally there are outbreaks of deadly encephalitis. This is a recent development, apparently due to the tiger mosquito, an overseas stowaway on a ship that docked in Jacksonville. Since encephalitis can be fatal, follow any published warnings and instructions carefully. Fortunately, tiger mosquitoes are most active around sunset, not during the day.

Lightning: Due to frequent thunderstorm activity, Florida ranks as one of the world's lightning capitals. In Florida, you're more likely to be zapped by lightning than fatally bitten by a rattlesnake (which are at their liveliest in summer). Lightning fatalities vary in any given year, but as many as ten people have been killed and three dozen injured in a single season.

Thunderstorms can usually be spotted from a good distance, unless you're surrounded by thick woods. A towering thunderhead is a dead-giveaway that a storm is in the vicinity.

When a thunderstorm approaches:

• Stay away from the beach or any type of water.

• Avoid tall trees in open fields, trees at the water's edge, or trees whose roots are in damp soil.

• Oaks and pine trees are among the best natural conductors of electricity because of their high starch content. Don't use them for shelter.

• If you're wearing an aluminum-frame backpack, take it off and stay well away from it until the storm passes.

• Stay away from wire fences or any pieces of metal that could conduct lightning to you.

• A tingling sensation in your scalp is a warning that a bolt may be about to strike: fall to the ground, quickly.

• Always try to get through the storm in a low spot under a thick stand of small trees.

• July and August are peak lightning months, but lots of thunderstorms appear in June and September, too.

• A person who is not breathing after being struck by lightning may be revived by quickly administering cardiopulmonary resuscitation (CPR). CPR is an essential part of emergency first aid training. It would be a good idea to contact your local Red Cross representative and enroll in a CPR course before going on your next hiking adventure.

• A person who is still breathing after being struck by lightning may recover on his own. A temporary loss of sight or hearing is common.

Hurricanes: Called "hurrican, the evil spirit" by the Indians, these storms sometimes affect hiking conditions. Hurricane season begins in June, with the greatest activity typically in August, September, and October. If you and a hurricane are headed toward Florida at the same time, change your path. Cancel or postpone. Heavy downpours always accompany these storms. A severe hurricane can disrupt Florida life for months at a time. Hiking trails

Cypress swamp.

are one of the last items anyone worries about clearing. The worst hurricane of this century was Hurricane Andrew, the costliest natural disaster in U.S. history. The saying about hurricane season goes: "June too soon, July stand by, August and September remember, October all over."

Considering all this, now you may understand why—from a Floridian's point of view at least—extended summertime hiking just isn't worth the effort. But short, early morning walks on nature trails are fun anytime.

Hunting Season: If this were a perfect world, all hiking problems would vanish with cool weather. But just as the weather turns cool, around mid-November, hunting season begins. Some of the best parts of the Florida National Scenic Trail pass through national forests and wildlife management areas open to hunting.

Hiking is forbidden in many areas during the first week of the hunting season and the period between Christmas and the New Year, when hunting is at its peak. The rest of the hunting season, hikers must wear a fluorescent orange vest (available at sporting goods stores). Weekdays normally see the fewest hunters in the woods. Never wear anything white—the white-tailed deer is the favorite target.

Trails located in hunting areas are clearly identified in the description section.

ARCHAEOLOGY & HISTORY

Little is known about Florida's first native inhabitants, who date back 10,000 to 12,000 years. However, it's believed that about 2,000 years ago the population began to group itself according to geographical environment. This resulted in three distinctive Indian groups: in the sub-tropical Everglades, the Central/North Florida St. Johns River Basin, and the Panhandle's northwest Gulf coast.

Unfortunately, artifacts from this long period of habitation are sparse due to Florida's acidic soil. Nearly all that remains are stone tools—knives, arrowheads, and scrapers—even some from the earliest periods.

Several of Florida's hiking trails cross sites of old Indian villages, and it's not unusual to find stone artifacts lying on the ground. Under the law, anything you find on the surface is yours to keep. You're not allowed to dig anywhere, especially in the big humps of dirt or shells known as mounds. The best time to find arrowheads and knives is immediately after a good rain, which washes away the top layer of soil to reveal either the whole artifact or edges of it sticking up through the dirt.

Hikes on the Florida National Scenic Trail in the Everglades will probably bring you into contact with Florida's remaining Indian tribe, the Seminoles. Furthermore, a number of Central and North Florida trails pass through plantations destroyed during the Seminole wars. Because you will be walking such historic grounds, it's helpful to find out who the Seminoles are.

THE SEMINOLES

Unconquered. Virtually unknown. And almost unchanged. That's how Florida's Seminole Indians have remained since the last of their three great wars with the United States ended in 1858.

By the end of that conflict, all the Seminole chiefs had been killed or removed to Oklahoma. Only about two hundred Seminoles, who refused to surrender under any conditions, remained in Florida. They were determined to stay free. That meant absolutely no interference from the outside, from non-Indians. To that end, their leaders forbade formal schooling until well into this century. Christianity was also held at bay until just a few decades ago.

Today, there are about 13,000 Seminoles on three reservations in Florida. Although their numbers are few, their proud spirit is still strong. Of all the Indians in the United States., they are the only ones who never signed a peace treaty, who never surrendered.

In recent years, however, the Seminoles opened giant Bingo halls and tax-free "smoke shops" on tribal lands in several parts of Florida. Those activities run counter to Florida law, but state law does not govern Indian lands.

In some other ways, however, the Seminoles are still in transition, adjusting to our multi-cultural society. For instance, only in the 1950s and 1960s was there a wholesale move from the traditional "chickee" to more conventional homes. The chickee was the shelter used when the Indians hid in the Everglades. A chickee will probably remind you of big grass huts from the South Seas, which isn't surprising since their purpose is much the same: protection against torrential rains and winds.

Seminole Indian village in the Everglades.

If you visit a Seminole village, you may be struck by how reserved or "stand-offish" the Seminoles appear to be. According to one Seminole, Alan Jumper, this is a misunderstanding.

He says what is mistaken for aloofness is something very different. "It is really a serious attempt by an Indian to get to know you. That takes time, and the Indian is standing back to see what kind of person you are. Our life is based on right and respect. And it is with these principles that a Seminole greets another."

Considering past history, it's understandable that a Seminole may want to take his time getting to know you—and getting to trust you.

EQUIPMENT AND TECHNIQUES

WHAT TO WEAR

The dress for Florida hiking is simple: hat, shorts, t-shirt, shoes, and socks. Florida hiking does not call for any investment in high-tech fabrics or equipment, just the good old basics. A few suggestions regarding the few items you will need:

Shoes: The most important item for any walk. Many hikers wear only an old pair of sneakers, but if you're going to do some serious hiking, you need to be equally serious about your footwear. A lot of trails are slippery and unstable; high-top hiking boots offer the most ankle support. These boots should also be comfortable when wet, because during some parts of the year you may have to do a lot of wading or walking through puddles. Flip-flops and sandals are disastrous.

Socks: Always wear them. They help prevent scratches and insect bites. They also should make walking a lot more comfortable. Be prepared to throw them away at the end of your Florida trip because they could be muddy beyond salvaging.

Shorts/Pants: Loose, quick-drying shorts are all you need unless mosquitoes are about or it's cold. An ideal compromise are the "convertibles." These cotton pants are essentially shorts that have legs you can zip on and off, as conditions change.

Shirts: Those with collars offer more protection against the sun. Long sleeves help prevent sunburn and can always be rolled up (or down) according to temperature.

Hat: Baseball caps help protect your nose but little else. Wide-brimmed hats protect your ears (which can burn surprisingly easily) and your neck against sun. Wide brims also keep the rain off your face.

Windbreaker/Poncho: Lightweight nylon that can be easily stuffed in a pack. Needed for protection against rain and chilly winds.

Hiking in Florida.

Coat/Sweater: Except for winter when a front passes through and temperatures fall as low as the popularity of tax collectors, winter temps rarely drop below forty or fifty degrees. During a real cold snap, temperatures may plummet into the teens even as far south as Central Florida; in Miami, it might briefly drop below freezing. However, these are extreme situations and when they occur, the unusually low temperatures last for only a few days. Layered clothing is often preferable since the temps may vary as much as thirty degrees in a day. A cool morning often becomes a warm, humid afternoon.

WHAT TO CARRY

Like the clothing, the necessary items for your pack are few but essential:

Repellent: Liberally spray your ankles and waist to repel ticks and mites. Also spray your clothes. Chemical preparations with deet or odorless "sportsman" formulas are available. Avoid sweet-smelling soaps, perfumes, and colognes, which sometimes attract insects.

Sunglasses: Essential for hiking. Constant exposure to bright sunlight can cause headaches and fatigue. Bright sun reflected off water is as much as ten thousand times brighter than is comfortable to the eye. Make sure the glasses block out harmful ultraviolet rays.

Liquids: Carry juices, water, or one of the replenishing liquids on the market intended to restore important electrolytes lost by sweating. You may drink a gallon of liquid on a long day's hike, so make provisions accordingly.

Snacks: You'll need to maintain your energy on the trail. For a day hike, dried fruit, candy, fruit (Florida oranges are terrific), and granola bars all supply good fuel. On overnight trips, freeze-dried dinners are easy and convenient, and some even can be prepared in the pouch simply by adding boiling water.

Vitamin Supplements: Notice how some people get eaten alive by insects while others just stand around and watch? Body chemistry appears to contribute to this. Vitamin B1 supplements and odorless garlic capsules do seem to work as natural insect repellents for some people.

Bug Bite Relief: Baking soda solutions help relieve itching. Papaya, the same ingredient in some meat tenderizers, is a good pain killer for nonpoisonous stings; the papaya enzyme breaks down the insect venom so it no longer stings. Regular antihistamine tablets taken for allergies or colds also help reduce swelling and itching; antihistamine in cream form may cause skin allergies. Cortisone cream also helps stop itching and rashes. One way to reduce the number of bites: always wear socks.

Plastic Garbage Bags: For wrapping clothes and cameras on rainy days. Also use them for ground cover to sit on to avoid chigger and ant bites; they're even good for transporting your damp and filthy hiking shoes home in your suitcase.

Camera: Be prepared to waterproof it instantly in case of liquid sunshine (rain). Plan to carry it in your sack or on a hip holster so your hands aren't encumbered the whole time. A flash may be needed in thick woods on overcast days.

Umbrella: Bring the small, collapsible kind that will fit into a day sack. This may seem like a strange item to take hiking, but when walking through exposed areas in direct sunlight mile after mile, nothing offers better protection or keeps you cooler than a light-colored umbrella. Further, nothing keeps rain off your face or out of your contact lenses better than an umbrella.

There's a checklist of these and other essential items at the back of this guide.

WHAT TO AVOID

Dehydration: By far, this is the greatest danger you'll probably face. You'll lose a lot of liquids walking around in high humidity, and not replacing it will make you feel tired and lousy. It takes about two weeks to adjust to high humidity, but you can maintain your energy by doing the following.

Consume liquids even when you're not thirsty: according to Orlando physician Dr. Christopher Conavay, you normally need a minimum of two quarts of liquid a day as a baseline. "But you may need to replace up to two gallons a day, or more, in a hot environment," he advises. "The best place to store water is in your body." The best way to do that is gulp a lot of it down so you can carry it camel-like on the trail.

• Potassium: Hikers sometimes develop cramps even if they have been drinking great amounts of water, and the problem is often due to potassium deprivation. Dr. Conavay continues, "The two most critical elements you need to replace are water and potassium. Besides potassium supplements available at health food stores, you can drink tea—which has a good amount of potassium—and it never spoils. Any acidic fruit will also contain potassium." Other potassium sources: single packets of ketchup and lite salt (salt containing half sodium chloride and half potassium chloride). Bananas are also rich in potassium. As for consuming extra salt, Dr. Conavay says not to worry "since salt is a fairly ubiquitous substance."

• Avoid colas and alcohol since they are diuretics which will dehydrate you even more.

• Air conditioning: you will probably feel more rested if you sleep in air conditioning following any extended hike.

Prickly Heat: When you're in constant humidity, it's easy to pick up a rash. Avoid it by powdering yourself in the morning and evening with talcum powder or powder containing zinc. Also, wear loose fitting pants. The most comfortable shirts are usually made of light-weight cotton.

Sunburn: Florida's sun is far more intense than anywhere else in the continental U.S. except for extreme elevations. Gradual exposure to the sun—only twenty to thirty minutes recommended the first day—is mandatory, to avoid painful sunburn unless you already have a base tan. The sun is at its worst between 10 a.m. and 3 p.m. Wear a water-resistant sun block (SPF20 or higher). It may be necessary to wear sun block even on your lips. Be particularly careful to cover ears, jaws, and the lower part of your neck.

The best protection of all is to cover your skin with a long-sleeved shirt and long pants and to wear a broad-brimmed hat. Not only do many sun block lotions come off when you perspire, some recent scientific reports claim clothing is the only truly safe sun block. Popular SPF lotions may be ineffective at preventing melanoma, the worst type of skin cancer. Scientists also say that wearing sun block provides a false sense of security since you don't realize the full bombardment your skin receives.

Clouds, too, create a false sense of security. Although the sun may be hidden, it still has the ability to inflict a severe burn. Beach hikers receive a double whammy: from the sun overhead and the rays reflected off the water and sand.

Sunstroke/Sun Poisoning: Symptoms of oncoming sunstroke are dizziness, vertigo, fevers, blistering, headache, nausea, sudden lack of sweat, and delusions. If these symptoms appear, take a cool bath or shower. Remain inside, in an air conditioned area, and drink fruit juices or replenishing drink mixes to replace lost body fluids. If you don't start to feel better, contact a doctor.

Water: As a general rule, no water along Florida trails is safe to drink unless it is designated as potable. Don't let clarity fool you: what you can't see can hurt you. If spring or river water will be used for cooking, boil it about five minutes to kill all parasites. Or use a filter designed to remove all parasites, including giardia. Some of these small filters work amazingly well and will remove almost everything from water but salt. One day, filters may be able to accomplish even that. In the meantime, never drink sea water!

Intestinal Problems: Usually the result of a bacterial infection or from consuming strange foods and drink. Always carry your own water and avoid drinking from streams, no matter how clear/clean they look. Diarrhea and its accompanying dehydration can be a serious problem: drink plenty of fluids other than alcohol and milk, which seem to prolong bouts of diarrhea. A bland diet of tea and toast seems to help some people. Although a bout with diarrhea usually resolves itself after a couple of days, the problem can really interfere with your hiking. Some medications will control attacks almost immediately; try loperamide and atropine.

Poisonous Plants: Poison ivy and poison sumac are a bother here as they are in much of the country. Touching either can produce a skin irritation that may develop small, itchy blisters. Poison ivy is a shrub that may be found upright or on the ground; it is characterized by three leaflets on each leaf and berries that are often whitish. Poison sumac is a bush with seven to thirteen leaflets and white berries. Cortisone cream is an effective remedy for both. Overall, Florida has about fifty poisonous plants such as oleander, and several types of mushrooms, but most are troublesome only if you ingest them. The best way to avoid poisoning is simply not to dine on anything you find in the wild.

Hypothermia: This dangerous condition most often occurs in the thirty to fifty degree air temperature range, so it's definitely a consideration even for sunny Florida. Hypothermia typically occurs when someone gets wet. Then, when the hiker is exposed to a cold and chilly wind, hypothermia sets in as the body loses heat faster than it is able to produce it. This initially causes exhaustion, mental confusion, fits of shivering, and reduced physical coordination. The person may then pass into unconsciousness and, if not properly attended, die.

The most effective treatment is to get the person out of wet clothes and into dry ones. Have them put on a hat: as much as eighty percent of a person's body heat is lost through the head. Give them warm liquids (but not coffee, tea, or anything containing caffeine) and have them sit by the fire. If a warm sleeping bag is available, have the person crawl into it. One of the most effective things to block out the cold even if the person is still in wet clothes is a space blanket, a lightweight, thin piece of fabric that has remarkable heat-reflecting capability. Space blankets are available at most Florida sporting goods stores. Lacking one, use a garbage bag, worn like a poncho, to block the wind and retain body heat.

Getting Lost: Most Florida hiking trails are clearly blazed, so getting lost may require some concerted effort. Always carry a map, compass, and whistle (three blasts is the universal call for assistance), plus a flashlight in case you are returning late. Let someone know where you've gone and when you expect to return. If you are completely lost and unable to find the trail, remain in one place until someone comes to find you. Wandering further afield could only make matters worse.

ANIMALS AND INSECTS: THE ROGUE'S GALLERY

Florida's subtropical climate has blessed it with an awful lot of creepy-crawlies. But with proper precautions it's easy to avoid them all: literally hundreds of thousands of Floridians hike the state every season without ever getting a scratch or a bite.

Knowing what to expect in advance is like taking a course in defensive driving. You'll rarely call on the knowledge, but having it available can be very helpful. Consider the following critters merely subjects of interest, not inevitable sources of irritation.

Rabid Raccoons: This designation isn't meant to be humorous but to drive home the point that in recent years rabies has been a considerable problem in Florida. At present, the only way to know for certain if an animal is rabid is to perform an autopsy. However, there are warning signs a hiker can watch for in raccoons. Animals that are overly friendly or aggressive and which seem to have no fear of humans are definitely suspect. So are those that appear bedraggled and wobbly on their feet. You're not likely to see a

Avoid any contact with raccoons no matter how cute they are.

raccoon foaming at the mouth. If you're approached by a suspicious-acting animal, retreat or chase it away and report it to authorities. Children may regard animals as playthings instead of wild creatures and want to play with any friendly furry animal. If they spot a raccoon before you do, they may be bitten as a result.

Chiggers: These are often more troublesome than mosquitoes because chigger bites may itch for days. Chiggers are small red mites fond of attacking around the ankles, waist, and wrists, where they burrow under the skin and cause severe itching. Putting clear nail polish on the chigger bites will often smother the critters. Calamine lotion also helps relieve the itching.

Chiggers are found almost anywhere outdoors: in the underbrush, tree bark, Spanish moss, and even wooden park benches. Fortunately, repellent sprayed in strategic body areas usually keeps them away. Another method is to lather your arms, legs, and neck with soap, then let it dry before you go into the woods. Another preventative is to sprinkle sulphur powder on your ankles, cuffs sleeves, and necklines; this also works well against ticks. With chiggers so prevalent, the best way to avoid them is to never sit directly on the ground but on a piece of plastic or poncho. And always tuck in your shirt tail.

Fire Ants: Their mounds are readily spotted—they look like a shovel-full of dirt. You may see as many as a dozen ant mounds in an area of high fire ant concentration. The ants generally won't bother you unless you bother their mound. Fire ants seem to stay in a state of constant alertness, and if their mound is disturbed, it's only a millisecond before hundreds appear. The danger is accidentally stepping on a mound and having the ants swarm up your legs. As many as half a million fire ants live in a colony. Anyone allergic to ant bites should carry medication, just in case.

Ticks: Because of Florida's warm weather, ticks are active almost year-round. Because of the danger of Lyme disease, it is essential to always use repellent in the woods and to check your clothing and body for ticks after a hike is over. Initial symptoms of Lyme disease are muscle aches, fatigue, and fever, all of which could easily be mistaken for flu symptoms. If the disease is not treated, the victim may develop meningitis, swollen joints, dizziness, fainting, irregular heartbeat, and headaches. If you find a tick on yourself while still in the woods, gently try to remove it with a pair of tweezers, gripping the body close to your skin. Be careful not to leave any of the mouth imbedded in the skin. If you discover a tick at home, the application of a tincture of iodine may induce the tick to let go as well as reduce the chances of infection. A drop of gasoline or kerosene will sometimes encourage a tick to loosen its grip.

No-see-ums: Only beach hikers at sunrise and sunset need to worry about no-see-ums. Also called midges and sand flies, no-see-ums are so tiny as to be invisible, but when they land they seem to be all teeth. In Spanish, they are known as mi-mis (pronounced "me-mees"), as in "a case of the screaming mee-mees!" Long pants and shoes/socks are the best protection.

Scorpions: Found most often in the dry regions of Central and North Florida, these have a nasty habit of crawling into hiking boots at night and making their presence known the next morning only after you put your boot on. Shake out your boots or keep them wrapped in your tent in a plastic bag (though the resulting smell may be worse than the bite). Scorpion stings are very painful, though they are rarely lethal.

Portuguese Man-of-War: When you're walking on the beach, be on the lookout for pale blue "balloons" about eight inches long in the tide line. These are the painful Portuguese man-of-war, a colony of animals functioning together as a single animal. The dangerous part of the man-of-war is its tentacles, which may be as much as thirty feet long. Therefore, it's possible to come in contact with the tentacles before you see the balloon, actually a gas-filled float topped by an irregular, inflated sail. The tentacles can cause a burning sensation or, in extreme cases, nausea, cramps, and breathing difficulties. First-aid consists of removing the tentacles and applying alcohol. A doctor may need to be contacted.

Snakes: It's true Florida has a larger snake population than any other state, but snakes are rarely a problem if you stick to the trails, don't haphazardly step over logs without looking, and exercise common sense. Six species are poisonous, and half of those are rattlesnakes. If someone is bitten, the best treatment may be to do nothing but take the person immediately to

Black bears may be seen throughout Florida.

a hospital. Cutting the skin and attempting to suck out the venom often does considerable harm, sometimes severing muscle tissue.

Thinking about a snake encounter is never pleasant, so it may be reassuring to know that, statistically, you are more apt to be killed by a hog than a snake.

Although it is unlikely you will encounter a problem, a little knowledge can save a lot of trouble:

• The Eastern Diamondback Rattlesnake, Florida's largest snake, lives in every part of the state. It is named for its pattern of yellow-bordered diamond shapes. This snake can be aggressive and does not need to be coiled to strike. If you disturb a diamondback and its coils, stay well away: the snake can strike from a third to one-half its body length. Its favorite haunts are pinewood trees, palmetto bushes, and brush areas.

• The Canebrake Rattlesnake is found mostly in North Florida in hammocks, flatwood forests, river bottoms, and swampy ground.

• The Pygmy Rattlesnake grows no more than eighteen inches and its rattle, which sounds like a buzzing insect, is audible only a few feet from the snake. Pygmies prefer wetlands, slash pine, palmetto brush, and wire grass. Bites usually cause only pain and swelling, not death.

• The Cottonmouth Water Moccasin can be surprisingly territorial and may attack accordingly. The nation's only poisonous water snake, it can bite either in or out of the water. It is distinctively marked by a dark band that runs from the eye to the jaw. Cottonmouths are found in marshes, streams, lake edges, and on tree branches overhanging the water.

• The Coral Snake is related to mambas and cobras and is said to be the country's most poisonous snake. Fortunately, it is rarely a problem since it must almost gnaw on a person to break the skin. Most bites occur when people pick up "the pretty snake" to examine it. Coral snakes make their homes in brush piles, rotting logs, and pine woods. The coral is sometimes confused with the harmless king snake, which also has colorful markings. The way to tell the two apart: "Red touch yellow, kill a fellow; red touch black, won't hurt Jack." Not great poetry, but it makes its point.

• The Copperhead is relatively rare, found only in the Panhandle. Not surprisingly, its head is copper-colored; it has a pinkish-tan body with reddish-brown crossbands.

Alligators: This is last on the list of hazards, and for good reason. Unless you swim in a remote lake during the spring mating season when alligators sometimes go a little crazy and attack swimmers, gators should be no danger at all. Alligators normally run or disappear when they encounter a human. The only exceptions: if they have been fed by people or you have a dog (a favorite snack of alligators) with you. Never get between an alligator and its lake or harass one: in a sprint, it can run far faster than you. In the unlikely event you should be chased by an alligator, run in a zigzag manner, a maneuver it can't duplicate.

TREADING LIGHTLY

Florida's warm weather and unique landscape are the main reasons so many people move to the Sunshine State—at the somewhat frightening rate of about one thousand persons each week. The outdoors (along with the many man-made theme parks) also attract tourists from all over, making Florida one of the world's top tourist destinations.

The result of all this attention: Florida is in danger of being loved to death. As more and more land is developed into sites for homes, schools, and shopping malls, the forests and preserves become ever more precious. Florida officials are attempting to buy up and protect as much land as possible, but their funding will never match that of the developers.

It is up to us, the present-day users, to serve as stewards of the parks and preserves to ensure that our children and grandchildren have the same hiking opportunities. Florida waters may become more polluted, and the fish population may dwindle further, but the land will endure.

This is how you can help:

• Always stay on the designated trails. Torrential rainfalls cause enough erosion, and hikers only make it worse by walking alongside the trails.

• Leave the wildflowers, bromeliads (air plants), and other plants where you find them. Not only might it be against the law to pick them, they probably wouldn't survive outside the Sunshine State, anyway.

• At the beach, never walk on the sand dunes but always use the boardwalks that pass over them. Sand dunes are the all-important barrier against the sea's erosion. Sea oats, the golden wheat-like grass that grows atop the dunes, are essential for the dunes to remain in place. Sea oats are protected by law.

• When hiking remote sections of any trail, camp only in designated areas.

• Be especially careful of campfires. Florida forests are sometimes tinder dry and it is incredibly easy to start a devastating forest fire. Campfires are usually forbidden at such times. Build fires only when and where permitted. Most areas prohibit cutting of trees, so you can use only "dead and down" material. Firewood can be picked up almost anywhere inside a forest. When possible, always use the location of a previous fire. Otherwise, rake all burnable material at least four feet away and dig a shallow hole for the fire. Place all the excavated sand to one side so it can be replaced when you leave. When breaking camp, douse the fire thoroughly and cover the hole with soil.

• If you are a smoker, be careful of your ashes. And please pack out your cigarette butts.

• Be careful of human waste. Bury it at least six inches deep, a minimum of 200 feet from any water and 100 feet from any campsite.

• Washing dishes with soap should be done well away from streams and lakes, at least 200 feet. Sand and pine cones are good for scouring pots and pans.

• Don't leave unwanted souvenirs for later hikers to discover. Everything you pack in, pack out.

The following phrase may not have originated in Florida, but it's become the motto posted on most public lands:

"Take nothing but pictures. Leave nothing but footprints."

HIKING WITH CHILDREN

Because the terrain has few ups and downs, Florida hiking is ideal for children. Finding suitable places for hiking isn't as much of a consideration as the length of the walk, weather conditions, and what you'll see.

In planning any outing with children, remember who it is you are hiking with: kids. So, don't be surprised or upset when they act like kids.

If you take toddlers on day hikes, plan on carrying them most of the way. Children aged five and six are often capable of hiking for short distances, but they, too, are not apt to be prepared for all-day trips. A walk of an hour or two is a good way to introduce them to the outdoors. It's amazing how a youngster who seems an endless bundle of energy at home, indoors, can tire surprisingly quickly outside, especially if it's warm or not interesting enough.

Careful planning may help keep children dry and from getting bored while camping.

The sea cow or manatee is one of Florida's most beloved creatures.

In Florida some of the best places to take young children are the state parks and nature reserves with boardwalks that span swamps and streams and go deep into the forest. Boardwalks usually lead to interesting places that may be full of bird life or unusual trees; perhaps a virgin stand of giant cypress wearing long swaying beards of grayish-white Spanish moss.

Or the boardwalk may reveal something truly marvelous. For instance, at the Blue Spring State Park near Orange City, just outside Orlando, the boardwalk offers the best land-based view anywhere in the world of the endangered manatee, or sea cow. The basis of the mermaid legend (conjured up by sailors obviously too long at sea), the manatee hardly resembles a beautiful woman. Instead, it is a hodgepodge of different parts. It has a flat tail like a beaver's, a huge elongated body like a sausage, and a bald and wrinkled head like a walrus or seal.

What child, boy or girl, could resist such a creature? Adults certainly can't; the manatee is one of Florida's most beloved animals, finishing close behind the dolphin.

This type of nature walk is going to have far more appeal than a simple two-hour jaunt through the woods where the fairly undramatic scenery doesn't change much. Interesting nature walks are the easiest way to create a life-long interest in the outdoors and all of its diversity. Plan walks designed to appeal to the children.

Careful planning that stresses safety will help make your outing an enjoyable one. Young skin is very sensitive to the sun, so always carry a strong sunscreen and apply it to your kids before and during your hike. A good bug repellant, preferably a natural product, should be a standard part of the first-aid kit. Also, consider a product that helps take the itch and sting out of bug bites. A hat helps keep the sun out of sensitive young eyes. And rain gear is also an important consideration. Kids seem to have less tolerance to cold than adults, so ample clothing is important. If your camp will be near a water consider bringing a life vest for your child.

Parents with infants must, of course, carry plenty of diapers, and be sure to pack them out when they leave. For children who get wet at night, so extra sleeping clothes are a must. A waterproof pad between the child and the sleeping bag should keep the bag dry, an important consideration if you stay out more than one night.

To sustain your child's interest, take them shopping and allow them to choose their own walking shoes, fanny packs, day sacks, water bottles, whatever. Of course, you may need to offer some guidance here and there, but let them feel they are making all the important decisions.

Encourage older children to carry their own packs, too. Some kids will want to bring favorite toys or books along. These special things they can carry themselves, thus learning at an early age the advantages of packing light.

Teach children as early as possible what to do if lost. Giving children a whistle and attiring them in bright clothing will also aid in finding them. Other survival skills, such as navigating and fire building, should be taught as early as possible. Get them accustomed to paying attention to where they are and where they're going by frequently noting things along the route.

Children learn from their parents by example. Hiking and camping trips are excellent opportunities to teach young ones to tread lightly and minimize their imprint upon the environment.

Note: If you leave your children with a baby sitter, leave notarized authorization for any needed medical treatment in case of an accident when you are out of contact. Doctors are reluctant to provide medical treatment without parental permission.

CAMPING

Almost all Florida state parks have camp sites. Most will accept reservations up to sixty days in advance of the check-in date. Even though the parks stay open until sunset year-round, you should check-in between 8 a.m. and 5 p.m. Fees vary according to park location, season, and whether you are using water and electricity.

Anyone traveling around the state by RV will probably find little fault with most park facilities. Tent campers, on the other hand, may find the close-together spaces a little claustrophobic. Fortunately, some state parks and the national forests offer camping at primitive sites deep in the woods.

Primitive sites require that you backpack everything in since the only facilities they may offer is a chemical toilet and possibly a rickety picnic table. It's best not to count on finding anything but a clear space.

If you're going to spend considerable time in Florida's state parks, you'll probably want to investigate the annual entrance passes for individuals and for families of up to eight people. They are available at the parks or through the mail by calling (904) 488-9872.

Any questions you have about Florida parks can be answered by calling the same number or by writing Department of Environmental Protection, Park Information, Mail Station #535, 3900 Commonwealth Boulevard, Tallahassee, FL 32399-3000.

BACKPACKING EQUIPMENT

The Pack: This sack on your back is what will transport virtually all of your gear into the woods. To make the experience a pleasant one, the pack must fit comfortably and have enough room for all your equipment. The best way to find your perfect pack is to try on a variety in a sporting goods store. Put some weight in a pack and wear it around in the store for a while.

The Tent: Don't plan on sleeping unprotected in the Great Outdoors except in cool weather. Mosquitoes, snakes, scorpions, and other assorted ground-dwelling beasties do not make this a viable alternative most of the year. Furthermore, dew can be heavy and soak you almost as much as a brief shower. Get the lightest tent possible—with a sewn-in floor—but make sure the fabric is well waterproofed. Most small tent manufacturers tend to be over-optimistic about how many people their shelters will comfortably fit. If two of you will be sharing the tent, buy a three person tent. Then, if it rains, the extra space will allow you to bring your gear inside.

Use a tent for protection from insects, snakes, and weather.

Plastic Ground Tarp: You'll want to place your tent atop the tarp, not only for added waterproofing, but to save wear and tear on the floor, usually the first part of the tent to give out.

Sleeping Bag: Except for winter in the Panhandle when the temperatures may drop below freezing, all you need is a light-weight bag. Down bags aren't needed and they can be less than satisfactory: down loses its insulating ability when it gets wet, and dampness is often a way of life for Florida campers.

Foam Pad: Sleeping directly on the ground seems easy—until you've tried it. Not even sand is comfortable. Since nothing ruins a camping trip more than a lousy night's sleep, take time to select the pad that will suit you best.

Gas Stove: The small single-burner gas stoves are ideal for backpacking. Since you'll probably be dining on freeze-dried food, you'll need boiling hot water; otherwise freeze-dried meals do not "cook" completely and may taste terrible. Pack a small aluminum cylinder with extra fuel.

Camp Light: Small gas units are efficient and will supply a considerable amount of light. They will also use the same fuel as your stove. However, they can also attract bugs.

THE FLORIDA TRAIL ASSOCIATION

This group of dedicated hikers is responsible for opening and maintaining the Florida Trail, which runs north-south through the length of Florida. The Florida Trail Association (FTA) each year sends volunteers to the woods to clear the way and preserve the vital system of tree blazes that lead hikers safely through the densest forest.

Trail Blazes

Most of the blazing on Florida trails have been placed there by the FTA. The blazes are at eye level and normally quite easy to spot. This is the FTA system:

• Orange blazes mark the main trail.

• Blue blazes designate side trails to developed campgrounds or a natural site of unusual interest.

• White blazes mark the trails in most of the state parks.

• A double blaze signals a change in direction. It could also mean the trail is no longer taking the most obvious route. Don't leave a double blaze until you've spotted the next single blaze.

Currently, the Florida Trail is interrupted in sections by holdings of private land. The FTA is continually adding land that eventually will form an unbroken path on public land for everyone to use. Currently, the longest uninterrupted stretch is 450 miles long, from the western border of the Apalachicola National Forest in the Panhandle to the southern end of the Ocala National Forest in North Florida.

In the meantime, it is possible to hike the entire trail—including private land—if you are an FTA member. In addition, you can participate in any of the approximately 500 different activities that take place throughout the state each year. Members are kept informed through a bimonthly newsletter.

For information about joining, write: Florida Trail Association, Box 13708, Gainesville, FL; 904/378-8823.

HOW TO USE THIS GUIDE

This book does not attempt to cover every trail in Florida. Instead, it is limited to the major hikes or those which offer the chance to observe unspoiled, natural Florida at its finest.

The maps are based on topographic maps issued by the state of Florida, those supplied by the USDA Forest Service (state and federal), and the state parks. Unless you are making an extended hike over weeks along the Florida National Scenic Trail, you should find these maps adequate. For long-range hikes you may want to purchase a map from the Forest Service or other appropriate agency.

Each trail is evaluated according to difficulty, but that is often based more on the length of the hike than the terrain conditions, which are normally quite flat. However, these estimates may not take into account muddy conditions resulting from prolonged rain or other natural events. These appraisals are only guidelines, subject to changing conditions, and should not be taken as unchanging gospel. Anytime the weather has been unusually wet or dry, consult with the appropriate on-site agency, which is listed with every trail.

Distances provided in the text are often rounded to the next highest number.

MAP LEGEND

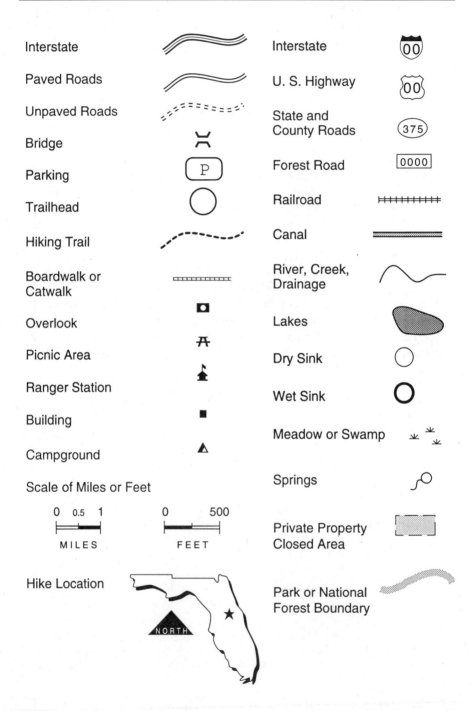

Interstate		Interstate
Paved Roads		U. S. Highway
Unpaved Roads		State and County Roads
Bridge		Forest Road
Parking		Railroad
Trailhead		Canal
Hiking Trail		River, Creek, Drainage
Boardwalk or Catwalk		Lakes
Overlook		Dry Sink
Picnic Area		Wet Sink
Ranger Station		Meadow or Swamp
Building		Springs
Campground		Private Property Closed Area

Scale of Miles or Feet

0   0.5   1
MILES

0   500
FEET

Hike Location

NORTH

Park or National Forest Boundary

Palm trees reach for the Florida sun.

PANHANDLE
COASTAL HIKES

The Panhandle is so unlike the rest of Florida that it seems a different state. In truth, the topography here has more in common with Georgia and Alabama than with Central or South Florida. This region also is not as well publicized and has suffered less development, so it offers some of Florida's best wilderness hiking.

The Panhandle's coast offers some of the best beach hikes in the country, with mile after mile of unspoiled shoreline.

Many coastal hikes run between the Gulf and a low rampart of beautiful, rolling sand dunes. The dunes are created when waves bring sand onto the beach and the wind pushes it inland. Slowly the sand piles up, and pioneer plants like sea oats take hold. The sea oat root system penetrates deep into the sand in search of water, also anchoring the plants against the wind.

As more sand piles up around the sea oats, the dunes grow. Eventually sea oats will cover most of the dune, protecting it from wind erosion. Walking on sea oats is the surest way to damage them. Without these plants, high winds and surging waves will cut through the dunes, causing damage inland. Because of their importance, sea oats are protected by law; you cannot pick them.

For a lengthy beach walk carry sunscreen and plenty of drinking water. A good beach hike prolongs itself with ample opportunities to photograph birds, pick up shells, take a swim, and enjoy everything the beach has to offer.

GULF ISLANDS NATIONAL SEASHORE

It's long been said that the beaches on Florida's Gulf Coast are the state's finest, even if they don't receive as much publicity as Daytona, Miami, or Fort Lauderdale. Gulf Islands National Seashore confirms that statement, without question. The sand is bright, clean, and sparkling. It even squeaks under your feet.

A cautionary note: pets are prohibited on all beaches in the National Seashore. Do not leave a pet confined in an unattended vehicle. Even with the windows ajar the interior of a car can reach a lethal 120 degrees.

Gulf Islands National Seashore is divided into four sections: Fort Pickens, Santa Rosa Recreation Area, Naval Live Oaks Reserve, and Perdido Key.

General Description: Florida's 65,816-acre share of the 137,598-acre national seashore that extends into Mississippi.

General Location: From Santa Rosa Island off Pensacola, to the Alabama border.

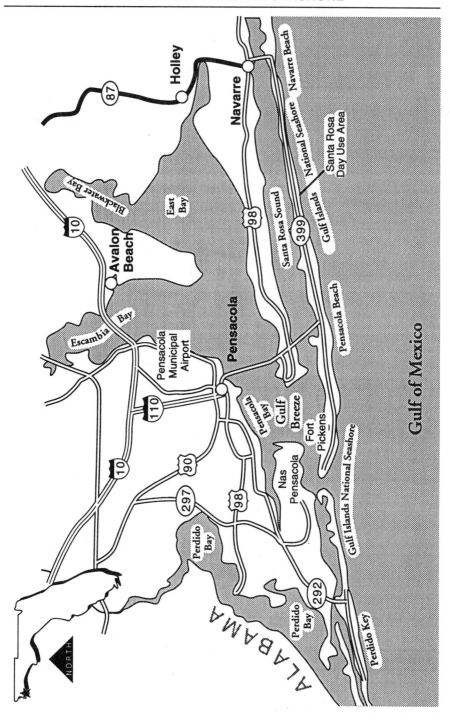

Maps: Florida highway map.

Difficulty: Easy.

Special Attractions: Numerous walks along the Gulf including the nation's top ranked beach, Perdido Key. Also, several historical exhibits, including old Fort Pickens.

Season: Summer is crowded. Spring and fall are best.

Camping: Fort Pickens has a popular campground with 165 sites, some with water and electricity. No reservations are taken, so arrive early to get on the day's waiting list. Primitive backpack camping is permitted on Perdido Key. Big Lagoon State Recreation Area, ten miles southwest of Pensacola off State Road 292, is on the way to Perdido Key. It has 104 sites, full hookups, and reservations are accepted. Big Lagoon also has three short nature trails through flatwoods and salt marshes on a boardwalk (wheelchair accessible).

Information: Gulf Islands National Seashore, Florida District, P.O. Box 100, Gulf Breeze, FL 32561; (904) 932-5302. Big Lagoon Recreation Area, 12301 Gulf Beach Hwy., Pensacola, FL 32507; (904) 492-1595.

HIKE 1 SANTA ROSA RECREATION AREA BEACHES

Finding the trailheads: To reach the Fort Pickens and Santa Rosa Recreation Area beaches, drive south from Pensacola on U.S. Highway 98 across the Pensacola Bay Bridge to Gulf Breeze. Turn right onto State Road 399 and cross the toll bridge to Pensacola Beach on Santa Rosa Island. A right on Fort Pickens Road leads two miles to the park's main entrance; it's another four miles to campgrounds and Fort Pickens. Or stay on State Road 399 and go east seven miles to the main parking and picnic area with beach access.

The hikes: The parking lot and picnic facilities here are open from 8 a.m. until sunset. Use the boardwalk to cross the fragile dunes to a superb beach. Once on the beach, you can hike four miles in either direction before meeting the sprawl of vacation homes from Navarre Beach or Pensacola Beach. Watch for sand crabs underfoot and dolphins offshore. Surf fishing is good; a fishing license is required.

While on Santa Rosa Island, take some time to tour Fort Pickens. The massive fortress was built between 1829-1834 and served as a prison for Geronimo, the famed Apache warrior, from 1886 to 1888. On summer Sundays, park rangers masquerade as Civil War soldiers to re-enact daily life at the fort in the 1860s. The surrounding beaches offer good hiking on both the Gulf and Bay sides. A public fishing pier near the fort is frequently packed with anglers.

HIKE 2 NAVAL LIVE OAKS RESERVE

Finding the trailhead: From Pensacola, drive south on U.S. Highway 98 across the Pensacola Bay Bridge. Continue about two miles east of Gulf Breeze on U.S. 98. Watch for signs and the access road on the left.

The hike: The Naval Live Oaks Reserve takes its name from the trees once highly valued by shipbuilders. Live oaks are the heaviest of all oaks and are highly resistant to disease and decay. The ship *USS Constitution*, better known as "Old Ironsides" from the war of 1812, was made of live oak. In 1827, Congress required the U.S. Navy to increase its plantings of live oaks. This site is one of the former oak plantations. A short hiking trail here wanders among sand pines as well as impressive, moss-draped oaks.

HIKE 3 PERDIDO KEY

Finding the trailhead: From downtown Pensacola, follow U.S. Highway 98 (Navy Blvd.) to State Road 292 (the Gulf Beach Highway). Continue about fifteen miles southwest to the Johnson Beach parking lot.

The hike: Seven-mile long Perdido Key has the nation's best beach according to a University of Maryland researcher. Its outstanding features are simple ones: sand, sea, sea oats. A true wilderness area, the Key can be reached only by foot or boat. Yet, ironically, you get a fine view of thriving Pensacola across the bay.

Primitive camping is permitted on the Key if you backpack everything in. The state of Florida also protects 247 acres as the Perdido Key State Recreation Area, another oasis of wilderness in this rapidly developing region. Since Perdido Key is undeveloped, contact neighboring Big Lagoon State Recreation Area (see above) for information. Either exploring or just relaxing on the superb beach is special here; you'll probably want to take the trouble to set up camp only if you're remaining in the area for several days.

GRAYTON BEACH STATE RECREATION AREA

At 400 acres, Grayton Beach is a relatively small park. Yet its nature trail, highlighting the coastal plant communities, is highly instructive.

Grayton Beach also offers the unusual opportunity to catch both fresh and saltwater fish. You can take saltwater species from the surf and catch both fresh and saltwater fish in brackish Western Lake. A fishing license is required for either.

General Description: A 0.75-mile nature trail that winds among dunes, pine flatwoods, and scrub communities.

General Location: Near Santa Rosa Beach and the township of Grayton Beach in Walton County.

Maps: None needed.

Difficulty: Easy.

Special Attractions: Because of its pristine nature, Grayton Beach's one mile of shoreline is considered one of the top five beaches in the nation.

Season: Spring through fall.

Camping: Thirty-seven campsites in pine scrub with complete facilities.

Information: Grayton Beach State Recreation Area, Route 2, Box 6600, Santa Rosa Beach, FL 32459; (904) 231-4210.

HIKE 4 GRAYTON BEACH NATURE TRAIL

Finding the trailhead: From Fort Walton Beach drive east 26 miles on U.S. Highway 98 to Santa Rosa Beach and turn right on County Road 30, which is about ten miles from the park entrance. The trailhead is located at the east end of the beach parking lot.

The hike: The walk begins in an area of shifting sand dunes. The sand settles only after plants and trees take root and hold it in place. In one spot, a shady hammock of live oaks, magnolias, and palmettos illustrates how effectively plant life can halt the sand.

HIKE 4 GRAYTON BEACH NATURE TRAIL

CR30A

ENTRANCE

0   300
FEET

NORTH

WESTERN LAKE

P

Barrier Dunes

P

Pine Flatwoods

Barrier Dunes

GULF OF MEXICO

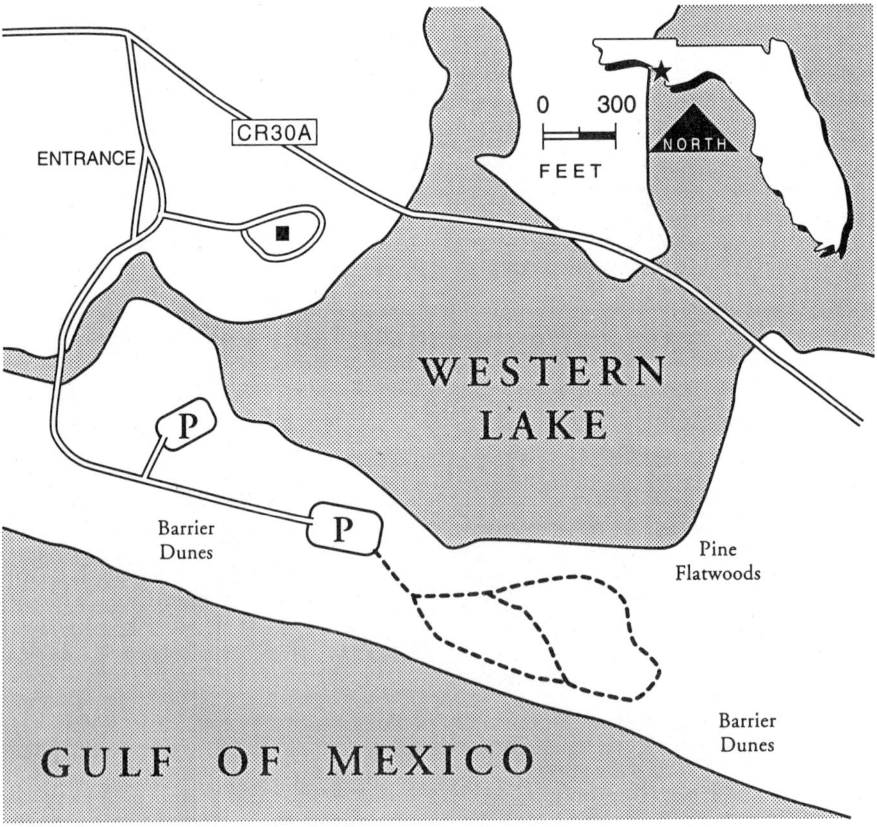

Next, the trail passes a scrub oak thicket, a dense and impenetrable tangle. But a few steps more and the scene bears witness to the power of nature's two main pruning forces: salt spray and wind. What appear to be bushes growing on the dunes are actually fully mature trees stunted by the wind and salt, and sometimes engulfed by drifting sand.

Farther on you'll pass an area where the sand shifts so fast vegetation can't take hold. Look for a variety of animal tracks here, evidence of lizards, skunks, snakes, raccoons, and ghost crabs.

A nearby stand of slash pine is a remarkable contrast to such barrenness. These pines have a natural resistance to fire and routinely survive flames that kill hardwoods and shrubs. A conspicuous plant here is the yaupon, with its small green leaves and, in the fall, red berries. Indians once used the leaves for a potion known as the Black Drink, using it to cleanse themselves.

The trail soon approaches a salt march near Western Lake. The march is an important nursery for fish and shellfish. Crabs are common here, attracting herons, otters, and raccoons, who dine on them amongst the black rushes.

The final exhibit on the nature trail demonstrates how turpentine was once drawn from the pines. The trees were slashed (hence the name slash pine) to yield large amounts of pitch, which was then taken to a turpentine still.

The trail ends at an intersection. Go right to return to the parking lot. Or go left to wander on the beach back to the concession building. Shore birds are usually numerous.

ST. JOSEPH PENINSULA STATE PARK

This remote, 2,516-acre park is bounded on three sides by St. Joe Bay and the Gulf of Mexico. The two sandy barrier islands that make up the peninsula were formed an estimated 5,000 years ago. About 1,000 years ago, the islands merged together at Eagle Harbor and joined the mainland, creating the present-day configuration. Stormy winds and waves have created mile after mile of huge sand dunes beautifully crested with golden sea oats.

If you're an avid birder try to be at St. Joe Peninsula a few days after the first cold front of autumn. Then you'll have a rare opportunity to view the annual migration of hawks, as birds fly in from as far away as Canada on their journey to Mexico and South America.

An accident of topography makes the St. Joe Peninsula a prime viewing site. Although hawks typically fly a wide corridor, they prefer not to fly over water. So, as they funnel over the St. Joe Peninsula—only a third of a mile wide—you can easily spot them in huge numbers. The sighting record is 600 hawks in a single hour, 10 per minute! A typical day's sighting is between 200 and 300 hawks, although 3,000 to 5,000 birds may be in temporary residence.

The most common migrant is the sharp-shinned hawk, followed by the Cooper's and broad-winged hawks. The St. Joe Peninsula is the only place

A red-shouldered hawk at St. Joseph Peninsula State Park.

in northwest Florida where the endangered peregrine falcon can be seen with some predictability, though their number is limited to a handful each season.

Prime places to spot hawks are Eagle Harbor at the marina (best in early morning) and the tip of the peninsula. Be sure to bring binoculars.

General Description: Nine miles of beach bordered by massive sand dunes and the Gulf of Mexico. Also, a separate walk through the peninsula interior.

General Location: Across from the town of Port St. Joe.

Maps: None needed.

Difficulty: Easy.

Special Attractions: A spectacular stretch of unspoiled beach populated by numerous shorebirds throughout the year. It is also a nationally-known site for observing hawks during the fall migration.

Season: Any time of year, though winter can be cold and blustery; summer is most crowded. Best time to view migrating hawks is late September through October.

Camping: 119 sites with water, electricity, and grills. One of the few Florida parks with rental cabins.

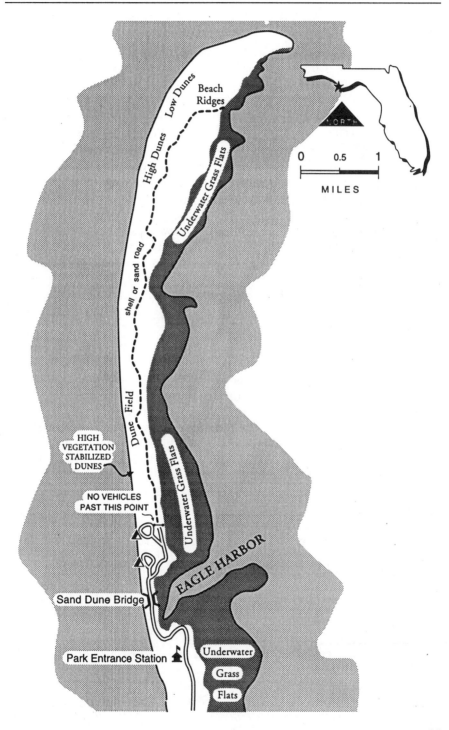

Low Dunes

Beach
Ridges

High Dunes

Underwater Grass Flats

shell or sand road

Dune Field

NORTH

0   0.5   1

MILES

HIGH
VEGETATION
STABILIZED
DUNES

NO VEHICLES
PAST THIS POINT

Underwater Grass Flats

EAGLE HARBOR

Sand Dune Bridge

Park Entrance Station

Underwater

Grass

Flats

Information: St. Joe Peninsula State Park, Star Route 1, Box 200, Port St. Joe, FL 32456; (904) 227-1327.

HIKE 5   ST. JOSEPH PENINSULA TRAIL

Finding the trailhead: From Port St. Joe, drive four miles south on U.S. 98 to County Road 30. Continue south for about five miles and turn right onto County Road 30E. This road leads eight miles to the park entrance and marina, and ends at the park's campground. Day-use hikers should park at the marina. The only beach access across the dunes is opposite the marina and is clearly marked. To hike the peninsula trail, park at the picnic area, a mile away from the trailhead, which is located at the rental cabins.

The hike: The fourteen-mile walk through the interior of the St. Joseph Peninsula provides a close look at sand pine scrub and pine flatwood habitats. Notice the ridges of sand behind the dunes. These long fingers of high ground are often divided by ponds, swampy areas, or grassy meadows. Such wet depressions are always good places to watch for bird life. Overnight camping in the wilderness area is limited to twenty people, but the number of day hikers is not restricted. You must hike in at least a full mile from the trailhead before setting up camp. The hike is about seven miles one-way, and you must retrace your steps: no chance of a return along the beach.

ST. VINCENT NATIONAL WILDLIFE REFUGE

This is one place you can walk for miles on the beach and never see anyone or any evidence of a man-made structure. The triangular landfall is quite large for a barrier island: four miles wide and nine miles long. Fourteen miles of beaches surround it and another eighty miles of sand roads crisscross it. Numbered roads run the width of the island (running north-south) while those labeled with letters of the alphabet extend its length (east-west).

St. Vincent has a long and interesting history. Pottery shards indicate human habitation on the island as far back as 240 A.D. Franciscan friars visiting the Apalachee tribes named the island in 1633.

In 1868, the first in a long string of private owners transformed St. Vincent into an exotic animal hunting preserve. In 1908 and again in 1948, the owners brought in zebra, eland, Asian jungle fowl, and some continental game birds, including ring-necked pheasants, bobwhite quail, and semi-wild turkey. All of this animal importation ended in 1968 when the U.S. Fish and Wildlife Service purchased the island and took over its management. You may see one of the remaining exotics, the sambar deer with its large ears.

Initially, the St. Vincent refuge was established for waterfowl. Now, perhaps of even greater concern is protecting the habitat of endangered species. Look for bald eagle nests in the pine trees near freshwater lakes and marshes. Loggerhead sea turtles nest here during the summer, but since the

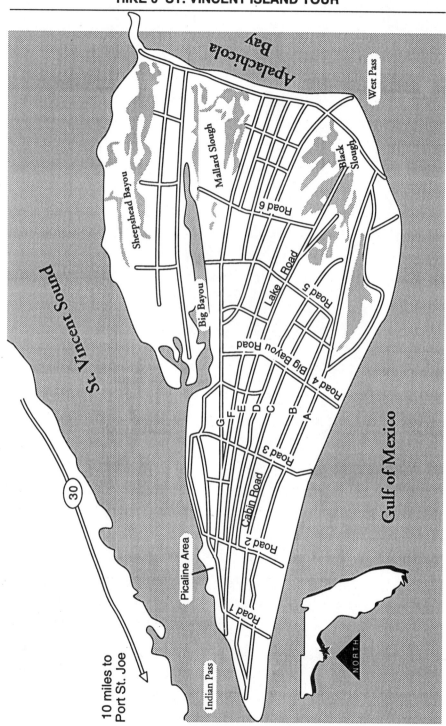

Apalachicola Bay

St. Vincent Sound

Gulf of Mexico

West Pass

Black Slough

Mallard Slough

Sheepshead Bayou

Road 6

Big Bayou

Lake Road

Road 5

Big Bayou Road

Road 4

G F E D C B A

Road 3

Cabin Road

Road 2

Picaline Area

Road 1

Indian Pass

10 miles to
Port St. Joe

30

NORTH

A great blue heron at St. Vincent National Wildlife Refuge.

refuge is open only during daylight, you'll probably never see the actual egg-laying process. Look for turtle tracks on the beach: they look like the treads of some earth-moving machine.

Indigo snakes—with a beautiful dark sheen—inhabit gopher tortoise burrows. Seasonally, wood storks and peregrine falcons pause here during their migrations.

Perhaps most interesting of all is the red wolf breeding program that began in 1990. After the wolf cubs are weaned and raised here, they are set free in the Great Smoky Mountains National Park and Alligator River National Wildlife Refuge. Red wolves once ranged all over the southeast, including Florida. Predator control and habitat loss annihilated them.

General Description: Ninety miles of beach front and dirt roads on a 12,358-acre undeveloped barrier island, which can be reached only by boat.

General Location: Just offshore from the Apalachicola River in Franklin County.

Maps: None needed.

Difficulty: Easy.

Special Attractions: Because of its limited access, this is a truly remote barrier island, with wildlife you're unlikely to see anywhere else in Florida, such as the sambar deer. These huge deer were imported from Southeast Asia and now roam wild here.

Season: Fall through spring.

Camping: Permitted only in conjunction with seasonal hunts.

Information: Refuge Manager, St. Vincent National Wildlife Refuge, P.O. Box 447, Apalachicola, FL 32329; (904) 653-8808. The visitor center is also located in Apalachicola, a considerable distance from the refuge. It is in the Harbour Master Building on Market St., open 8 a.m. to 4:30 p.m., Monday through Friday only.

HIKE 6 ST. VINCENT ISLAND TOUR

Finding the trailhead: From Apalachicola go west about five miles on U.S. Highway 98 and turn left on County Road 30; the turnoff is ten miles west of Port St. Joe if you happen to be coming from the direction of Panama City. Continue just past the town of McNeils, turn southeast onto County Road 30B, and drive to the end of the road. You can launch a canoe, john boat, or large pleasure craft at the public ramp at Indian Pass just across from the western tip of St. Vincent Island. The refuge, about a quarter-mile offshore, looms large from this point.

The hike: Although St. Vincent is an island of sand, you'll discover an unusually varied habitat. Many of the sand roads going east-west follow ridge lines that are actually ancient beaches created by fluctuating sea levels over the last 5,000 years. Walking around, you'll also find marshes and freshwater lakes, four different slash pine communities, pure stands of cabbage palm, dunes among both live and scrub oak, and mixed hardwoods.

The wetlands are where you're most apt to spot the exotic sambar deer. This is actually an elk from Southeast Asia and is quite easy to recognize. It has huge, paddle-shaped ears and weighs between 500 to 600 pounds. The refuge's white-tailed deer are puny by comparison: only 130 pounds, tops. The native white-tails do not compete with the sambar since they prefer quite different habitat. The white-tailed deer are in the drier, upland sections.

Since sand roads are the only trails throughout the interior, it's easy to feel totally isolated, even cut off from civilization, an unusual feeling in much of Florida. The roads are well canopied, and the brush is often thick. This is one of the most beautiful wilderness places in all Florida. On a weekday, when boaters are few, the only sounds you may hear are the cries of birds. It is so quiet, so peaceful, your ears may ring. Disturbing this hushed tranquility by talking seems almost a sacrilege.

ST. GEORGE ISLAND

Until 1965, St. George Island could be reached only by boat. Today, the toll bridge crossing Apalachicola Bay from the mainland passes over a rich fishery famous for its oysters. The bridge ends on the rapidly developing central part of the island.

St. George's sands are brilliantly white. During a full moon, the light reflecting from the sand is bright enough to read by. Let your imagination wander and the whole landscape seems cloaked in a pure, fresh snow. A cool breeze off the Gulf often adds to the illusion.

Like all the Gulf barrier islands, St. George is a prime birding area in fall and winter when numerous migratory species visit. As many as thirty-three species of warbler have been sighted, along with dark-eyed junco, northern gannet, red-breasted nuthatch, and savannah sparrow.

General Description: Hikes of three to nine miles in Dr. Julian G. Bruce St. George Island State Park on a beautiful barrier island no more than a mile wide.

General Location: In the Gulf of Mexico, near the town of Apalachicola.

Maps: None needed.

Difficulty: Easy.

Special Attractions: Incredibly beautiful beaches bordered by high sand dunes and the Gulf of Mexico. Good winter bird watching.

Season: Fall to spring. Biting flies can be a bother in summer.

Camping: Sixty developed campsites plus a primitive camping area for backpackers.

Information: St. George Island State Park, P.O. Box 62, East Point, FL 32328; (904) 927-2111.

HIKE 7 SAINT GEORGE ISLAND PARK BEACHES

Finding the trailhead: Take the four-mile toll bridge off U.S. 98 at Eastpoint, just east of the town of Apalachicola. After reaching St. George Island, turn left and follow County Road 300 to the park entrance. Beach access is available at several of the picnic pavilions facing the Gulf, and via an undeveloped road requiring four-wheel drive near the park's eastern tip.

The hike: Hikers can enjoy nine miles of beach walks on the Gulf front at St. George Island State Park, which covers 1,884 acres at the island's eastern tip. Large dunes with bonnets of golden sea oats border most of the shoreline.

In some places dunes have migrated across the island from the Gulf side to the bay, stopped only by the tree line. The boardwalk near the middle of the island illustrates how futile it is for man to try to control such forces: the boardwalk is often obliterated by sand, so you must walk in designated areas where the wood slats were intended to be high above ground. At least the observation platform at the end remains above the sand.

St. George Island State Park is one of the best public parks for collecting seashells on the Gulf coast. Nesting birds are also common on the beach and grass flats. Look for snowy plovers, least terns, black skimmers, and other shore birds.

Dunes with sea oats.

HIKE 8 PRIMITIVE TRAIL

Finding the trailhead: Park at the split rail fence at the back of the designated campground. A sign points the way.

The hike: A good backpacking trail begins near Sugar Hill on a winding path that is actually an old turpentine road. The 2.5 mile trail leads to a primitive campground at Gap Point overlooking Eastern Cove with Goose Island just offshore. Return on the same trail.

ST. MARKS NATIONAL WILDLIFE REFUGE

St. Marks is probably the best place in Northwest Florida for general bird watching. Founded in 1931 and one of the nation's oldest refuges, St. Marks encompasses 65,000 acres of land and another 31,500 acres of adjacent Apalachee Bay. It also includes a designated Wilderness Area of 18,000 acres.

Natural salt marshes, tidal flats, and freshwater impoundments attract up to 150,000 migrating waterfowl in winter. Alligators thrive in the open marshes and swamps, while turkey and white-tailed deer occupy the pine woods. Fall typically sees an explosion of butterflies, some migrating as others are just hatching. Monarchs, swallowtails, and skippers are among the most common butterflies found on the refuge.

Two sets of short hikes located at widely separated parts of the refuge offer strikingly different views of this vast habitat. Trails near the visitor center pass through swampy terrain, while those farther west traverse higher ground.

General Description: Trails from 0.3 mile to 43 miles on a wildlife refuge that offers important habitat for wintering waterfowl, attracting as many as 300 bird species. A public hunting area.

General Location: The office/visitor center is three miles south of the fire tower at the town of Newport.

Maps: None needed for the five short hikes, but very helpful for the section of the Florida Trail that also crosses the refuge.

Difficulty: Easy to moderate.

Special Attractions: A huge variety of wildlife: alligators, 50 species of mammals, more than 100 types of reptiles and amphibians.

Season: Waterfowl begin arriving in September, but December through February is best.

Camping: None in the refuge itself, unless you are hiking the Florida National Scenic Trail. During hunting season you may camp at Newport Park at U.S. Highway 98 and County Rd. 59; also the Ochlockonee River State Park on U.S. Highway 319, about four miles south of Sopchoppy. These fill rapidly on weekends during hunting season.

Information: St. Marks National Wildlife Refuge, Box 68, St. Marks, FL 32355; (904) 925-6121.

HIKE 9 PLUM ORCHARD POND TRAIL

Finding the trailhead: Take U.S. Highway 98 to Newport, turn south on County Road 59. A sign marks the turnoff.

The hike: This 0.3-mile loop begins just north of the visitor center. The trail skirts the marshy shores of the pond, with interpretive signs that identify many of the native plants and trees. In dry weather, the trail is wheelchair accessible, but check trail conditions at the visitor center.

HIKE 10 STONEY BAYOU AND DEEP CREEK TRAILS

Finding the trailhead: These two routes begin at the same trailhead on Lighthouse Road (County Road 59) just south of the visitor center going toward the lighthouse. The trailhead is on the left. The Stoney Bayou Trail is sometimes closed to protect migrating species.

The hikes: The Stoney Bayou and Deep Creek trails are open to hiking year-round but are restricted to day-use only. Both are loop trails, overlapping at the beginning. They start along the high roadbed of the old Aucilla Tram that leads into a dense coastal swamp. The Stoney Bayou loop is six miles; the trail veers off to the right from the trailhead. The Deep Creek Trail covers twelve miles, venturing farther east along the tram roadbed. It too turns left and

Feeding alligators is prohibited.

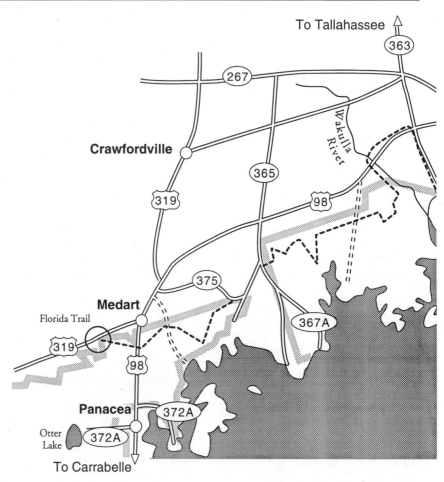

eventually rejoins the Stoney Bayou loop, returning along the Stoney Bayou Field.

Wetlands like these are remarkably fertile, producing more plant matter per acre than the finest farmland. These wetlands are also important in filtering and purifying water, replenishing the underground water supply, and even acting as a natural "sponge" during periods of flooding.

Although these are mostly open trails atop impoundments, the wildlife viewing can be quite good, depending on time of year. March sees the migration of white pelicans and ibis; September enjoys a burst of swallowtail butterflies; October the monarchs; by the end of November, migrating waterfowl are in profusion; in December, bald eagles may be nesting.

If your feet are still willing, try the Mounds Pool Trail, which begins about five miles south of the visitor center on County Road 59. This one-mile

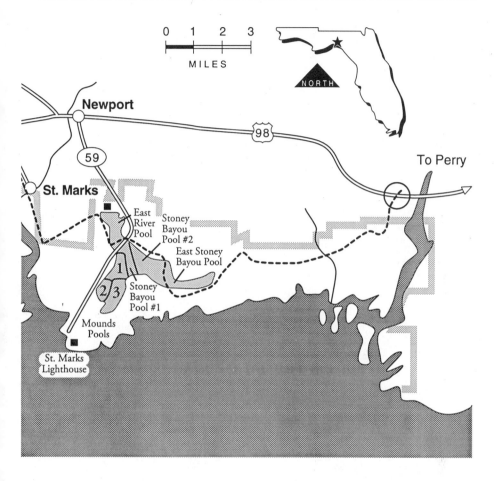

interpretive trail traverses an old turpentine forest. The main attraction is an observation tower offering a fine view of the slash pines and marshes.

HIKE 11 OTTER LAKE TRAILS

Finding the trailhead: Take U.S. Highway 98 west toward Panama City. Just before the town of Panacea, look for the brown Otter Lake Recreation Area sign by the First Baptist Church. Turn right onto County Road 372A; the road is poorly marked, but watch for the recreation area sign at the turnoff. Several hundred yards down this road is the Otter Creek Recreation Area. The hiking trails begin almost immediately inside.

The hikes: The Ridge Trail and Otter Lake Loop are loop trails with a common trailhead. Both the Ridge Trail, marked in yellow blazes for 4.6

miles, and the Otter Lake Loop, almost eight miles and blazed in blue, use forest roads to lead you through sand hills of longleaf pine and turkey oaks.

Although the longleaf once was the dominant species in this area, logging allowed oaks to grow and flourish. Prescribed burns help restore the pines. Wildlife common here are fox squirrels, fence lizards, gopher tortoises, and blue jays.

HIKE 12 FLORIDA TRAIL EXTENSION

Finding the trailhead: The western trailhead is off U.S. Highway 319, just north of U.S. Highway 98. After only a few hundred yards on U.S. 319, look for a dirt road (Carraway Cut Off) on the left; you should also spot a small Florida Trail sign on the opposite side of the road. Take Carraway Cut Off a short distance to a small parking area.

The hike: A forty-three-mile section of the Florida National Scenic Trail, this extension runs west-east into the heart of the St. Marks Refuge, through places that can be reached only on foot. This hike is recognized as the best in all Northwest Florida for its great variety of wildlife zones and forest types.

The trailhead is an important juncture for the Florida Trail. The leg going north enters the Apalachicola National Forest; this trail is known as Apalachicola East (described later under Inland Panhandle Hikes). The southern route leads into St. Marks.

Camping is permitted at six primitive sites for through hikers only. The campsites are Marsh Point (at 4.5 miles); Wakulla Field (at 13 miles); River Hammock (at 15 miles); East River (at 28 miles); Ring Dike (at 30 miles); and Pinhook River (at 40 miles).

A use permit is mandatory and must be obtained by telephone, mail, or in person at the visitor center at least fifteen days in advance. No fires are allowed anywhere, including at the campsites, and only a single night's stay is allowed at any one site. Still, with six sites, backpackers could stay a week inside the refuge if desired.

Traveling west to east, the St. Marks trail goes only a short distance before crossing U.S. 98. In fact, the trail crosses roads, paved and unpaved, on and off at the beginning, including a part of the old Tallahassee-St. Marks railroad corridor. In use from 1837 until 1984, the Tallahassee-St. Marks was the longest operated railroad in Florida. Its founding was financed by planters and merchants in Georgia and Florida to take their cotton to the port at St. Marks. The tracks are now torn up and the corridor transformed into the first Rails to Trails project in Florida. This is a multi-use trail; you may encounter cyclists and riders on horseback.

Supply stops are possible at mile nine, and mile twenty-four, the town of St. Marks (with several good, inexpensive seafood restaurants). At St. Marks, hikers must arrange for someone to ferry them across the St. Marks river to rejoin the trail.

Once on the other side, the route follows an old railroad grade to Port Leon, a ghost town that has been abandoned since an 1843 hurricane. It's not far from there to the East River campsite. Just beyond the campsite is a blue-blazed side trail to the refuge visitor center, only 0.8 mile away.

The next major landmark is County Road 59, where the trail turns north (left). If you want to take a long diversion toward the coast, the St. Marks Lighthouse is 4.3 miles distant to the right. Stay on the paved road and you can't miss it.

From County Road 59, the main trail follows the Stoney Bayou and Deep Creek trails. The Ring Dike campsite is at the south end of the East Stoney Bayou impoundment.

From the campsite, you'll join the Aucilla tram road after a junction with the blue-blazed Deep Creek Trail. After about two miles you'll cross the Pinhook River on a wooden bridge and locate the final campsite. It's now only another few miles to the end at U.S. 98. Your hike is capped off with one last look at forests of pine, oak, gum, and palmetto. If you stop seeing trail blazes at the end, not to worry. The last stretch is on private land.

Except for periods of heavy rain, this is a fairly dry trail. During wet weather, follow the alternate dry routes blazed in blue about thirty-five miles into the hike.

INLAND
PANHANDLE HIKES

BLACKWATER RIVER STATE FOREST

The largest of the Florida state forests, Blackwater River seems more like Georgia than Florida. The terrain is hilly, the soil is red, and the stands of longleaf pines here are among the finest in the United States. Turkey oaks, laurel oaks, and live oaks are scattered among the pine; the ground cover is mostly wiregrass.

This is a multiple-use forest; be prepared for occasional clear-cuts from timber harvesting. These denuded sections, looking like the aftermath of a tornado, contribute to the 25 million board feet of timber removed from Blackwater State Forest annually. In a good year, the forest produces as much as $5 million in revenue. Selected seed trees are saved to start a new forest. In sixty years this new growth is ready for harvesting.

In spring, millions of wildflowers decorate the forest. One of the most common is black titi, which blossoms in low wet areas; the nectar of these fragrant flowers makes a good honey. Adding to the spring colors are wild azaleas with white, pink, or yellow-orange petals.

The Blackwater River from the Jackson Red Ground Trail.

General Description: Hikes of 4.5 miles and 21 miles through one of the most scenic, but least known parts of Florida, the 183,185-acre Blackwater River State Forest. A public hunting area.

General Location: Between Milton and Munson, near the Alabama border.

Maps: Available from the forestry office just south of Munson.

Difficulty: Easy to moderate, depending on weather conditions.

Special Attractions: One trail retraces General Andrew Jackson's route during his 1818 campaign in Florida.

Season: Fall through spring.

Camping: Several campgrounds offer numerous sites. Or try nearby Blackwater River State Park, 15 miles northeast of Milton off U.S. 90, with 15 sites.

Information: Blackwater Forestry Center, 11650 Munson Hwy., Milton, FL 32570; (904) 957-4201. To locate the center and obtain a map, take State Road 191 from Interstate 10. The forestry office is near junction of 191 and State Road 4 just south of Munson.

HIKE 13 JACKSON RED GROUND TRAIL

Finding the trailhead: Located northwest of Crestview at the Karick Lake Recreation Area, off County Road 189, three miles south of Blackman.

Note: You'll need to arrange a pickup at the Red Rock picnic area following the hike. The turnoff from State Road 191 to Red Rock is easy to miss. Look for a road flanked by two churches: a Baptist church and the Springhill Assembly of God Church. Turn east and proceed 3.5 miles to the Red Rock Picnic Area. The trail ends/begins another 0.3 mile beyond the picnic area.

The hike: The twenty-one-mile Jackson Red Ground Trail is named for the striking red soil, uncommon in Florida. Originally an old Indian trading path, the route was used by General Andrew Jackson in 1818, when he marched 1,200 men from the Apalachicola River to Pensacola, a distance of 225 miles, in eighteen days.

Avid hikers can easily walk this section (another part of the Florida Trail) in one long day. Camping is available at both ends of the trail.

From the north, the trail begins along an earth dam bordering the southeastern end of Karick Lake. It quickly leads into swamps, streams, oaks, and stand after stand of longleaf pine. Several small hiking shelters—a godsend on rainy days—are scattered along the trail.

Whenever the trail intersects with forest roads look for orange blazes. The route also crosses several streams on wooden bridges or railroad ties. Tread carefully on the railroad ties if it has been raining; they can be as slick as ice.

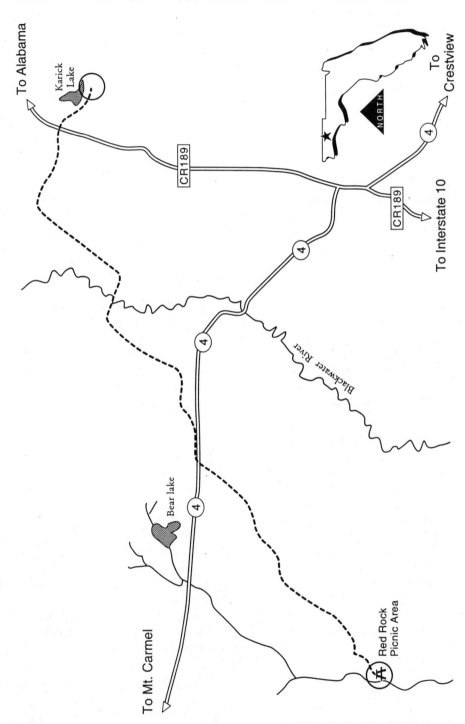

The southern end of the trail emerges from the forest and crosses the Juniper Creek bridge. Look north from the bridge to see a series of sandbars that seem more characteristic of the ocean than a freshwater stream. Juniper Creek is a tributary of Blackwater River, considered one of the purest sand bottom rivers in the world, and this is a fine sample of it.

HIKE 14 SWEETWATER TRAIL

Finding the trailhead: At the Krul Recreation Area, located off State Road 4, just east of 191.

The hike: At 4.5 miles one-way, this trail provides a short, pleasant walk through a microcosm of the terrain found on the Jackson Trail. It ends at an intersection with the Jackson Red Ground Trail. Sweetwater Trail begins at the Krul Recreation Area, then crosses Sweetwater Creek via a swinging bridge. At about mile three, it passes the Bear Lake Recreation Area, which has camping and showers. Once the trail intersects with the Jackson Trail, you'll have to retrace your steps or continue on the main trail to the northern or southern ends of the Jackson Red Ground Trail.

FRED GANNON ROCKY BAYOU
STATE RECREATION AREA

Because Rocky Bayou is one of the smallest hiking locations in Northwest Florida, it's often ignored by walkers seeking longer, better-known trails. A pity, because this park is a real gem with a tremendously diverse landscape in just a small area. It's well worth a day or an overnight stay.

General Description: A small, 357-acre park with three short nature hikes of up to a mile each.

General Location: Just outside the town of Niceville.

Difficulty: Easy.

Special Attractions: The opportunity to fish in Rocky Bayou, an arm of Choctawatchee Bay.

Season: Fall through spring.

Camping: Forty-two campsites with hookups.

Information: Rocky Bayou State Recreation Area, 4281 State Rd. 20, Niceville, FL 32578; (904) 833-9144.

HIKE 15 ROCKY BAYOU TRAIL

Finding the trailhead: Take State Road 20 about three miles east of Niceville. Follow the park road to campsites 25 and 26. The access trail begins just opposite. Park at the gate or beside one of the campsites if they're empty.

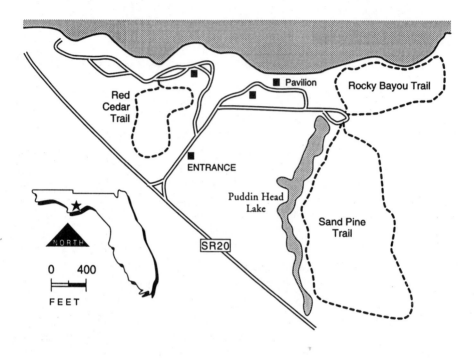

The hike: The Rocky Bayou Trail skirts a bayou, as expected. But it begins in thick forest where the ground is covered with balls of green deer moss, one of the heaviest concentrations of it seen anywhere. Then the trail winds through the woods until it reaches the bayou banks.

Rocky Bayou, like all bayous, is a shallow, curving channel with slow-moving water. The term bayou—the French word for gut or channel—apparently was first used by French settlers on the lower Mississippi River and adjacent drainage areas of Louisiana, Texas, and Mississippi.

HIKE 16 SAND PINE TRAIL

Finding the trailhead: Rocky Bayou and Sand Pine share the same trailhead (see Hike 15).

The hike: The mile-long Sand Pine Trail offers an opportunity to watch the beavers that reside in the long finger of water known as Puddin Head Lake. The trail follows the lake almost to its tip, then turns inland. There, mature sand pines tower over the scrub vegetation of rosemary and scrub oak.

A footbridge crossing a small stream above the Rocky Bayou Trail.

A third, shorter path, the Red Cedar Trail, provides a close up look at a grove of red cedars and their habitat. To find the trailhead, take the road that veers left just beyond the entrance station and look for the trailhead on the left, near the end of the second median.

FLORIDA CAVERNS STATE PARK

Much of Northwest and North Florida is honeycombed with limestone caves, but most remain flooded because of the state's high water table. The multitude of dry caverns in this park are an unusual exception. A remarkable variety of formations decorate the caverns: soda straws, stalactites, stalagmites, columns, rimstones, flowstones, and draperies.

The caves were created over many millennia. When Florida was covered by sea water, living organisms deposited thick layers of calcium on the ocean floor. It gradually hardened into limestone, and as the sea receded, this limestone became the state's land base. Rainwater slowly seeped into the limestone, dissolving it and forming many small tunnels and caves.

Some caves are now dry only because the groundwater dropped below cavern level. But new cavities are still being fashioned by groundwater in this ongoing process. So far, twenty-three dry caves have been mapped in the park, and another thirty surface holes have been discovered but not explored. The public is permitted to explore only one of the caverns.

General Description: A 1,280-acre park containing one of Florida's most elaborate dry cave systems.

General Location: The town of Marianna near the Chipola River.

Maps: None needed.

Difficulty: Easy.

Special Attractions: An underground tour of approximately one-hour through Florida's version of Carlsbad Cavern and Mammoth Cave.

Season: Anytime. Waters may rise after prolonged heavy rains, flooding parts of the cave system used for tours. If in doubt, call ahead.

Camping: Thirty-two sites in the park.

Information: Florida Caverns State Park, 3345 Caverns Road, Marianna, FL 32446; (904) 482-9598.

HIKE 17 FLORIDA CAVE TOUR

Finding the trailhead: Drive three miles north of Marianna on State Road 167. The park is on the left.

The hike: There is a cave tour fee in addition to the standard park admission. No flashlight is needed since the state provides all necessary illumination (some quite moody and beautiful) of the striking limestone configurations.

Some of the more unusual patterns resemble more above-ground objects such as pipe organs, wedding cakes, and various animals. In several spots you'll find rimstone pools of clear water, which make some of the most dramatic photos. A good flash or high speed film is mandatory.

At one time, special tours were led into several additional caves but this practice has been ended to better protect delicate underground formations and the bat colonies. Intentionally or not, spelunkers often disturb the resting bats. The endangered gray bats here are easily awakened by voices and lights. Once alert, the hibernating bats use valuable energy they may need to survive long cold winters.

A plan is underway to open caves that are not inhabited by endangered species or that do not contain numerous delicate geological formations.

In the single open cave, you may see as many as five different bat species on the tour. Bats have always been important in controlling insects. At one time, when the population was undisturbed and undiminished, these bats locally consumed an estimated 858,880 pounds of insects per year. Personally, I find it difficult to visualize how many thousands of mosquitoes it must take to make just a single pound. That's a lot of bugs the bats were putting the bite on.

The tour is one-way and ends well away from the entrance. As soon as you step outside, you're presented with the option of taking several short trails (each under thirty minutes) that penetrate the Chipola River floodplain. The trails pass hardwood hammocks containing American beech, southern magnolia, white oak, and dogwood as well as limestone outcroppings.

TORREYA STATE PARK

The park is named after the torreya, or Florida yew, the largest bigleaf magnolia found in the United States. It grows only in this park. The torreya is one of more than 100 rare and endangered species living in this small protected area.

Many of the hardwoods and plants growing in Torreya are more commonly found farther north in the Appalachian chain. The plants apparently moved into Florida during the last glacial period when the climate was wet and cool. As the climate warmed and became semi-tropical, most of the plants died off, except in a few isolated locations like Torreya, where conditions remained almost unchanged.

The vegetation and landscape of Torreya are so distinctive they inspired (or deluded?) an attorney from nearby Bristol to proclaim the park the lost Garden of Eden. He even published a book supporting his thesis. One can only hope he was better at law than archeological theory.

The ranger station is unusually grandiose for a state park. It is actually a plantation house built around 1840, later moved to Torreya and restored. Known as the Gregory House, it is fully furnished in antiques. The house is

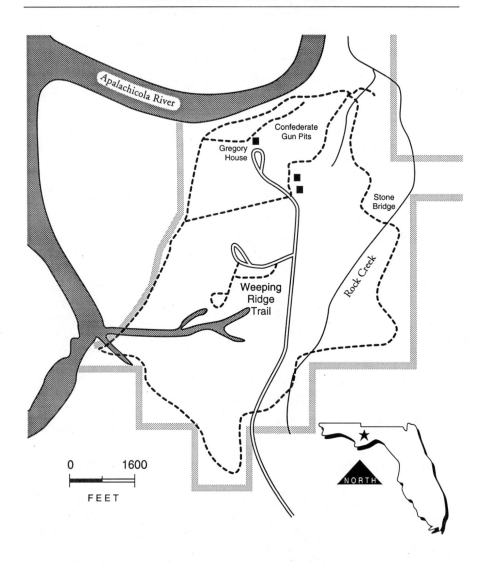

a reminder of the long-ago days when scores of steamboats traveled the Apalachicola River with cargoes of cotton and supplies for the settlers.

General Description: Because of the park's high bluffs, deep ravines, and unusual vegetation, many consider this seven-mile walk one of the most unique in all Florida.

General Location: Thirteen miles northeast of the town of Bristol.

Maps: None needed.

Difficulty: Easy to moderate.

Special Attractions: This is more like the Appalachians than semi-tropical Florida. Not only is the terrain hilly, but Torreya contains many of the same plants found farther north in the Appalachians.

Season: Fall to Spring.

Camping: Thirty-five developed sites plus a primitive camping area.

Information: Torreya State Park, Rt. 2, Box 70, Bristol, FL 32321; (904) 643-2674.

HIKE 18 TORREYA LOOP TRAIL

Finding the trailhead: Take State Road 12 to State Road 270 or 270A between Bristol and Greensboro. Park in front of the old Gregory House. Access to the loop trail begins at the south end of the Gregory House parking lot on a short path and is blazed in blue. The loop trail is blazed in white.

The hike: The trail skirts the perimeter of the park. However, it is not necessary to walk the entire length to see the torreya trees or walk the banks of the Apalachicola: a secondary loop trail of about forty-five minutes is also located behind the Gregory House. Consult the park map.

Walking clockwise on the main loop trail, you initially pass through streams and over hills for almost 0.75 mile. You'll encounter the cliffs between miles three and five, and the bluffs overlooking the Apalachicola River at about mile six.

Out-of-state visitors may not be impressed by the "high" bluffs and "deep" ravines here, but they are quite unusual for Florida. The 150-foot high bluff over the Apalachicola River, or the "towering" 300-foot high Logan's Bluff are vistas of high drama to Florida flatlanders.

During the Civil War, Confederate gun batteries were set up along the bluffs overlooking the Apalachicola River. Today, these are nothing more than depressions in the ground marked by signs. The Apalachicola River is best known as the boundary that marks the change from the Eastern Time Zone to Central.

Although this is a relatively short walk, there are two primitive camping areas: Rock Creek, almost at the beginning, and River Bluffs, about five miles in. Campers are limited to twelve persons at each site and must register in advance. If all spaces are taken, use the park's regular campground.

APALACHICOLA NATIONAL FOREST

Apalachicola is an Apalachee Indian term meaning "friendly people living on the other side." To walk to the other side of this forest, you'll pass through territory still remarkably abundant in wildlife: an estimated 10,000 deer, 2,000 turkey, and 175 black bear all thrive here. As many as 600 red-cockaded woodpeckers' nests are scattered throughout the tall pines. Parts

The fox squirrel is a common resident of Apalachicola National Forest.

of the forest are almost impenetrable. The 24,000-acre Bradwell Bay, in particular, boasts some of the most inhospitable terrain in all Florida.

Yet amid this wilderness is an outdoor area reserved for the physically challenged. Trout Pond, open from April to September, has a special nature trail that is wheelchair accessible. A pier extending into the lake provides an excellent fishing. Trout Pond, located off State Road 373, is about ten miles southwest of Tallahassee.

General Description: Trails of thirty-three and twenty-one miles through one of the largest national forests in the East, covering 557,000 acres. A public hunting area.

General Location: Between Tallahassee and St. Marks National Wildlife Refuge.

Maps: This is a remote region. Obtain the USDA Forest Service map available at any district ranger station.

Difficulty: Strenuous if heavy rains have flooded some sections. In Apalachicola East, it may be necessary to wade through waist-deep water. Otherwise, walking is easy to moderate.

Special Attractions: Among the state's longest trails, by Florida standards these trails offer true wilderness hiking. It is possible to combine the two Apalachicola forest trails with the St. Marks National Wildlife Refuge hike and also the Aucilla River extension, without interruption. This is total distance of 127 miles.

Season: Fall to spring.

Camping: Several primitive sites exist along the hiking trails. Ochlockonee River State Park is near the middle of the forest and is a favorite hiking campsite for those finishing Apalachicola West, or those about to begin Apalachicola East. Contact Ochlockonee River State Park, P.O. Box 5, Sopchoppy, FL 32358; (904) 962-2771.

Information: National Forests in Florida, P.O. Box 13548, Tallahassee, FL 32308; (904) 878-1131. District Ranger West, (904) 643-2477. District Ranger East, (904) 926-3561. The most accessible Forest Service office is on U.S. Highway 319 near Crawfordville.

HIKE 19 APALACHICOLA WEST

Finding the trailhead: Located off State Road 12, about ten miles south of Bristol. Marked by a Florida Trail signpost.

The hike: A distance of almost thirty-four miles, this is one of the most remote trails in Florida. A map and compass are mandatory. Of the two forest trails, this is the drier. After heavy rains you shouldn't find water much deeper than your ankles in even the wettest parts.

The trail first enters a wet savannah, home to numerous wildflowers and orchids, then passes through pines and cypress. At mile three, you'll reach Memery Island, a piece of higher ground. Here you'll also find a blue-blazed

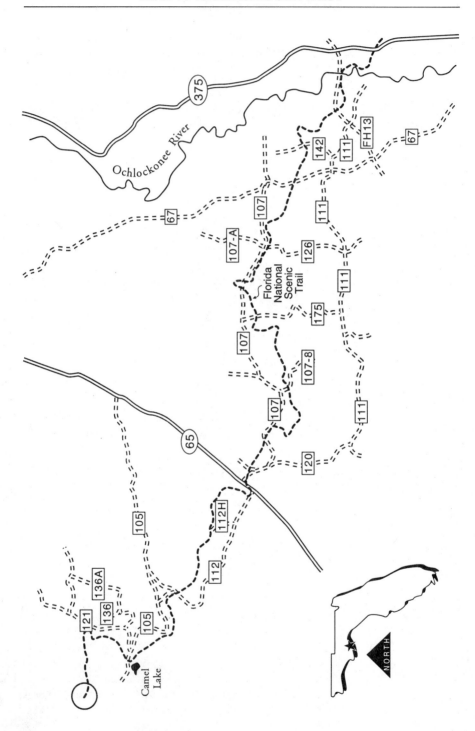

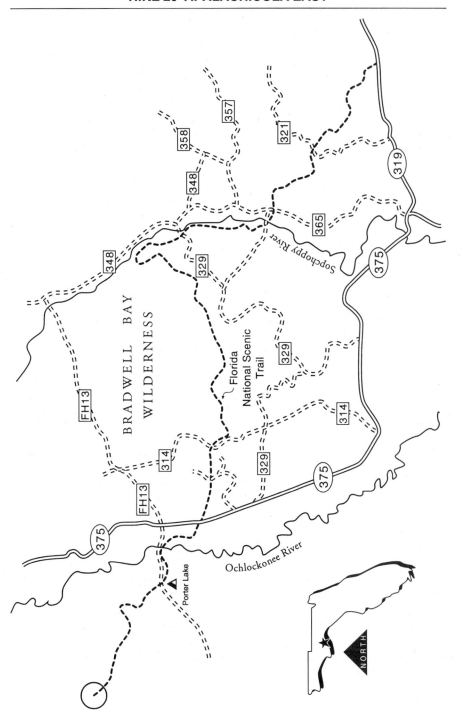

side trail to Hidden Pond, which then rejoins the main route about five miles farther down the path at Forest Road 108.

Continuing on the main trail, you'll soon come to Forest Road 105; the Camel Lake Campground is a tenth of a mile to your west. From 105, you'll periodically cross other forest roads: 108, 112-H, and 112, which joins with State Road 65 to take you across the New River bridge.

From State Road 65 take Forest Road 120, then enter the woods, mostly pine and palmetto. For about the next ten miles, Forest Road 107 will be a constant companion as you cross and recross it, finally hiking the dirt road in the open for more than two miles. You'll have one final junction with FR 107, cross Forest Road 177, then use the County Road 67 bridge to cross Indian Creek.

Forest Road 142 provides the last water crossing as the trail then takes you to a circular clearing, across Forest Road 13 and leads you to the Ochlockonee River and the nearby Porter Lake Campground, where potable water and other facilities await you.

If none of this seems too arduous, you're correct. The really nasty stuff is on the other side of the forest.

HIKE 20 APALACHICOLA EAST

Finding the trailhead: One mile west of County Road 375 on County Road 368, also known as Forest Road 13. Look for the Florida Trail signpost.

The hike: This twenty-nine-mile stretch of Florida National Scenic Trail includes swampy forest and fearsome Bradwell Bay, a low expanse where the water sometimes rises waist-deep after heavy downpours. Since Bradwell Bay is about seven miles from the official trailhead, you'll have the opportunity to call it quits fairly quickly if conditions are more than you care to handle.

The hike begins mildly enough along County Road 375, then moves onto Forest Road 314, which takes you to the edge of Bradwell Bay, a saucer-shaped depression that holds standing water most of the year.

Bordering Bradwell Bay are virgin stands of slash pine, saw palmetto, grasses, and oak clusters. A dense thicket of buckwheat tree (titi) grows in the middle; the titi blooms in March and April, transforming the bay into a strikingly scenic place.

How Bradwell Bay got its name is quite a story. It's named for a hunter lost for days in the titi thicket. Hopelessly disoriented, Bradwell supposedly left his rifle behind in the crook of a tree to reduce his load. Either Bradwell was awfully fond of that gun or dead certain that no one else could ever find his rifle: he offered a $10,000 reward to anyone who could retrieve it. No one ever collected. Should you find the rusted weapon, you're out of luck. Bradwell is long dead and so is the reward offer.

As long as you stick to the blazed trail, you should have little problem. The trail joins and follows the north side of Monkey Creek, then meets Forest Road 329, which leads to the Sopchoppy River. A little over two miles later you'll cross Monkey Creek by footbridge; another 3.5 miles you'll cross the Sopchoppy on Forest Road 343.

Still headed southeast, you'll encounter pine and oak forest, crossing Forest Roads 365, 321, a power line corridor, and finally Forest Road 356. At this point it's only another mile to the trail's end at U.S. 319, signified by a Florida Trail sign.

If your appetite for the Florida outdoors has yet to be satisfied, you can continue on the forty-four mile long St. Marks trail (see Hike 12), then onto the Aucilla River trail (see Hike 23).

LEON SINKS GEOLOGICAL AREA

The term karst refers to a limestone terrain that has been shaped and changed by both rain and groundwater. Although quite pure to drink, rain drops become weakly acidic as they absorb carbon dioxide from the air and from decaying vegetation. This mild acid then has the ability to eat away and dissolve the limestone bedrock that lies under much of Florida.

Over time, the large hollows, caves, and fissures created by the erosion may cause the ground surface to collapse, forming a sinkhole or a crater-like depression. The Leon Sinks are situated in the Woodville Karst Plain that extends from Tallahassee to the Gulf of Mexico. The plain is still evolving, which means new sinkholes may appear at anytime.

Along the three available walks, you'll have an excellent chance of spotting a white-tailed deer, a wild turkey, a fox squirrel, a gopher tortoise, or a red-shouldered hawk. Unfortunately, you won't have the chance to see the most unusual inhabitants, the cave crayfish and the insect-like cave amphipods; they reside underground, in the water-filled holes you'll be walking over.

Despite all the dramatic geologic activity, plant life thrives around the sinks: longleaf and slash pines; ash, maple, beech, and oak trees; plus an underbrush of wiregrass, gallberry, and fetterbush.

On a hot day, you can only look longingly at this series of natural swimming pools. To protect the sinkhole walls from erosion, swimming is not allowed.

General Description: Three trails through an unusual geological area featuring wet and dry sinkholes, and swampland. The longest trail is three miles.

General Location: In the Apalachicola National Forest just south of Tallahassee.

Maps: None needed.

Difficulty: Easy.

Special Attractions: The opportunity to see a karst plain where sinkholes may still appear at anytime.

Season: Anytime.

Camping: At Ochlockonee State Park, four miles south of Sopchoppy off U.S. 319; thirty sites.

Information: Wakulla Ranger District, USDA Forest Service, Route 6, Box 7860, Crawfordville, FL 32327; (904) 926-3561. Leon Sinks is open from 8 a.m. to 8 p.m.

HIKES 21, 22 SINKHOLE AND GUMSWAMP TRAILS

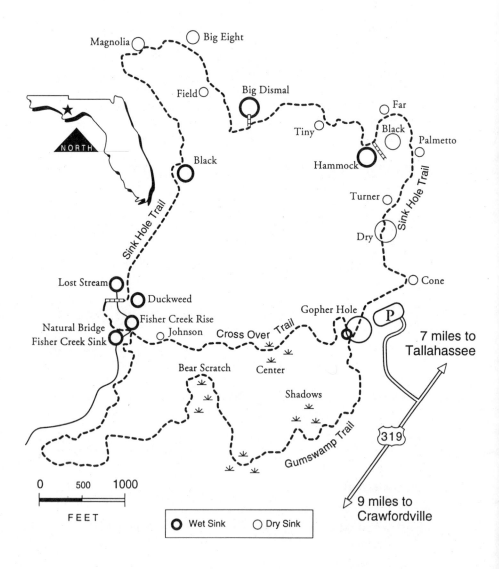

HIKE 21 SINKHOLE TRAIL

Finding the trailhead: Take U.S. Highway 319 seven miles south of Tallahassee; look for the well-marked turnoff.

The hike: This trail is marked with blue blazes and covers a distance of 3.1 miles, the longest and most complete of the three hikes in this area. One of its most interesting stops is the observation platform at Big Dismal Sink, which showcases more than seventy-five different plant species growing on its steep sides.

HIKE 22 GUMSWAMP TRAIL

Finding the trailhead: Take U.S. Highway 319 seven miles south of Tallahassee; look for the well-marked turnoff.

The hike: This trail is blazed in green, extends for 2.3 miles through a very different terrain. You can return by way of the white-blazed, 0.5-mile Crossover Trail.

AUCILLA RIVER

The now-you-see-it, now-you-don't phenomenon of the Aucilla River is quite unique. Like Florida Caverns State Park and the Leon Sinks, it illustrates the remarkable nature of the porous limestone rock found throughout much of Florida.

Equally as impressive is the incredibly thick forest of large magnolias, oaks, and gums, the branches often intertwined with long coils of grapevines. You needn't worry too much about wandering from the trail when the underbrush is this dense: you probably couldn't push your way through it if you had to.

General Description: Starting at the eastern boundary of the St. Marks National Wildlife Refuge, this seventeen-mile extension of the Florida Trail borders limestone sinks and the Aucilla River in the Aucilla Wildlife Management Refuge. Traverses a public hunting area.

General Location: The southwestern tip of Taylor County between Perry and Newport.

Maps: Not needed.

Difficulty: Easy to moderate, depending on rainfall. The trail skirts the edges of sinks and the Aucilla River; high water can obliterate these boundaries and could make walking dangerous.

Special Attractions: Like something out of a fairy tale, the Aucilla River disappears underground for the first half of the hike, emerging only as sinkhole formations. It re-emerges and flows above ground for the last half of the hike.

An Aucilla River sinkhole.

Season: Fall and spring.

Camping: Available in the town of Newport on U.S. 98 west of the Aucilla, or at the primitive site at Goose Pasture, closed during the hunting season.

Information: No offices of any agency are on site. Contact the Florida Division of Forestry in Perry 61A Plantation Rd, Perry, FL 32347 (904) 584-6121.

HIKE 23 AUCILLA RIVER TRAIL

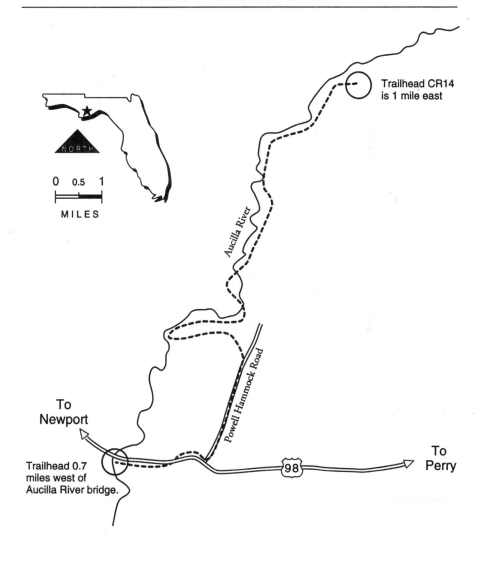

HIKE 23 AUCILLA RIVER TRAIL

Finding the trailhead: From the town of Perry, take U.S. Highway 98 west to the Aucilla River. From the river bridge, go another 0.75 mile west to the official trailhead on the right.

The hike: Going west to east, the trail begins on U.S. 98 just west of the Aucilla River bridge. You'll follow the shoulder of U.S. 98 for three miles to Powell Hammock Road, where you'll turn left. If you want to avoid the monotonous highway walk, simply park at Powell Hammock Road and start your walk there.

Once on Powell Hammock, the trail stays on this graded road to pass huge dolomite pits that are still being excavated. The trail next turns west to reach the forest edge, then continues on jeep tracks and dirt roads.

At about mile eight, you encounter the first of the sinkhole formations: Twin Sinks and Sarasinks. Most sinks are circular, steep-sided holes in the ground with water—from the Aucilla River—at the bottom. The holes may be as much as forty or fifty feet deep, depending on the water level.

After the first set of sinks, the trail crosses a dirt road and proceeds another 0.5 mile north to an even greater concentration of sinks. None of the names are posted but you'll be able to guess how some received their titles: Chocolate Sink, New Sink, Mosquito Slap Sink, and Hurry Up Sink.

Cross another dirt road to Kitchen Sink, Long Suffering Sink, Ryan Sink, Dragonfly Sink, and Watts Sink. Crossing another dirt road puts you at Frink Sink, Sunshine Sink, and Long Sink; after yet another dirt road, you'll arrive at Breakdown Sink. The trail comes out on Goose Pasture Road, crosses a cattle guard, and returns to the woods and Roadside Sink, Overflow Sink, and Vortex Sink.

If you're interested only in exploring sinkholes, arrange for a pickup at Goose Pasture Road. That cuts out the last half of the hike but shows you all the sinkholes. However, you'll want to walk the trail 0.2 mile beyond Goose Pasture Road itself since this short segment passes three of the sinks. Or, to see a sink without doing any walking, take Goose Pasture Road to the FTA sign located just beyond the cattle crossing; a sink is visible from the road, to your right. To reach Goose Pasture Road directly stay on the Powell Hammock Road for 4.3 miles, turn left onto Goose Pasture Road, and go one mile to the first cattle crossing.

To finish the hike beyond Goose Pasture Road continue seven more miles to the trail's end. Heading north, the trail borders the river, which is finally visible as an uninterrupted flow.

At about mile seventeen there's a camp site at a river bend, after which the trail uses a jeep road and ends at the Florida Trail sign on a forest road. County Road 14 is almost two miles farther east.

An alligator suns itself in Wakulla Springs State Park.

WAKULLA SPRINGS STATE PARK

Wakulla Springs is not only large, it is majestic. The spring run is one of the most scenic spots in all Florida, loaded with incredibly diverse wildlife living in and around the water. On a warm, sunny day, you may see more alligators here per square foot than anywhere else in Florida, including the Everglades.

The spring bowl (covering almost three acres) is the source of a tremendous water flow, as much as 14,325 gallons per second, or 1.2 billion gallons per day. The water is crystal clear, which allowed a visitor in 1850 to spot the bones of a prehistoric mastodon on the bottom, almost 100 feet below. The mastodon is now displayed at the Florida Natural History Museum in Tallahassee. Scientists have also identified the remains of nine other Ice Age mammals, some as far as 1,200 feet back in the spring cave. The cave is at least 4,300 feet long and 300 feet deep, but the source of the spring has yet to be found.

Ranger-led snorkeling trips are offered during summer months, when the constant seventy-degree spring water is apt to feel more refreshing than chilly. Swimming is permitted in several restricted areas and these boundaries should be observed because of the large gator population. Glass-bottom and jungle cruise boats make a two-mile trip down the spring run year-round. The park offers three short nature trails through this incredibly diverse habitat.

Vegetation along the short trails is remarkably diverse, including old-growth floodplain forests, longleaf pine forest, and upland hardwood forest, including sassafras, American beech, and American basswood. A sizable wild turkey and white-tailed deer population thrives in this protected habitat.

In the shallow marshes look for native birds such as anhingas, ospreys, limpkins, herons, egrets, both black and turkey vultures, and even bald eagles. In winter, the bird population mushrooms with the arrival of migratory waterfowl, including hooded merganser, American widgeon, and the always abundant American coot.

It's unlikely you will encounter an alligator, but if you do, stay far removed. Remember, in a sprint it can run faster than you can.

General Description: Short hiking trails bordering the world's largest and deepest fresh water spring.

General Location: South of Tallahassee.

Maps: None needed.

Difficulty: Easy.

Special Attractions: Scenic boat tours on the jungle-like spring run.

Season: Anytime.

Camping:: None, but Wakulla Springs Lodge (built in 1937 and still decorated in 1930s style) offers overnight accommodations.

Information: Edward Ball Wakulla Springs State Park, 1 Spring Drive, Wakulla Springs, FL 32305; (904) 224-5950.

HIKE 24 SALLY WARD AND BYPASS TRAILS

Finding the trailhead: Take either State Road 365 or State Road 267 south from Tallahassee; turn onto State Road 61 to the park entrance. The Sally Ward Trail starts from the main lodge building.

The hikes: The main 0.75-mile Sally Ward trail leads from the Lodge to Sally Ward Spring. It parallels Sally Ward Creek, one of the sources of the Wakulla River.

The Bypass Trail makes a ten-minute detour from Sally Ward and goes through a small swamp—wet much of the time—and then rejoins the main Sally Ward Trail.

HIKE 25 HAMMOCK TRAIL

Finding the trailhead: This hike branches off at 0.75 mile on the Sally Ward Trail (See Hike 24).

The hike: This is the longest nature trail at Wakulla Springs, providing a forty-minute walk through old-growth hardwood forest. Hikers can join this

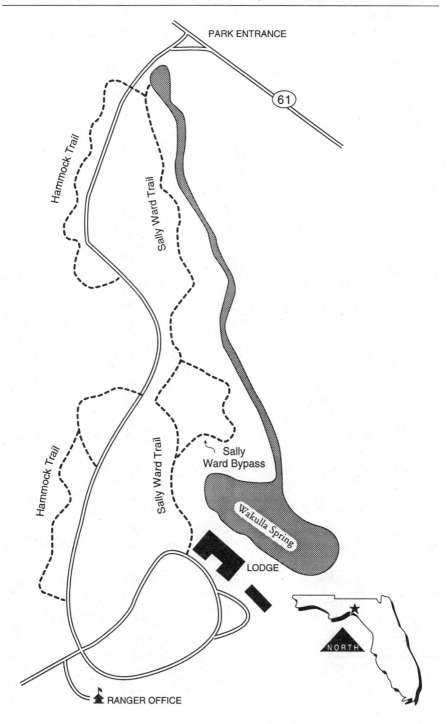

PARK ENTRANCE

61

Hammock Trail

Sally Ward Trail

Hammock Trail

Sally Ward Trail

Sally Ward Bypass

Wakulla Spring

LODGE

NORTH

RANGER OFFICE

1.25-mile trail at Sally Ward Spring, then follow it almost to the ranger office. The ranger office borders a sandhill pine forest, a remnant of the longleaf pine savannah that once occupied 70,000,000 acres throughout the South.

Lighthouse near Pensacola.

PANHANDLE CITY WALKS

PENSACOLA

Pensacola has an old, remarkably diverse downtown area divided into three different sections, some of which reflect the nationalities of the city. Five different flags have flown over this city, including Spanish, French, English, and Confederate. The occupiers were all drawn here because of the excellent natural harbor.

Two of the downtown neighborhoods are on the National Register of Historical Districts, and a third is considered a historic district by the city. A stroll through all three may take half a day or more if you stop in the museums and a few of the shops. This is one of Florida's most pleasant city walks, but few people seem aware of it. Instead, Pensacola is best known for its military installations and as the home to the Navy's precision flying team, the Blue Angels.

Although St. Augustine generally is regarded as the nation's oldest city, Pensacola can claim the distinction of being the first city settled. Spanish explorers apparently discovered Pensacola's deep-water harbor as early as 1519, and Spain quickly claimed this spot, at a place named Panzacola. Several later expeditions visited briefly, but in 1559 a colony of about 1,500 settlers arrived in the area. Founder Tristan de Luna reported to King Phillip that this was "the best port in the Indies."

Unfortunately, the colony did not fare well. It had to struggle throughout its two-year existence after a hurricane almost destroyed the settlement. Spain decided to abandon the site in 1561. St. Augustine was founded four years later, in 1565, and has been permanently settled ever since.

General Description: Walking tour of more than 100 city blocks in one of Florida's oldest and most historic port towns.

General Location: Downtown Pensacola.

Maps: Be sure to obtain a copy of "A Historical Guide to Pensacola" from the Visitor Information Center.

Difficulty: Easy.

Special Attractions: Remarkable examples of numerous architectural styles of the past two centuries; also several museums of West Florida history.

Season: Anytime.

Camping: Big Lagoon State Park, ten miles southwest of Pensacola on State Road 292; 104 sites.

73

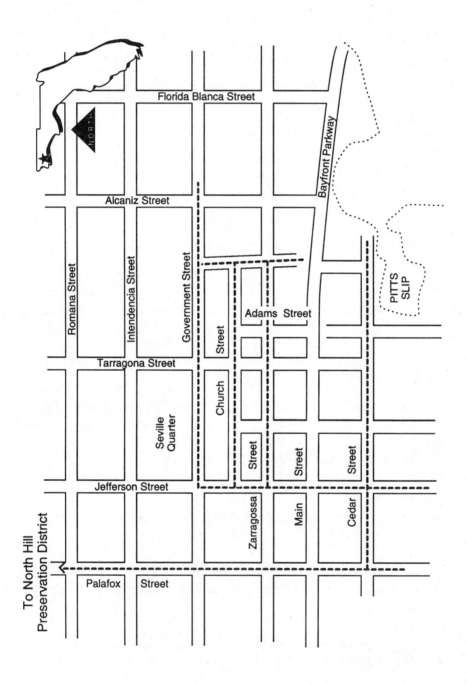

Information: Pensacola Convention & Visitors Information Center, 1401 East Gregory Street, Pensacola, FL 32501; (800) 874-1234 outside Florida; (800) 343-4321 within the state.

HIKE 26 PENSACOLA HISTORIC DISTRICTS

Directions: From Interstate 10, take Exit 1C to the first traffic light and turn left at the first stop light on South Tarragona Street, which has railroad tracks. Follow South Tarragona four blocks to Church Street; you are now at Historic Pensacola Village in the Seville Historic District.

The walk: The North Hill Preservation District was where lawyers, physicians, and businessmen built their homes between 1870 and the 1930s. Queen Anne, Neoclassical, Tudor Revival, Craftsman Bungalow, Art Moderne, and Mediterranean Revival are among the architectural styles in this fifty-block area. Homes of note are: 1215 North Reus Street (Mediterranean Revival, 1928); 204 West Brainerd (Neoclassical, 1910); 904 North Baylen Street (Queen Anne, circa 1900); 823 North Baylen (Queen Anne/Victorian, 1896); 1125 North Spring Street (Tudor Revival, 1929); and 10 West Wright (a Mission Revival Episcopal church, 1902).

The Palafox Historic District was the commercial heart of Old Pensacola where more than a dozen foreign consulates had their offices. Many of the wooden buildings were lost to fire and hurricanes. But quite a few remain, and some have been restored. Among the more noteworthy sites are the San Carlos Hotel at Palafox and Garden Streets, considered one of the South's finest hotels when completed in 1910. The Plaza Ferdinand VII was where Andrew Jackson formally received the state of Florida from Spain in 1821.

The Seville Historic District boasts an unusual abundance of Creole, Folk Victorian, and Frame Vernacular homes. But the most interesting section, known as Historic Pensacola Village, is a cluster of museums dedicated to the history of West Florida. Located on Zaragora Street between Adams and Tarragona, the museums (industry, commerce, Black history) are open from 10 a.m. to 4 p.m., closed Sundays.

TALLAHASSEE

Many people believe the name Tallahassee means "beautiful land" or "natural beauty." The Apalachee Indian name means something far different: "land of the old fields," "abandoned villages," or "old town." Paleolithic Indians roamed the area more than 12,000 years ago, but the name is more likely from the Mississippian Indians who moved into the area between 1250 and 1500.

In 1539, Spanish explorer Hernando de Soto set up a winter encampment in Tallahassee, using it as the starting point for the first European exploration of this new land. De Soto is believed to have held the first Christmas celebration in North America at Tallahassee.

In the 17th century, the Spanish created Franciscan missions among the Apalachee Indians. Skirmishes between the Indians and settlers resulted in the dispersal of the Indians and destruction the missions by 1704.

Tallahassee became Florida's capital city through a fluke of fate. In 1823 William Pope DuVal, first civilian governor in Florida, wanted a central location for the legislature to meet. He sent a horseman from St. Augustine and another by boat from Pensacola, and the two rendezvoused at the place the Indians called Tallahassee. That's how the city, only fourteen miles from the Georgia border and more than 400 miles from the state's southern tip, became the capital city.

Three log cabins served as the first government buildings. A two-story stone masonry capitol was erected in 1826; periodic expansions through the following decades always countered attempts to move the capital to a more centrally located city.

Tallahassee grew as a trade center with the arrival of the first railroad: a mule-drawn, rail trolley that connected Tallahassee with the port at St. Marks, sixteen miles distant. So much wealth flowed into the city that Calhoun Street was dubbed "Gold Dust Street." Park Avenue was first known as "200 Foot Street" and the name was changed because one of the town's leading ladies wanted a more sophisticated name on her son's wedding invitations. The oldest standing residence is "The Columns," a columned brick building from the 1830s; it's rumored to have a nickel embedded in every brick.

General Description: A stroll through Florida's capital city with its government buildings, former mansions—and a few rolling hills!

General Location: Near the eastern Panhandle boundary, in Leon County.

Maps: Available at the Visitor Information Center in the New Capitol Building.

Difficulty: Easy.

Special Attractions: The old Capitol Building, Florida State University campus, Museum of Florida History.

Season: Anytime.

Camping: None available.

Information: Tallahassee Area Visitor Information Center, P.O. Box 1369, Tallahassee, FL 32302; (800) 628-2866 or (904) 413-9200. Located in the New Capitol Building, the center conducts free, hourly tours of the Capitol building daily.

HIKE 27 TALLAHASSEE HISTORIC TRAIL

Directions: Follow Interstate 10 from the east or west, or U.S. Highway 27 from the south to downtown Tallahassee.

The walk: The Tallahassee Historic Trail offers fifty-nine historic buildings, an impressive eight-mile hike that takes four hours to complete. Obtain a copy of the "Downtown Tallahassee Historic Trail" from the Visitor Center located in the new Capitol Building, West Plaza Level on Duval Street. The brochure provides an excellent map and a brief description of each site.

A shorter tour—about an hour—is all that's needed to see the major government buildings. The Old Capitol building, which has undergone four major alterations, dates from 1845. Restored to its 1902 look, its Classical Revival style is overshadowed by the high-rise New Capitol towering just behind it.

HIKE 27 TALLAHASSEE HISTORIC TRAIL

NORTH

Boulevard St.
Brevard St.
Duval St.
Adams St.
Monroe St.
Dewey St.
Virginia St.
Calhoun St.
Meridian Rd.
Woodward St.
Tennessee St.
Call St.
Park Ave.
Bronough St.
College Ave.
Jefferson St.
Pensacola St.
St. Agustine St.
Apalachee Parkway/US 27
Gaines St.

✪ Indicates
Points of Interest

The First Presbyterian Church on North Adams Street built in 1838 is the only territorial church remaining in Tallahassee. It served as a town refuge during the Seminole raids of 1838 and 1839. The church's north gallery was set aside for slaves, who were allowed to join but had to sit apart from their masters.

Tombstones personalize the past by giving us names to ponder, so don't miss the Old City Cemetery (1829) and St. John's Episcopal Cemetery (1840). The Old City Cemetery holds a true cross-section of early Tallahassee society, from slaves to soldiers to governors. St. John's contains notable royalty: Prince Achille Murat, nephew of Napoleon Bonaparte, and his wife Catherine, great-grandniece of George Washington.

Most of the historic homes are on Park Avenue and Calhoun Street. Park Avenue, originally Tallahassee's northern boundary, is the city's oldest neighborhood. Listed on the National Register of Historical Places, it also includes a number of churches (including St. John's Episcopal) and government buildings. Calhoun Street developed during the 1840s strictly as a residential area.

NORTH FLORIDA INLAND HIKES

Although these hikes are all inland, none are far from water. Florida is veined with sizable and fascinating rivers. The riverside hikes are among the state's most interesting and most scenic.

SUWANNEE RIVER STATE PARK–ELLAVILLE

This 1,838-acre park contains both the Withlacoochee and Suwannee Rivers within its boundaries. The name Withlacoochee is uncommon enough, but Florida manages to have two rivers with this name. One is farther south between Ocala and Tampa. This Withlacoochee begins in Georgia and ends here in the Suwannee River.

This river junction was the site of several settlements though little evidence of them remains. The town of Columbus once stood here; it is completely obliterated except for a graveyard. A Florida governor once owned a stately mansion here, close to where the two rivers meet; the great house later turned into a decaying ghost house.

The Confederates built earthworks here to protect a railroad bridge sought by Union troops as they advanced from Jacksonville. The earthworks, at least, still exist.

General Description: A 4.6-mile extension of the Florida Trail inside the park, another seventeen miles of pathway bordering the Suwannee and Withlacoochee Rivers.

General Location: Thirteen miles west of the town of Live Oak and fifteen miles east of the city of Madison on the north side of U.S. Highway 90. The appropriate exit is well marked on Interstate 10.

Maps: Not essential.

Difficulty: Easy to moderate, depending on rain.

Season: Fall to early spring.

Camping: Thirty-one sites.

Information: Suwannee River State Park, Route 8, Box 297, Live Oak, FL 32060; (904) 362-2746.

HIKE 28 SUWANNEE RIVER STATE PARK-ELLAVILLE

Finding the trailhead: Take County Road 141 to the Withlacoochee River Bridge near the state park. Look for the Florida Trail sign. You now have the option of hiking east into the park or going southwest on the longer Ellaville route.

Suwannee River State Park.

SUWANNEE RIVER STATE PARK

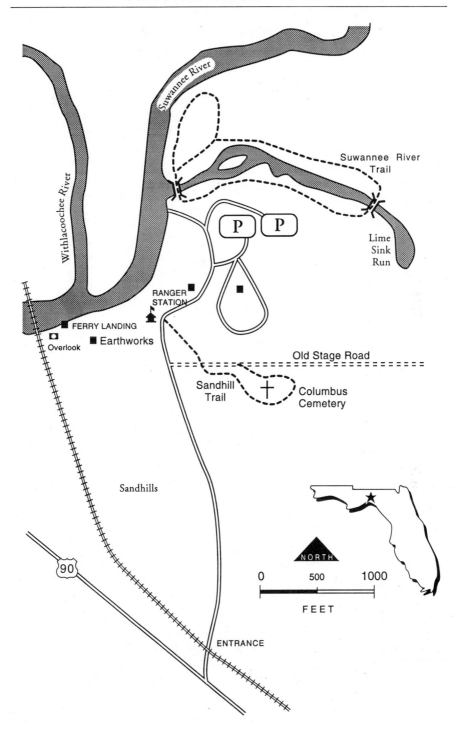

Suwannee River

Withlacoochee River

Suwannee River Trail

Lime Sink Run

P   P

RANGER STATION

FERRY LANDING

Overlook

Earthworks

Old Stage Road

Sandhill Trail

Columbus Cemetery

Sandhills

90

NORTH

0   500   1000

FEET

ENTRANCE

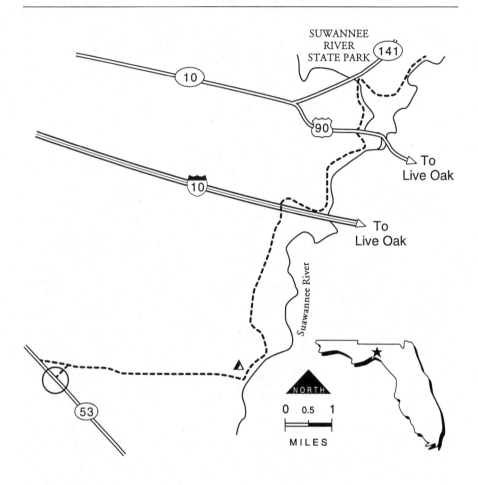

The hike: It could be argued that the park section, the shortest, is also the most scenic, since a considerable stretch at the western end of the Ellaville leg is mostly paved county roads.

Going west to east into the state park, begin at the white blazes at the state park boundary. The trail passes under power lines, by an underground stream that surfaces as a pair of sinkholes and by a public boat ramp. You'll have to retrace your steps back to the Withlacoochee River Bridge on County Road 141, where the Ellaville route begins.

The following distances for the Ellaville leg are computed from the trailhead on County Road 141 and do not include the 4.6-mile state park section. You'll find an old campsite on the Withlacoochee after about a mile, but look for the main campsite after crossing railroad tracks and old Route 90, at almost two miles. Less than a 0.5 mile farther, after crossing U.S. 90, there's a bluff campsite overlooking the Suwannee.

The trail then goes under some power lines, leaves the river to parallel I-10, and then crosses the interstate at the River Ranch Road overpass. You're soon off the thoroughfare as you pass an abandoned homestead, follow a fire lane, and reach another river campsite (mile 11.3). From here the route follows a graded road for four miles, or almost until the end at State Road 53.

STEPHEN FOSTER STATE FOLK CULTURE CENTER

Songwriter Stephen Foster, born July 4, 1826, wrote such American classics as "Oh! Susanna," "Camptown Races," "Jeanie With the Light Brown Hair," and "My Old Kentucky Home." Known as America's Troubadour, he also immortalized the Suwannee River (as in "way down upon") in "Old Folks At Home," which Florida adopted as its official state song in 1935.

As you stroll the grounds, keep in mind you are not following in Foster's footsteps. He never saw the Suwannee, but liked the sound of it. He never saw any part of Florida, for that matter.

The Folk Culture Center, on the banks of the Suwannee, is intended to memorialize Stephen Foster and to serve as a gathering place for those who perpetuate the crafts, music, and legends of early Florida. You may hear the carillon tower chiming out Stephen Foster songs on the hour and half-hour

Stephen Foster State Folk Culture Center.

almost anywhere you happen to be in the park. The tower rises directly in back of the plantation-styled Visitor Center where you can see the desk Foster used to write "Old Folks At Home," a piano on which he often played, and scenes from some of his most famous works.

A Folk Culture Celebration (Memorial Day Weekend) and an Old Fashioned Fourth of July are held here each year.

General Description: A four-mile leg of the Florida National Scenic Trail along the bank of the Suwannee River. This is the only section of trail that continuously borders such a large river.

General Location: In the town of White Springs between Jacksonville and Tallahassee.

Maps: None needed.

Difficulty: Easy to moderate riverbank hike, depending on the amount of rain. The Folk Center is wheelchair accessible.

Special Attractions: A folk culture center dedicated to Foster.

Season: Anytime except periods of sustained heavy rain.

Camping: Not available.

Information: Stephen Foster State Folk Culture Center, P.O. Drawer G, White Springs, FL 32906; (904) 397-2733.

HIKE 29   STEPHEN FOSTER FOLK CENTER

Finding the trailhead: Take the U.S. Highway 41 exit off Interstate-10, follow to White Springs. The folk center is on the left, at the bottom of a hill. The trailhead is near the large white building (known as the spring house) also on the left, just outside the center entrance, that overlooks the Suwannee River.

The hike: This four-mile riverside hike runs from one end of the park to the other, right along the river bank, leading east to west. The trail is blazed in white. The walk provides an excellent look at Florida's most famous, cypress-lined river. Near the folk center you'll notice high water marks posted several places on the banks. As these show, the trail is sometimes several feet underwater and not passable then. White lilies, dogwood, redbud trees, sparkleberries, and azaleas in bloom can turn the pathway into a beautiful garden walk. At the end of the trail, you'll need to retrace your steps to the park entrance.

Returning to the spring house and following the blazes west to east, you can link up with the thirty-five mile long National Scenic Trail that passes through the Osceola National Forest (see Hike 30).

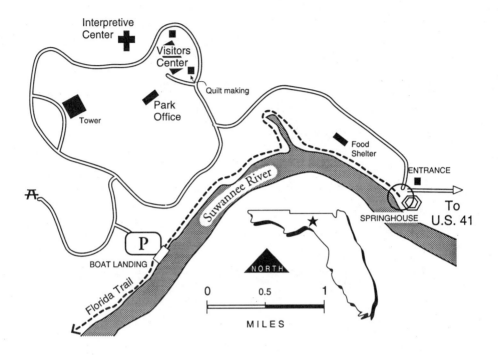

OSCEOLA NATIONAL FOREST

This forest, made up primarily of pine flatwoods, has long been in the middle of the struggle over what constitutes proper "public use." Mining companies holding leases to a considerable portion of the forest wanted to strip mine it for phosphate. That, of course, would destroy the ecosystem along with its aesthetic qualities. The Florida Wilderness Bill now restricts that.

In late spring, visitors can pick blueberries and blackberries in any number of places. Old "borrow pits," where soil was removed to fill in low lands elsewhere, are also found throughout the forest. Many of these are now filled with water and make excellent places for "lakeside" camping or sacking out.

The southernmost trailhead at Olustee Battlefield State Historic Site is also the location of Florida's largest Civil War battle. The monument built in 1912 commemorates the meatgrinding battle that took place February 20, 1864, when Union and Confederate forces of about 5,500 men clashed from noon to dark. The casualties were staggering: 1,861 on the Union side and 946 on the Confederate. Union forces withdrew to Jacksonville for the rest of the war and never made a major foray here again. The battle is re-enacted with costumed participants every February.

General Description: A thirty-five mile leg of the Florida Trail through the 157,000-acre Osceola National Forest, a public hunting area.

General Location: Just west of Jacksonville.

Maps: Available from the forest service.

Difficulty: Easy to moderate.

Special Attractions: Site of Florida's largest Civil War battle.

Season: Fall to spring.

HIKE 30 OSCEOLA NATIONAL FOREST

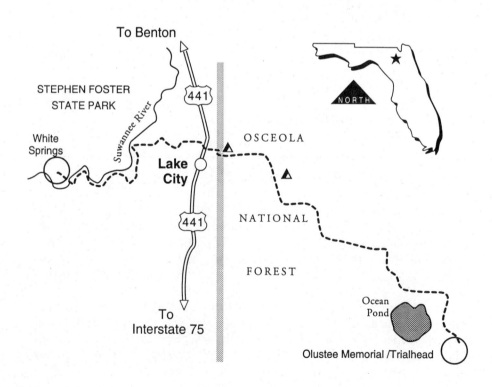

Camping: Available at Ocean Pond near the Olustee Battlefield.

Information: District Ranger, U.S. Forest Service, P.O. Box 70, Olustee, FL 32072; (904) 752-2577.

HIKE 30 OSCEOLA NATIONAL FOREST

Finding the trailhead: From Interstate -10 take U.S. Highway 90 south at the Lake City or Sanderson exits to the Stephen Foster State Folk Culture Center. The trail begins near the white spring house just outside the park gate.

The hike: Overall, the entire trail is much more user-friendly these days since the U.S. Forest Service constructed almost three dozen catwalks and crossings over streams that once had to be waded.

Leaving the Stephen Foster Folk Center, the first four or five miles of the hike run atop some of the steepest banks on the Suwannee River. At first, the trail follows U.S. 41 and crosses the Suwannee on the State Road 136 bridge. The track follows the Suwannee's south bank, passes Waldron Landing, and leaves the river at Bell Springs.

After crossing Robinson Creek on a log bridge, the trail arrives at Big Shoals, Florida's only whitewater rapids—also a popular campsite (mile 8.5). Then it's along a fence line to junction with Old River Road, which in turn joins St. James Church Road. From St. James the trail moves onto Trash Pile Road, which leads to U.S. 441 and eventually the Osceola National Forest boundary (mile 14.5). After following a jeep road, and Forest Road 237, you'll arrive at the West Tower campsite, which also has drinking water (mile 18.5). The next ten miles of trail cross forest roads, following jeep trails. Watch for the 0.5-mile blue-blazed side trail to Ocean Pond, one of the most pleasant campsites in the forest (swimming!).

From Ocean Pond to Olustee Battlefield is only another six miles. The trail meanders through cypress swamps and pine flatlands, passing two primitive campsites before the hike's end at U.S. 90 at Olustee.

One of the more unusual creatures you may see on this long hike is the gopher tortoise, which lives in burrows in the earth. Gopher tortoises belong to a group of twenty-three species of land tortoises that originated about sixty million years ago. All but four species are extinct, and the gopher tortoise itself is in serious trouble.

These tortoises play an important role in forest ecology. Their burrows (which may be twenty-eight feet long and ten feet deep) provide a comfortable constant temperature throughout the year for themselves and many other animals—it sometimes seems that all the forest critters able to fit inside, do.

Gopher tortoises may live as long as forty years. About the only place you'll see a gopher is when he is sunning just outside his burrow, ready to hide at a moment's notice. If you see one sunning, observe or photograph it quietly. At the least, you'll certainly see the burrow holes scattered throughout the woods.

O'LENO STATE PARK

This 6,000-acre park sounds like a place that could have been named after some obscure Irish clan, but O'Leno has a far more colorful and bizarre history. In a roundabout way, the name derives from the small settlement established here on the banks of the Santa Fe in the early 1800s. It was first called Keno, after a form of lotto gambling. Religious leaders found the name unsuitable and managed to have it changed to Leno, perhaps because "L" is the next letter after "K."

The lumber town grew and prospered, with its own mill, hotel, and general store. Leno also marked the farthest southern point of Florida's first telegraph line. However, Leno faded into obscurity when the railroad passed it by, and the town died forever shortly after 1900. The site came to be called Old Leno, then shortened to O'Leno (a Southern contraction, like y'all).

A wonderful old suspension bridge, built in the 1930s, crosses the Santa Fe.

General Description: Several hikes totaling thirteen-miles along the banks of the Santa Fe River, a tributary of the Suwannee.

General Location: Between Gainesville and Lake City.

Swinging bridge at O'Leno State Park.

O'LENO STATE PARK

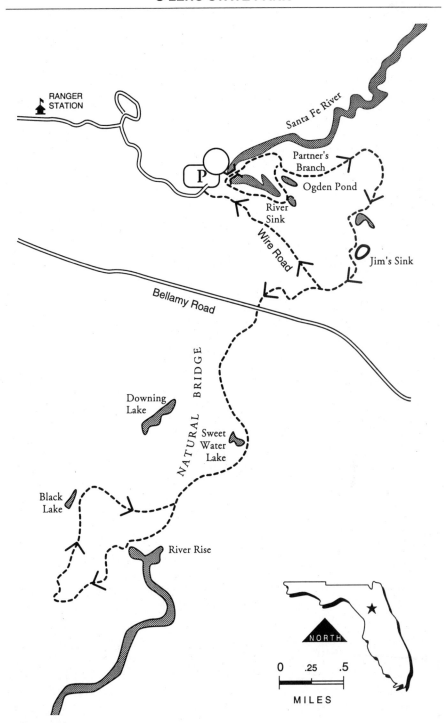

RANGER STATION

Santa Fe River

Partner's Branch

Ogden Pond

River Sink

Wire Road

Jim's Sink

Bellamy Road

NATURAL BRIDGE

Downing Lake

Sweet Water Lake

Black Lake

River Rise

NORTH

0   .25   .5

MILES

Maps: Obtain at the entrance gate.

Difficulty: Easy.

Special Attractions: The Santa Fe River flows through the park, disappearing underground for three miles before returning to the surface. Sinkholes, hardwood hammocks, and sandhill communities line the trail.

Season: Fall to spring.

Camping: Sixty-four sites in two separate areas, most with facilities; plus primitive camping, and eighteen rental cabins of varying capacities.

Information: O'Leno State Park, Route 2, Box 1010, High Springs, FL 32643; (904) 454-1853. To hike the full length of the trail, register at the park entrance.

HIKE 31 LIMESTONE TRAIL

Finding the trailhead: To reach the park, follow U.S. 41 from Lake City; the park is twenty miles south of Lake City. The Limestone Trail is just inside the entrance gate, on the left.

The hike: This short loop trail meanders through a transitional forest of hardwood and pine.

HIKE 32 RIVER SINK TRAIL

Finding the trailhead: Park near the suspension bridge that spans the Santa Fe. The trailhead is to the right of the bridge before you cross.

The hike: This forty-five-minute loop trail circles around the place where the river goes underground. Begin on the right branch of the loop, which borders the fast-flowing Santa Fe, gurgling and foaming before it disappears from sight. This spot, called the river sink, looks like someone constructed an earthen dam to block the river. The pool where the river ends is often filled with green duckweed, and sunning turtles frequently line the bank. This is a truly deceptive appearance, since the river continues to flow underground for the next three miles, showing itself occasionally in the form of narrow fingers of water. Boardwalks and overlooks provide a closeup look at the river sink.

HIKE 33 PARTNER'S BRANCH LOOP

Finding the trailhead: This hike branches off the River Sink Trail. The path is on the right after you pass Ogden Pond, marked by an interpretive sign and bench.

The hike: Partner's Branch wanders along a series of depressions, ponds, and sinks—all reminders of what is pouring through the ground underfoot. Note the sections of hardwood and sandhill areas that have been burned, a natural and necessary process for this type of habitat to survive. The return loop is known as the Old Wire Road, filled with ruts from the wagons of pioneer settlers. This is where the first telegraph line in the state was strung. This final leg of the Partner's Branch Loop can become something of a quagmire after heavy rains.

HIKE 34 RIVER RISE TRAIL

Finding the trailhead: The path splits off from the Partners Branch Trail shortly after Jim's Sink.

The hike: This longest section crosses the rest of the land bridge or "natural bridge" formed where the Santa Fe River disappears for three miles. Early explorers also took advantage of this phenomenon: the old Spanish Trail also crossed the natural bridge, as well as a stagecoach road in the 1800s. Hiking here, it's a strange and sobering thought to imagine the Santa Fe flowing beneath your feet, rushing through a series of dark, flooded subterranean passageways. The trail passes the river rise where the Santa Fe gushes back out of the ground and continues its course as a normal surface river. The trail makes a loop shortly after the rise, then retraces itself back to the Partner's Branch Loop.

PAYNES PRAIRIE STATE PRESERVE

Paynes Prairie is one of the most unusual natural areas in Florida. The prairie is a constantly changing place; sometimes a wet marsh, sometimes a fire-ravaged plain. This huge basin was formed thousands of years ago, when rain dissolved the underlying limestone and the terrain sank. For this reason, most of the plain is covered by marsh, wet prairie, and areas of open water. The uplands surrounding it are considerably more diverse, with pine flatwoods, lush hammocks, swamps, and many ponds, which attract a variety of wildlife.

Indian artifacts found here date back as far as 10,000 years ago. The Seminoles were the prairie's last Indian inhabitants, and it is thought the prairie may have been named for King Payne, a Seminole chief. In the late 1600s, this basin was the largest Spanish cattle ranch in Florida.

The state intends to keep the area as natural as possible, which means nature is allowed to take care of itself.

Left alone, nature has played some strange tricks here. The most bizarre occurred in 1881, when nearby Alachua Sink clogged up and Paynes Prairie turned into a lake. This gave paddlewheel steamers a new passageway into the interior, and they quickly capitalized on it as an important cargo route. Then, in 1891, the sink opened up and the lake drained almost overnight, leaving the steamboats high and dry.

What are bison doing here? They were once a natural part of Paynes Prairie, so the state introduced a small herd, which roams free in a 6,000-acre area. There was never more than a small population in the past, but the re-

A wildfire in the distance in the Paynes Prairie State Preserve.

introduction of the animals coincides with the state plan to restore the area to its original status. The animals are most frequently seen near the visitor center observation tower, Cone's Dike, or the platform at Alachua Lake. But these bison are shy, and you'll be fortunate if you do see them.

Should bison appear while you are on foot, keep your distance. Bison can be quite brutal, as injured tourists in Yellowstone National Park learn every year. If an bison raises its tail, retreat immediately—it is a sign the animal may charge.

Bison are certainly the largest animals of Paynes Prairie, but many other species live here. The trick is being able to spot them in the grass. Paynes Prairie is home to white-tailed deer, wild turkey, white ibis, pileated woodpeckers, hawks, egrets, and meadowlarks.

It is also one of the most important wintering grounds for East Coast sandhill cranes. Sandhill cranes, sometimes called "rusty nail birds," have a piercing cry similar to a nail being pried from a board. Paynes Prairie also has a reputation for its many species of snakes, so in summer look before you step when you're out on the grassy plain.

Paynes Prairie is divided into two districts, the North Rim Interpretive Center and the Southern Visitor Center. The Visitor Center is just off U.S. Highway 441, ten miles south of Gainesville, or one mile north of Micanopy.

PAYNES PRAIRIE STATE PRESERVE

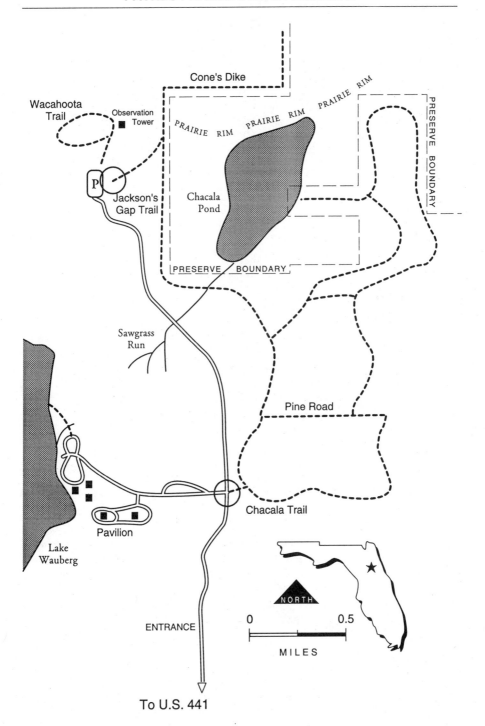

General Description: A series of short hikes through the 18,000-acre preserve, a mostly grassy, treeless expanse.

General Location: Just south of Gainesville.

Maps: Obtain at the visitor center.

Difficulty: Easy to moderate.

Special Attractions: The chance to see American bison (buffalo) roaming Florida's own version of the Great Plains. Organized overnight backpacking trips and wildlife walks are held regularly, particularly during the winter months. **Note:** the headquarters of the Florida Trail Association is located on U.S. 441 just north of Paynes Prairie. Their small white building is well marked and easily visible from the road.

Season: Fall to early spring.

Camping: Fifteen tent sites and thirty-five RV sites.

Information: Paynes Prairie State Preserve, Route 2, Box 41, Micanopy, FL 32667-9702; (904) 466-3397.

HIKE 35 GAINESVILLE-HAWTHORNE STATE TRAIL

Finding the trailhead: At Boulware Springs Road in the city of Gainesville.

The hike: This is a Rails-to-Trails project that passes through part of Paynes Prairie. The seventeen-mile walk traverses Paynes Prairie and Lockloosa Wildlife Management Area, and ends at the city of Hawthorne. The trail features several overlooks with good views of the prairie.

Hiking, cycling, and horseback riding are all permitted on this old railbed. The trail is open from 8 a.m. to sunset daily. Don't wander from the trail—much of the adjacent land is off limits to the public.

HIKE 36 LA CHUA

Finding the trailhead: Begin at the North Rim Interpretive Center located off U.S. Highway 441 just south of Gainesville. The entrance is marked. La Chua also intersects with the Gainesville-Hawthorne Trail, about 1.7 miles from the Gainesville trailhead.

The hike: The buildings at the La Chua trailhead were once bunkhouses or warehouses of the Camp Ranch that operated from the beginning of the 20th century to 1970, when the state acquired the property. This three-mile trail leads into the prairie for a close-up look of the habitat.

Sections of both the La Chua and Gainesville-Hawthorne trails are sometimes closed due to high water, fire management, or nesting birds and alligators.

HIKE 37 BOLEN BLUFF

Finding the trailhead: Begin off U.S. 441 at the southern end of the prairie. A sign marks the start.

The hike: A one-mile walk through both mixed forest and prairie habitat.

HIKE 38 WACAHOOTA

Finding the trailhead: Starts from the visitor center parking lot in the park's southern section. Look for the sign.

The hike: At 0.5-mile, this is the shortest walk at Paynes Prairie. It wanders through mixed forest and prairie.

HIKE 39 CONE'S DIKE

Finding the trailhead: Also begins from the visitor center parking lot in the southern section. Look for sign.

The hike: This six-mile hike offers a longer look at mixed forest and the prairie.

HIKE 40 CHACALA

Finding the trailhead: This well marked trailhead is located at the first main intersection inside the southern part of the park.

The hike: Through a series of loops, you can travel up to eight miles through pine flatwood, mixed forest, and scrub sandhill communities. This is a popular trail for local horsemen.

GOLD HEAD BRANCH STATE PARK

It seems people panned for gold everywhere, including Gold Head Branch, a small stream created by freshwater springs that flow into Little Lake Johnson. Miners actually found some color, though in limited quantities.

The park itself is one of the oldest in the Florida park system, dating back to 1939. Its 1,562-acres were developed as a Civilian Conservation Corps project. The lakes here hold bass, bream, and speckled perch (fishing license required), and you can swim in Lake Johnson.

General Description: A three-mile section of the Florida Trail, plus several short hikes of a mile or less through extremely diverse habitat in an area that once produced gold.

General Location: Between the cities of Palatka and Starke.

Maps: None needed.

Difficulty: Easy, unless you have difficulty climbing stairs.

Special Attractions: A walk through a deep ravine, where the air is always cooler and the vegetation markedly different from topside.

Season: Fall to spring.

Camping: Seventy-four sites with all facilities; also a primitive camping area. Fourteen rental cottages are available at Lake Johnson.

Information: Gold Head Branch State Park, 6239 State Road 21, Keystone Heights, FL 32356; (904) 473-4701. In addition to the marked trails, you'll find throughout the park numerous dirt roads, open only to foot traffic, that lead off from the entrance road. These allow you to explore more of the sandhill habitat where you may see gray squirrels and foxes.

HIKE 41 RIDGE TRAIL

Finding the trailhead: Take State Road 21 six miles northeast of the town of Keystone; the park is on the right. The well marked path begins at the Ravine, the park's most prominent natural feature.

The hike: This mile-long trail meanders along the ravine's upper ridge. At first, the trail descends on a boardwalk into the steep, water-carved ravine, a remarkably shady and cool place, perfect for a stroll on a warm day. This lowland oasis with its canopy of hardwoods is different from the rest of the park, which is a dry, scrub sandhill community, mostly high pineland.

The ravine's cooler, moist climate, with thick ground covering, provides ideal conditions for large, curving hickory trees, cinnamon ferns three to four feet high, shiny-leafed Southern magnolia, and American holly. As the trail climbs the slope, oak trees dominate, then longleaf pines. Keep an eye out for barred owls and woodpeckers, quite common throughout this area. The trail ends at the site of an old mill.

HIKE 42 LOBLOLLY TRAIL

Finding the trailhead: Start across the bridge at the old mill site, as an extension of the Ridge Trail.

The hike: This 0.5-mile loop trail features the loblolly pine, a large, fast-growing tree that may reach 90 to 110 feet. They grow best in a wet basin, which early colonists called a "loblolly"; hence the tree's name.

Many more plant species line the trail: white-flowering dogwoods, a favorite ornamental that occurs throughout the state; tallowwood, the bark of which is used to tan leather; red bay, with long aromatic leaves that add flavor to soups and stews; and the green, fan-shaped saw palmetto, bearing black fruit that was once a staple food for the Indians.

Many of the longleaf pines still carry scars of the turpentine industry that flourished here before this became a park. The trees were cut with diagonal grooves and metal strips were nailed on to divert the gum or sap into red clay

GOLD HEAD BRANCH STATE PARK

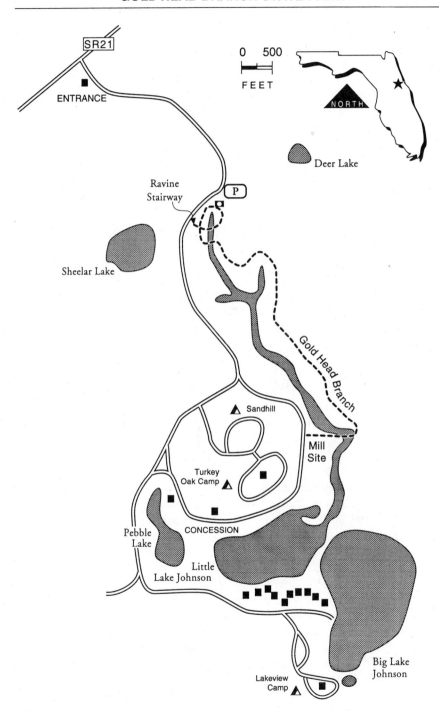

pots. Because these scars often resemble a cat scratch, the trees are sometimes referred to as "cat face."

The trail ends at the site of the old combination grist mill and cotton gin that in the late 1800s diverted water from Gold Head Branch for its operation.

HIKE 43 FLORIDA TRAIL

Finding the trailhead: The trail starts near the park entrance; ask at the gate.

The hike: Although this trail extension totals more than thirty miles, the general public is permitted on only a three-mile segment; the rest is on private land and open to the public. The short trail passes Deer Lake and goes through the ravine to end at the park's southern boundary.

OCALA NATIONAL FOREST

The 360,000-acre Ocala National Forest was the first designated national forest east of the Mississippi River. The Big Scrub, as it is affectionately known, is the world's largest stand of sand pine scrub forest. It also contains one of the most scenic extensions of the Florida National Scenic Trail, what the Florida Trail Association calls the "crown jewel" of the 1,300-mile system.

Ocala's seventy-five-mile leg passes through rolling hills and longleaf pine forests, skirts as many as sixty ponds, and ventures into numerous cypress and gum swamps. Usually, hikers don't need to worry about soaked feet in the swamps since many of the wet spots are spanned by boardwalks.

Ocala is an outdoor paradise. Scores of tiny lakes are hidden away in the forest, many of them ideal for fishing and primitive camping. Developed camping areas are found at Alexander Springs and Juniper Springs, two fresh water springs that double as natural swimming pools.

At Alexander Springs, the bottom slopes away to a depth of thirty feet near the middle, which makes it an ideal training ground for scuba diving classes. Fish life along the right bank is prolific and easily accessible to snorkelers. Canoes can be rented from a concessionaire on the grounds.

Nearby Juniper Springs, which is much smaller, doesn't attract the same crowds as Alexander Springs because of the lack of diving and swimming opportunities. Juniper's spring boil, where the water gushes out of the ground, has been modernized into a huge concrete-lined swimming pool.

And Ocala is perhaps the only place in Florida where you can plumb the depths of a 100-foot sinkhole and never get wet. Most deep sinkholes are filled with water because of the state's high water table, but this one is dry.

The scrub jay, a threatened species that is one of Florida's most interesting and attractive birds, is frequently sighted in the Ocala forest. A

A young angler displays his catch, a largemouth bass taken in one of the lakes of the Ocala National Forest.

member of the crow family, scrub jays are common throughout the south-western United States; east of the Mississippi, they live only in Florida.

As the name implies, scrub jays live around the thickets of short bushy oaks known as scrub. They feed on acorns and, just like squirrels, sometimes bury the acorns for future use.

Scrub jays are wary when feeding. Normally, one bird will act as a sentinel while the others eat. Yet scrub jays also become quite accustomed to people and often visit the most heavily used parts of the forest.

General Description: Two legs of the Florida National Scenic Trail totaling almost seventy-five miles are considered the prettiest part of the entire system. A public hunting area.

General Location: East of the town of Ocala.

Maps: Obtain from Forest Service office for two dollars.

Difficulty: Easy to moderate.

Special Attractions: The pathway penetrates the world's largest stand of sand pine.

Season: Late fall to spring.

Camping: Available as primitive sites or developed campgrounds.

Information: Lake George District, 17147 East Highway 40, Silver Springs, FL 34488; (904) 625-2520.

HIKE 44 OCALA NORTH

Finding the trailhead: Take State Road 19 about eight miles south of the town of Palatka. Look for a side road that leads to a lock of the Florida Barge Canal. Park at the lock.

The hike: This forty-six-mile hike starts at a lock of the now-abandoned Florida Barge Canal. The trail crosses the barge canal lock, which is open from 8 a.m. to 5 p.m. Hikers may need to use a whistle to attract the attendant's attention. At about mile seven the trail arrives at the spillway of Rodman Dam, built as part of the barge canal project. Environmentalists now want to remove the dam so the Oklawaha River can be returned to its natural state. In the meantime, the spillway is a popular place to fish.

Continuing south, the trail crosses forest roads 77, 31, 88, and 75, then to the shores of Lake Delancey (mile fourteen), a good spot for water and camping. A second campsite is at mile 18.5, at Grassy Pond.

From Grassy Pond, the trail crosses Forest Road 88, County Road 316, County Road 318, Forest Road 88 again, and Forest Road 51. Shortly afterwards (mile thirty), comes a junction with a three-mile side trail leading to the Salt Springs Recreation Area, which has complete facilities and a swimming-pool-like natural springs.

Back on the main trail continue across forest roads 90 and 65 to Hopkins Prairie, which offers complete facilities and lakeside camping at mile thirty-five.

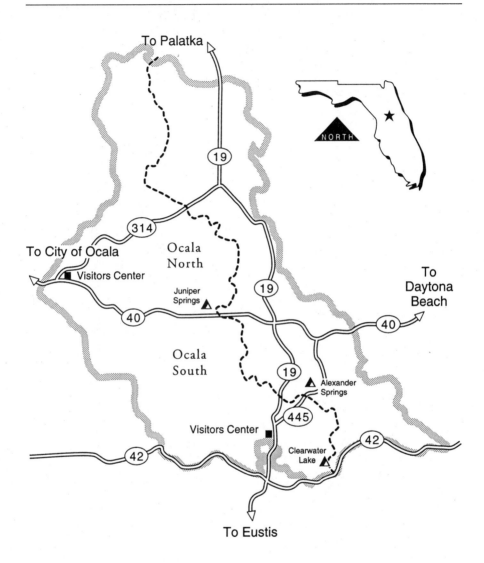

From Hopkins Prairie, the trail crosses Forest Road 86 and then the north side of Pat's Island. Now the trail enters a wilderness area where hunting is never permitted. Cross forest roads 10 and 76 to arrive at Hidden Pond, with primitive sites and another chance to swim (mile forty-one).

From here, the trail crosses Whiskey Creek and Whispering Creek (you may have to wade during high water). It then skirts the south edge of Juniper Prairie and arrives at Juniper Springs Recreation Area, one of the two largest campgrounds in the forest.

HIKE 45 OCALA SOUTH

Finding the trailhead: Going north to south, begin at Juniper Springs Recreation Area off State Road 40, just west of the junction with State Road 19.

The hike: This hike traverses almost twenty-eight miles of pine and hardwood forests, offering one of Florida's drier hiking routes. Leaving Juniper Springs Recreation Area, the trail crosses State Road 40, then follows a boardwalk over a stretch of marshland. After crossing Forest Road 599, the trail arrives at Farles Prairie (mile 5.5), a huge grassy expanse that's often an excellent place for spotting wildlife. Hikers can camp here.

Crossing Forest Road 595, follow the blue-blazed trail (mile eight) that goes 0.1 mile east to a campsite with water and latrines.

Continue two more miles to another blue-blazed side trail that loops around Buck Lake, one of Ocala's more popular "wilderness" campgrounds. Then the trail crosses County Road 9277, State Road 19, Forest Road 525, and State Road 445 to reach the blue-blazed half-mile trail that leads to the Alexander Springs Recreation Area (mile 16.5).

Back on the main trail, follow a series of boardwalks: a long one before Forest Road 539, and several short ones through another swamp. At mile twenty-two, the trail cuts through a power line right-of-way, then follows a boardwalk over a creek. Go across Forest Road 538, then a backwoods dirt road. Almost at the end of the hike, look for the Golden Blaze Tree. Marked in 1986, it commemorates the twenty years that went into establishing the Ocala Trail.

Walk a few hundred more yards to a blue-blazed trail to Clearwater Lake Campground. Officially, the Ocala Trail ends at County Road 42, just east of the campground entrance.

HIKE 46 LAKE EATON SINKHOLE

Finding the trailhead: From State Road 40 near Mill Dam, take Forest Road 79 and follow the winding road until the sinkhole sign appears on the right.

The hike: This 0.5-mile walk to the sinkhole is a scenic one, through a forest of sand pine, scrub oak, and green palmetto fronds. Scrub jays, gray squirrels, and woodpeckers are the most obvious animals.

A sinkhole is created when water erodes the limestone base beneath the soil and the land collapses. In most places this huge hole—it's 122 feet deep and 450 feet wide—would have filled with water to become a pond or small lake, but the water table here is too low.

Vegetation inside the sink itself is not common to this type of forest. Closer to the water table and growing in heavy shade, magnolia trees, live oaks, loblolly pine, and sabal palms occupy the side and bottom of the great pit. The size of these trees and the small amount of organic material at the base of the sinkhole indicate the sinkhole is probably less than a 100 years old.

A sandhill crane in the Ocala National Forest.

Protected from the drying effects of wind, these trees are usually spared from the periodic fires that occur in the upper story sand pine forest. The last time the sand pine here was burned (intentionally, by the Forest Service because the short-lived pines were dying) was 1983.

You won't be able to stand in the deepest part of the sink because the boardwalk doesn't extend that far. The boardwalk was built to prevent erosion created by curious climbers scrambling up and down the sinkhole sides.

BULOW PLANTATION RUINS
STATE HISTORIC SITE

The once-magnificent Bulow Plantation was built in 1821 by Charles Bulow of Charleston, South Carolina, who also cleared much of the 2,500 acres for sugar cane, cotton, rice, and indigo.

Charles died after only three years of working the estate. The property was taken over by his son John, who fashioned it into one of the finest and wealthiest plantations in Florida. The sugar mill was one of the largest ever built in the state. Famed wildlife artist John James Audubon visited the estate in 1831, during a painting trip in Florida.

The Seminole Wars ended the prosperous plantation days. Ironically, John Bulow was opposed to the government's plan to send the Seminoles to reservations in the far west. Bulow went as far as firing a four-pound cannon at the state militia when it came on his land.

However, realizing the Seminoles were becoming increasingly hostile, Bulow and his slaves abandoned the plantation. In January 1836, the Seminoles attacked and burned every plantation built on land the Indians claimed belonged to them, including Bulow's. Disheartened, Bulow gave up and moved to Paris; he died before the age of twenty-seven.

Altogether, there were three Seminole Wars in Florida. The Seminoles were never defeated and never signed a peace treaty with the U.S. government. No other Indian tribe can make that claim.

All that remains today are the extensive coquina ruins of the sugar mill, a spring house, and the crumbling foundation of the great house. Interpretive signs at the sugar mill explain the entire process for making syrup from sugar cane. A small building adjacent contains artifacts found on the grounds.

General Description: A very short but striking section of the Florida Trail that encompasses ruins of Florida's largest sugar mill.

Maps: None needed.

Difficulty: Easy.

Special Attractions: Ruins of the old plantation; one of the best stands of live oak on Florida's east coast, including trees more than two hundred years old.

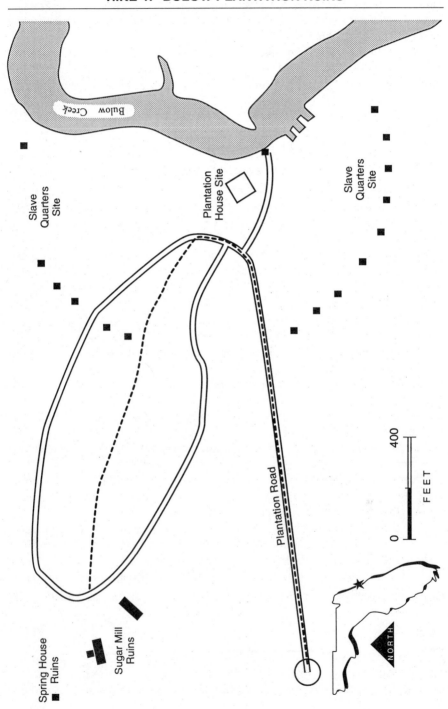

Bulow Creek

Slave Quarters Site

Plantation House Site

Slave Quarters Site

Plantation Road

Spring House Ruins

Sugar Mill Ruins

NORTH

0   400

FEET

Bulow Plantation ruins.

Best Season: Fall through spring.

Camping: Not available on site. Try Tomoka State Park (below).

Information: Bulow Plantation State Historic Site, P.O. Box 655, Bunnell, FL 32010; (904) 439-2219. Open 9 a.m. to 5 p.m.

HIKE 47 BULOW PLANTATION RUINS

Finding the trailhead: Take Exit 90 off Interstate 4 and go east less than a mile to County Road 2001, on the left. Follow the county road to the brown and white state marker at Plantation Road and turn right.

The hike: The plantation hike can be done several ways. The easiest is to drive the Plantation Road, park at the Plantation House site and walk the quarter mile to the sugar mill ruins. It is far more scenic to park at the beginning of Plantation Road and walking this beautifully canopied, narrow dirt route, something few people take the time to do.

Statue at Tomoka State Park.

TOMOKA STATE PARK

This state park boasts a forty-foot statue depicting Chief Tomokie defending a sacred golden cup. This brightly colored statue is impressive, but Chief Tomokie apparently never existed. The Fred Dana Marsh statue is based mostly on the artist's imagination.

Real or contrived, Chief Tomokie looms too large to ignore, so here is his legend. Once upon a time, there was a sacred spring from which a messenger of the "Great Spirit" would drink every evening, using a sacred gold cup. The dew from the messenger's wings gave the spring miraculous powers similar to Ponce de Leon's Fountain of Youth. Tomokie did not believe this story and so drank from the spring himself, using the sacred cup which had never before been touched by human hands.

This sacrilege caused war to break out between Tomokie's warriors and other Indian tribes. During battle, enemy arrows were unable to harm Tomokie until the beautiful Indian maiden Oleeta sprang forward and fired an arrow into his heart, killing him. Oleeta rushed forward and grabbed the cup, only to be killed by a poisoned arrow. Tomokie's followers were all killed, Oleeta was buried near the sacred spring, and the gold cup supposedly is still in the possession of the Indians today. The statue depicts Oleeta aiming her arrow at Tomokie, who is brazenly pouring water from the sacred cup while holding a spear. Her bow is drawn back, the arrow ready to fly.

If you're interested in Florida's early Indians be sure to take a look inside the Fred Dana Marsh Museum at some point. It contains a rare six-inch wooden statuette found in the bottom sediment of the Tomoka River in 1960. Wood artifacts normally rot quickly in Florida's humidity, so a find like this is a significant one. It is made from the Brazilwood tree, which today grows only in Central America. The source of the wood has generated endless speculation.

General Description: A fifteen-minute nature walk through the former Timucuan Indian village of Nocoroco, situated on a spit of land separating the Tomoka and Halifax rivers.

General Location: Just north of Daytona.

Maps: None needed.

Difficulty: Easy.

Special Attractions: A museum displaying rare wooden Indian artifacts, outdoor sculpture by artist Fred Dana Marsh depicting the legend of Chief Tomokie, canoeing in the Tomoka River, and fishing from shore.

Season: Fall to early spring.

Camping: 100 sites.

Information: Tomoka State Park, 2099 North Beach Street, Ormond Beach, FL 32174; (904) 676-4050.

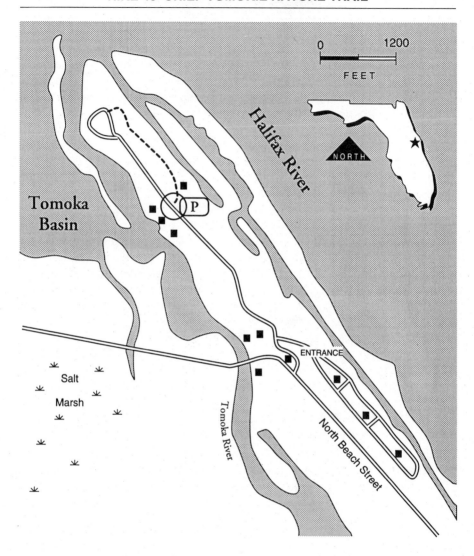

HIKE 48 CHIEF TOMOKIE NATURE TRAIL

Finding the trailhead: Follow County Road 2001 south from the Bulow Ruins (above). Or take the Ormond Beach exit off Interstate-4 just north of Daytona, go east to Beach Street and turn left at the brown and white sign pointing to the park. The walk begins at the Fred Dana Marsh Museum.

The hike: This nature walk through a rich coastal hammock is all too brief. From the museum, the shady trail leads to the picnic area and statue. In dry weather, the trail may be wheelchair accessible, but check with the park ranger at the entrance to be certain.

The sandy banks of the Tomoka River, visible from the statue, can be an excellent spot for bank fishing. Simply pick your spot and cast out; a fishing license is required.

But if you feel like walking farther—and there is something invigorating about this place—try a stroll on the road back to the park entrance, then retrace your steps to the museum parking lot. There are several shaded turn-offs, including one to the canoe concession, so this can be a nice thirty-minute walk each way.

HONTOON ISLAND STATE PARK

Hontoon may not be Robinson Crusoe's island, but in the mushrooming Central Florida region, it's the next best thing. Hontoon Island has no land access—visitors arrive by boat. The park service provides free ferry service, every fifteen minutes, across the narrow river channel separating Hontoon from the mainland. Just stand on the dock to attract the boatman's attention. The ferry boat is large enough to carry people only, no cars. The only motorized vehicles on the island belong to the parks people.

To camp here, visitors must lug their gear to the truck that hauls it to the campsite. Wise campers pack lightly. Or avoid the exertion altogether and stay in one of the handful of cottages located near the tent sites. The cottages come virtually complete, except for bedding and food. Plan meals carefully—there are no stores on the island. What you come without, you do without.

General Description: A wooded island hike of about three miles to a large Indian shell mound.

General Location: On the St. Johns River near the town of Deland.

Maps: None needed.

Difficulty: Easy.

Special Attractions: Indian mound; eighty-foot observation tower over-looking the St. Johns River.

Season: Fall through early spring.

Camping: Twenty-four campsites; also primitive cabins for rent.

Information: Hontoon Island State Park, Box 2096, Deland 32720; (904) 736-5309.

HIKE 49 HONTOON INDIAN MOUND

Finding the trailhead: Take U.S. Highway 17/92 to Deland from Interstate-4. Turn left onto State Road 17. Stay on 17 for several miles until reaching State Road 44; turn left. Follow the park signs to the parking lot. Walk to the end of the pier to board the park's ferry boat.

The hike: Start at the large owl totem pole near the dock. This is a replica of a Timucuan Indian totem pole found in the park, the only one like it discovered in the entire southeast. The original is now locked away safely in the Museum of Natural History in Tallahassee. One theory behind totem poles is that totems similar to these were used to identify a particular clan. Canoes approaching the island would be able to spot the totem from the water.

Next, walk through and beyond the children's recreation area and climb the eighty-foot high observation tower that provides an excellent overview of the region. From the top, you'll see the channel of the St. Johns you crossed to get to Hontoon Island. The 1,650-acre island spread out below includes a large open savannah; hammocks of pine, oak, and palms; and a cypress swamp.

The hike to the Indian shell mound takes about ninety minutes, roundtrip. Begin on the marked trail to the right of the dock and behind the administrative offices.

The trail ends on the bank of Snake Creek, a tributary of the St. Johns. Surrounded by lush growth, the shell mound is immense: 300 feet long, 100 feet wide, and thirty-five feet high.

Supposedly used either ceremonially or as a trash heap (depending on whose theory you believe), this mound and others like it probably served another important purpose: during periods of high water caused by hurricanes, they were the safest high ground available. There are several other shell mounds that form small islands in the St. Johns just to the north. Considering the tiny size of the snail shells that comprise this mound, it probably would have taken generations to build it.

This trail is an easy walk, but it can be wet in spots after heavy rains.

Hontoon Island Ferry.

BLUE SPRING STATE PARK

The West Indian Manatee is believed to be the basis of the mermaid legend because of its human-like face and broad beaver-like tail.

Manatees, which may weigh as much as a ton, eat up to a hundred pounds of vegetation every day. They once ranged from North Carolina to Texas, but destruction of their habitat through development and pollution has resulted in their almost complete extinction. Only Florida has a resident population of the animals, believed to number somewhere between 1,800 to 2,200.

The manatee, once a four-footed land creature, is a close relative of the elephant. A manatee's front flippers still have vestiges of what would have been nails. Manatees have no natural enemies, although human progress has certainly endangered their chances for survival.

General Description: A boardwalk skirting a wintering home of the endangered manatee. Also a four-mile forest hike.

General Location: Between Daytona and Orlando.

Maps: None needed.

Difficulty: Easy.

Special Attractions: This is the only place in the world where a herd of thirty to forty endangered manatees is so easily visible from shore.

Season: During the coldest parts of the year, from mid-December to early March. This is a popular park, often extremely crowded on weekends.

Camping: Fifty-one campsites; vacation cabins available for rent.

Information: Blue Spring State Park, 2100 West French Avenue, Orange City, FL 32763; (904) 775-3663.

HIKE 50 SPRING RUN BOARDWALK

Finding the trailhead: From Interstate-4 between Orlando and Daytona, take the Deland exit and follow the brown and white signs to the state park in Orange City.

The hike: This half-mile walk borders the edges of the clear spring run. Easily wheelchair accessible, the boardwalk has several platforms overlooking the water to provide excellent views of the manatees, who winter in the constant seventy-two-degree spring run which empties into the St. Johns River. As mammals, manatees are susceptible to cold and need to spend the winters in such refuges. Once the St. Johns River warms up, the manatee herd disperses until the following November or December. There is no vegetation growing in the spring run, so manatees will make short forays into the river for food.

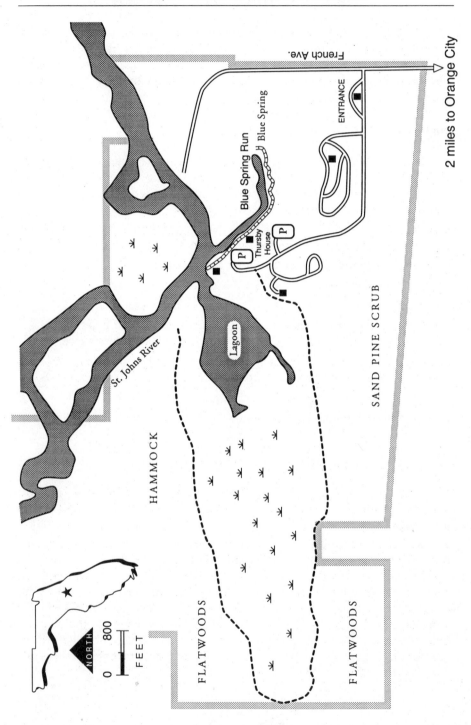

The best time to see manatees is early in the morning, shortly after the park opens, when between twenty-five and forty animals rest on the bottom, rising to the surface to loudly inhale breaths of fresh air.

And make it a weekday, unless you are there as soon as the park opens at 8 a.m. Manatees are an extremely popular attraction and the park often fills on winter weekends. Cars line up and wait until parking spaces empty again. Even weekdays can be crowded, with busloads of school children, but they typically do not arrive before 10 a.m.

The boardwalk also passes through a heavily wooded hammock and ends at the boil of Blue Spring. Fish life in the immediate vicinity of the boil is scarce, due to the water's low oxygen content. However, it can become quite abundant just a few hundred feet down the run—particularly garfish and big tilapia.

HIKE 51 FOREST HIKING TRAIL

Finding the trailhead: This trail departs from the main parking lot next to the Thursby House, a large white wooden building.

The hike: The four-mile trail skirts the boundaries of the park, passing through sand pine scrub, pine flatwoods, and marsh hammock. The trail ends on the opposite side of a freshwater lagoon connected to the St. Johns River. You must retrace your steps back to the parking lot. Since most people will be at the spring run, you'll have the trail all to yourself unless an organized hiking group happens to show up the same day.

MANATEE SPRINGS STATE PARK

The highlight of 2,075-acre Manatee Springs State Park is a first-magnitude spring that produces 81,280 gallons of water every minute, or about 117 million gallons each day. This never-ending supply of fresh water attracted many inhabitants, including the Weedon Indians.

From 1773 to 1778, naturalist William Bartram traveled through the southeastern United States. In 1774, he was in Florida, and his description of Manatee Springs is as accurate today as when he wrote it.

"It is amazing and almost incredible what troops and bands of fish and other watery inhabitants are now in sight, all peaceable; and in what variety and gay colours and forms, continually ascending and descending, roving and figuring amongst one another, yet every tribe associating separately. We entered the grand fountain, the expansive circular bason, the source of which arises from under the bases of the high woodland hills, nearly half encircling it. The ebullition is astonishing, and continual, though its greatest force of fury intermits, regularly, for the space of thirty seconds of time; the waters appear of a lucid sea green colour, in some measure owing to the reflection of the leaves above...

"The bason is generally circular, about fifty yards over; and the perpetual stream from it into the river is twelve to fifteen yards wide, and ten or twelve feet in depth; the bason and stream peopled with prodigious numbers and variety of fish and other animals; as the alligator, and the manatee or sea cow, in winter. Part of a skeleton of one, which the Indians killed last winter, lay upon the banks of the spring....

"The vegetable productions which cover and ornament these eminences, are generally Live Oak, Magnolia grandiflora, in the Creek tongue Tolochlucco, which signifies the Big Bay, Laurus Borbonia or Red bay, in the Creek tongue Etomico, that is King's tree, Olea Americana and Liquidambar, with other trees, shrubs, and herbaceous plants common in East Florida.

"The hills and groves environing this admirable fountain, affording amusing subjects of inquiry, occasioned my stay here a great part of the day."

Little has changed since Bartram's time, except that manatees are infrequently seen these days. Scuba diving and snorkeling are permitted in the spring boil. A boardwalk flanks the southern end of the run, passing through a thick cypress swamp to the Suwannee River.

General Description: Two short nature trails through hammock and sandhill habitats, and a boardwalk tour along a clear spring run.

General Location: On the Suwannee River just west of the city of Chiefland.

Maps: None needed.

Difficulty: Easy. A boardwalk that borders the spring run and which extends out into the Suwannee is wheelchair accessible.

Heron feeding in Manatee Springs State Park.

Special Attractions: The opportunity to swim in the clear, constant seventy-two-degree spring.

Season: Anytime.

Camping: One hundred sites inside the park, all with grills, picnic tables, and water; some with electricity.

Information: Manatee Springs State Park, Route 2 Box 617, Chiefland, FL 32626; (904) 493-6072.

HIKE 52 NORTH END TRAIL

Finding the trailhead: Take U.S. Alt. 27 to Chiefland and look for the prominent park signs in the middle of town. Go a quarter-mile beyond the entrance gate. The path is on the right.

The hike: This short loop trail traverses hammock and sandhill communities where white-tailed deer roam. Also watch for wading birds such as the limpkin, often heard calling out as it searches for apple snails in the swamp.

HIKE 52 NORTH END TRAIL (Manatee Springs State Park)

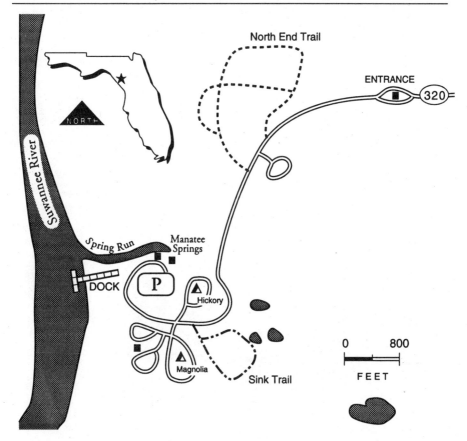

CITY WALKS OF NORTH FLORIDA

ST. AUGUSTINE

St. Augustine is unique among Florida attractions. It has no thrill rides, no audio-animatronic robots, and no theme parks. Instead, it is an entire community devoted to a single subject, the reconstruction of the first permanent Colonial Spanish town in America.

St. Augustine is a kind of Williamsburg South, a collection of authentically restored buildings where people in costume explain and demonstrate Spanish life of the 1700s.

Ponce de Leon was the first European to explore this part of northeast Florida, arriving in 1513 in search of the fountain of youth. Although he obviously failed in his quest (Ponce de Leon is buried in Puerto Rico), his landing did grant immortality to the site.

St. Augustine was permanently settled in 1565—forty-two years before Jamestown and fifty-five years before the Pilgrims ever saw Plymouth Rock. Today, it is recognized as the nation's oldest city, though Pensacola also claims that title.

San Marcos Castillo at St. Augustine.

For the early Spanish explorers, St. Augustine was one of New World's most important outposts. It not only guarded the northeastern frontier of Spain's empire, it also helped protect treasure-laden galleons that stopped at the port city before sailing across the Atlantic with their rich cargoes.

In those days, where there was gold, there were pirates. And because of repeated pirate attacks on the city, work began in 1672 on the massive Castillo de San Marcos, the oldest masonry fortification in the United States. and one of the finest remaining Spanish battlements in the Western Hemisphere. Overlooking Matanzas Bay, the fort took fifteen years to complete and was never taken in combat.

However, St. Augustine did temporarily become British property in 1763, when Spain traded it for the newly conquered Havana, Cuba. Spain took repossession of the town in 1784, finally relinquishing the city in 1821, when Florida was sold to the United States.

St. Augustine has been a popular tourist destination since the late 1800s, when Standard Oil co-founder and railroad magnate Henry Flagler extended his rail service into Florida and built great hotels like the Ponce de Leon and Alcazar, to entice wealthy families to vacation there.

In 1959, work was begun to re-create the old Spanish colonial city to make the area more attractive year-round. Old St. Augustine now consists of more than thirty restored or reconstructed examples of both Spanish and British architecture. Most buildings have overhanging wooden balconies and walled garden patios, a faithful re-creation of the period between 1750 and 1845.

General Description: The oldest continually-occupied city in North America, settled by the Spanish in 1565.

Maps: Available from the tourist office at 10 Castillo Drive.

Difficulty: Easy. Note: The streets are flat and wheelchair accessible. In addition, forty-five minute tours by horse-drawn carriage depart from directly in front of the Castillo. Sightseeing trams stop at the several ticket booths bordering the historical district. Both carriages and trams follow the same 7.5-mile route, stopping frequently so passengers can disembark, look around, then reboard. Train riders can stay as long as they like since trains come along about every fifteen minutes.

Special Attractions: A five-block restored Spanish settlement and the largest Spanish fort in the Continental U.S.

Camping: Anastasia State Park on nearby Anastasia Island.

Information: The St. Augustine Chamber of Commerce, 10 Castillo Dr., St. Augustine, FL 32084; (904) 825-1000; (800) OLD-CITY.

HIKE 53 ST. AUGUSTINE HISTORICAL WALK

Directions: Off Interstate 95, forty-five miles south of Jacksonville and fifty miles north of Daytona Beach.

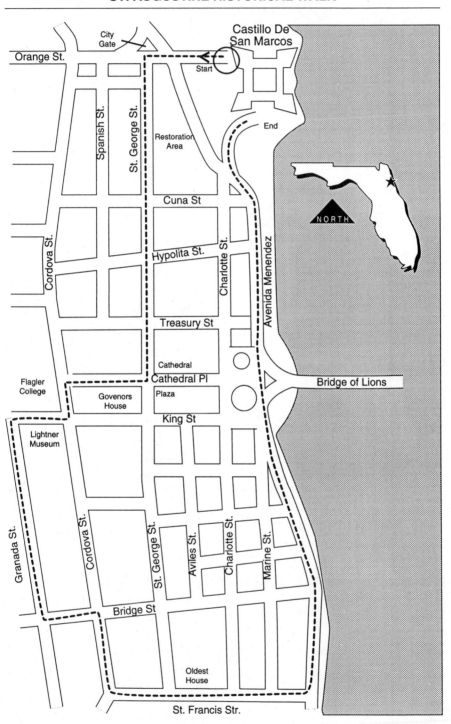

The walk: Every visitor's first stop should be the St. Augustine Visitor Information Center at 10 Castillo Dr. This remarkably complete center offers orientation movies and stacks of brochures describing the various attractions.

With this introduction, the next obvious stop is the Castillo, St. Augustine's most imposing and most visited site. Originally built at a cost of $30 million—an enormous sum for its time—this national monument has walls thirty feet high and nine to twelve feet thick, surrounded by a moat forty feet wide. Demonstrations of cannon firing are held on weekends periodically throughout the year by personnel dressed in authentic Spanish military garb.

Across from the Castillo is San Augustin Antiquo, a narrow five-block section of St. George Street closed to modern traffic. People in Spanish costumes conduct tours and engage in various crafts such as furniture, candle, and cigar making. In several reconstructed homes you can see period artifacts and demonstrations of activities like wool dyeing and old-time food preparation.

Some of the nation's oldest buildings are also located in the historic district. One is The Oldest Wooden School House, built during the Spanish occupation before the American Revolution. The Oldest Store Museum contains a varied collection of more than 100,000 mementos of yesteryear.

Mixed in with the historic buildings are small bakeries, ice cream shops, and a variety of restaurants. The huge Columbia Restaurant is almost an attraction in itself. Ranked one of the state's best restaurants, it features Spanish and Cuban dishes, most notably its rich chorizo soup (garbanzo beans, ham, and Spanish sausage) and paella (rice, saffron, seafood, and chicken). The elaborate Sunday brunch is superb.

Just a short distance from old St. Augustine is the incredible Lightner Museum on Cordova Street. Formerly the 300-room Alcazar Hotel, the Lightner Museum buildings and gardens cover three full city blocks. It houses an amazing collection of the old and the odd, including fine Oriental art, Tiffany glass, and mechanical musical instruments and other artifacts from the 19th century. An antiques mall is located on the first floor in what was formerly the hotel's giant indoor pool.

Across the street from the Lightner Museum is Flagler College, also once a great hotel. Not an official tourist attraction, the ornate buildings of this private college are quite beautiful.

Farther afield is the Oldest House on St. Francis St., a National Historic Landmark that dates back to at least 1727. The house is furnished in eighteenth and nineteenth century antiques, and the adjacent museum (open 9 a.m. to 5:30 p.m. daily) highlights the city's history.

Another famous landmark is the Fountain of Youth at 115 Magnolia Avenue. One of the more notorious tourist attractions, the Fountain of Youth is also an important archeological site, a twenty-one-acre park where St. Augustine's first fort was established.

CEDAR KEY

When most people hear the term Florida Keys, they think only of the island chain extending from South Florida toward Cuba, a series of coral-encrusted mounds rapidly developing into a South Miami subdivision.

But Florida has a second set of keys, a group of 100 small islands several miles off the state's west coast about midway between Tampa and Tallahassee. Known collectively as the Cedar Keys, the region retains far more of the pure old-time Keys flavor than you'll find in their more famous southern counterparts.

Although several of the islands have been home to various settlements, a lumber mill, an army hospital, and even a detention camp for Indian prisoners, all but one were abandoned long ago. Today, only Way Key is inhabited, and it boasts a permanent population of only about a thousand. Way Key also is home to the small town of Cedar Key, an old-fashioned fishing village that has gallantly clung to the rustic charm of Florida in the 1920s, a reminder of what Key West must have been like before the Navy base, the night clubs, and the hordes of tourists.

Like many other Florida locales, Cedar Key once had its prosperous boom period, but following its bust in the late 1800s, it has remained almost unchanged. An accident of geography helped Cedar Key retain its past. It is

Pelicans at Cedar Key.

literally in the middle of nowhere surrounded by nothing. The nearest town is Otter Creek, twenty-two miles away on U.S. Highway 19. So out-of-the-way is Cedar Creek, there isn't a single open place of business along the stretch of State Road 24 that connects Cedar Key to Otter Creek. Only tall pines, cypress, cabbage palms, and palmettos border the thoroughfare that eventually pokes three miles out into the Gulf to Way Key.

The first glimpse of Cedar Key reveals that fishing is not a sport here but the most important means of survival. The mounds of discarded oyster shells are piled so high around some of the sheds they've almost become a second foundation.

It doesn't take long to reach the center of things: Way Key itself is only one square mile, in the shape of an "L," and no wider than a half-mile at any point. The town of Cedar Key occupies much of the island.

The main reason most people come to Cedar Key is to eat, and the focal point of that activity is just offshore, a curving block-long roadway built on pilings. Adjacent to this aerial roadway are several restaurants that specialize in both seafood and spectacular views of the Gulf.

The seafood offered is sometimes adventurous: a special pate made of fresh mullet, or mulletburgers, crabburgers, shrimpburgers, and oyster burgers. Or eat your seafood fried or broiled.

General Description: A brief walk of several blocks through an old, picturesque fishing village.

General Location: On the Gulf of Mexico west of Gainesville.

Maps: None needed.

Difficulty: Easy. This entire route is wheelchair accessible.

Special Attractions: Some of the freshest, tastiest seafood found anywhere in Florida.

Season: Anytime; a seafood festival is held each fall.

Camping: Contact the Chamber of Commerce.

Information: Cedar Key Area Chamber of Commerce, P.O. Box 610, Cedar Key, FL 32625; (904) 543-5600.

HIKE 54 CEDAR KEY WALKS

Directions: From Chiefland, drive thirteen miles south on U.S. 19/98. Turn right on State Road 24 and drive twenty-one miles to Cedar Key.

The walks: You'll have to leave the table at some point and work off your seafood meal to start making room for the next one. The easiest place to take a walk is the long pier extending off restaurant row. A combination fishing pier and dock, this is where the big shrimpers tie up and where quite a few anglers come to wet a line. A small squadron of pelicans usually stands on the pier posts, hoping for a scrap of fresh bait.

Cedar Key's other area of interest is along Second Street, two blocks off the waterfront. Second Street harbors the real soul of the town: a cluster of weathered frame buildings adorned with gingerbread carvings and wonderful New Orleans-style balconies.

Several of the oldest structures are only deserted shells. They seem decayed and haunted-looking, buildings still struggling to make the transition from Cedar Key's boom days of the past century.

Although you would never guess it from the almost ghost-town appearance of Second Street, this was once the pride of a thriving port city that threatened to rival Mobile and New Orleans. In 1885, Cedar Key had 5,000 residents, more than five times today's population. The busy port shipped locally produced lumber (primarily cedar), fish and oysters, as well as imported fruit, sponges, and other commodities brought directly to the docks by railroad and boat. In addition, both the Farber and Eagle pencil companies had large operations on nearby keys because of the plentiful cedar supply.

But by 1890, the boom was over: no thought was given to selective cutting or reforestation, and the timber supply began to run out. Overfishing brought about a simultaneous decline in marine resources, and Cedar Key's population dropped by three-fourths. Next was the hurricane of 1896—which destroyed the main lumber mill, tore away all the wharves, damaged the railroad, and swept away all bridges leading to Way Key—putting a permanent end to the prosperous times.

Yet some of that former grandeur still remains in the show place of Cedar Key, the old Island Hotel, built in 1836. The ten-room, two-story structure is built of hand-hewn cypress boards that appear so weathered they could be planking from the Mayflower.

Just down the street from the hotel are two particularly good stops. One is a small crafts shop where the locals display their handicrafts; the other is the wonderfully stocked old Country Store. The Country Store is crammed with antiques of every variety and description: bottles, tools, dolls, and furniture.

One of Way Key's most beautiful places is one that few tourists ever see: the colorful old cemetery located on a hill overlooking the water. With markers dating back to the early 1800s, it—better than anywhere else—chronicles the history of Cedar Key, noting those who were victims of epidemics or lost at sea.

The locals continue a burial custom today that, from the appearance of several of the graves, is an old one. It involves covering the grave from the marker to the foot with a thick bed of pink clam shells. In time, the shells lose their color and become a dingy gray, but until they fade, these shell mounds provide a colorful and fitting monument to people who spent their lives working the sea.

CENTRAL COASTAL HIKES

Thanks to Disney World, Universal Studios, Sea World, and other theme park attractions, Central Florida considers itself the vacation capital of the world. Not nearly as well known are the hundreds of miles of hiking/walking opportunities.

CANAVERAL NATIONAL SEASHORE

The distance from the Florida/Georgia border to Key West is more than 500 miles. For all that distance, the longest stretch of undeveloped beach remaining on the Florida's East Coast is the twenty-five-mile strip of barrier island known as Canaveral National Seashore.

When the Kennedy Space Center was developed on Merritt Island in the early 1960s, NASA found it had far more land than it needed. So, NASA invited two other government agencies to help manage the area. The U.S. Fish and Wildlife Service established the Merritt Island National Wildlife Refuge as a sanctuary for wintering waterfowl in 1963, and in 1975, the National Park Service created Canaveral National Seashore.

Today, the Seashore's close ties to the space program are still obvious: the southernmost boundary is in plain view of one of the space shuttle launch pads.

General Description: Short nature hikes and an extended twenty-five-mile beach hike where you may not see another person for hours. The park opens at 6 a.m. year-round and closes at 8 p.m. in summer, 6 p.m. in winter.

General Location: Situated between New Smyrna Beach and the town of Titusville.

Maps: None needed.

Difficulty: Walking the entire seashore is moderate to difficult, depending on heat and mosquitoes. The nature trails offer easy walking.

Special Attractions: The longest deserted beach walk on Florida's East Coast. A beach wheelchair is available at the Information Center in Titusville.

Season: Fall through early spring. Mosquitoes can be incredibly fierce at sunset; carry repellent.

Camping: Primitive backpacking only. Call for the latest regulations.

Information: Canaveral National Seashore, 308 Julia St., Titusville, FL 32796; (407) 267-1110. Also 7611 South Atlantic Ave., New Smyrna Beach, FL 32169; (904) 428-3384.

An uncrowded beach at Canaveral National Seashore.

HIKE 55 BEACH WALK

Finding the trailheads: North district: seven miles south of New Smyrna Beach on A1A. South district: twelve miles east of Titusville on State Road 402; this district is closed prior to space shuttle launches.

The hike: Canaveral National Seashore actually is made up of three beaches: Playalinda, Klondike, and Apollo. The tips of both Playalinda and Apollo can be reached by car, but Klondike is open only to hikers, a rare chance for a long walk without any man-made intrusions.

At the northern end of Playalinda Beach, hikers may encounter nude sun bathers. Technically, nudity here isn't legal, but authorities often overlook it as long as there aren't too many complaints.

Those planning to hike the full twenty-five miles of the Seashore must factor in both time and tide. A combination of high water and rough surf can leave little or no beach to walk on. This stretch has no stops for water and other facilities; a canteen, insect repellent, and sunscreen are a must to prevent the experience from becoming a "march-or-die" ordeal.

The beachfront is far more than just a strip of sand, and what you'll view along the seashore walk changes with the seasons. In summer, the seashore is a vital nesting ground for endangered loggerhead and green sea turtles. Only daylight hiking is permitted, but special night-time tours are conducted by the park service so visitors can watch the turtles lay their eggs. Early morning hikers may see a few stragglers. More likely all you'll spot are the turtle flippers' tread-like tracks leading down to the sea.

The turtles, particularly loggerheads, emerge from the sea to nest here between May and September. A female deposits as many as 120 eggs in the hole she digs with her hind flippers. She may repeat this procedure several times during the nesting season, yet only about one turtle from each of her nests will survive to adulthood.

Raccoons often eat the eggs, sometimes as soon as the turtle lays them. Shore birds pick off many of the hatchlings as they scamper toward the sea. Fish kill off many more.

But this natural selection process is not what endangers the sea turtle population. Instead, bulkheads and beach developments have closed off old nesting grounds. Hatchlings, confused by street lights and other artificial illumination, go inland instead of toward the sea. As a result, many die of starvation or are killed by cars. Canaveral National Seashore is one of the most important turtle nesting grounds remaining on the east coast.

The sand dunes here house raccoons, armadillos, and several species of harmless snakes. Plants inhabiting the dune area include sea oats; the large, round-leafed seagrape (raccoons frequently feed on the edible fruit, which can also be made into a delicious jelly); bayonet-leafed yuccas; prickly pear cactus; and saw palmetto. None of this is very soft or tender and is best left untouched.

From early fall through winter, migrating waterfowl appear in truly staggering numbers. As many as 280 species of birds have been recorded, and

CANAVERAL NATIONAL SEASHORE, MERRITT ISLAND WILDLIFE REFUGE

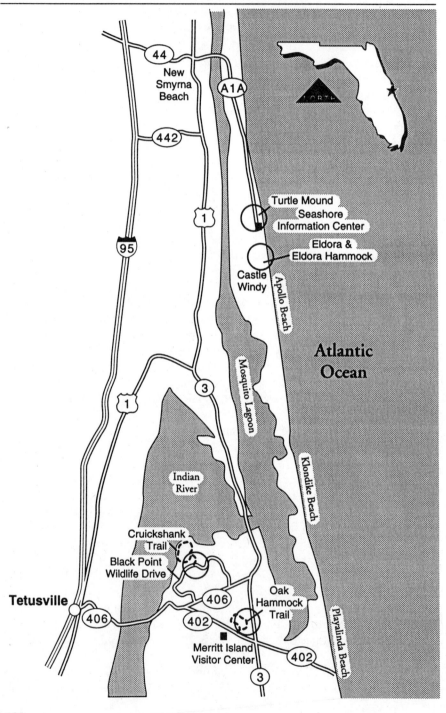

a good winter bird count goes something like this: 50,000 to 70,000 ducks; 100,000 coots; 12,000 to 14,000 gulls and terns; 2,000 raptors, and enormous numbers of songbirds. The only other Florida site that supports a bird population anywhere near this size is Lake Okeechobee to the south, and it is second-best.

Surf fishing can be excellent from late fall to early spring. Bluefish, redfish (channel drum), whiting, and other popular species come close to shore. When conditions are right, you may sight hundreds of bluefish attacking baitfish on the surface. They look like a huge voracious school of piranha. Angling can become frenzied at such times, since the fish will hit virtually anything that swims and flashes. Feeding bluefish are so fierce that swimmers and surfers have sometimes mistaken their nibbles for shark bites.

The surf line is sometimes rich in shells, one of the few items you're allowed to collect here. The best time for shelling is immediately after one of the fall storms, when a fresh supply is washed ashore. The greatest varieties are found then, including razor clams, lightning whelks, calico scallops, and angel wings.

HIKE 56 TURTLE MOUND

Finding the trailhead: North district: seven miles south of New Smyrna Beach on A1A.

The hike: Turtle Mound is an ancient hillock of oyster shells left by the Timucuan Indians. A quarter-mile, self-guided trail leads to the top of the two-acre shell pile. It apparently was created by oyster-eating Indians between 600-1200 A.D., possibly as a high-ground refuge during hurricanes. A popular daytime activity here is catching blue crabs using chicken necks and a small sinker tied to a stout piece of twine. The crabs become so involved in dining on the chicken necks they don't mind being reeled in like a fish— until they're scooped up in a long-handled net.

HIKE 57 CASTLE WINDY

Finding the trailhead: Begins at parking area #3 on A1A inside the seashore boundary.

The hike: This one-mile loop trail crosses the island from the beach to Mosquito Lagoon. An interpretive brochure available from the north end Visitor Center explains the coastal vegetation. A Timucuan Indian midden is visible along the Lagoon shoreline.

HIKE 58 ELDORA

Finding the trailhead: Starts from parking area Number 8 on A1A.

The hike: This half-mile trail leads to what once was a turn-of-the-century settlement. Only one of the old wooden buildings still remains, and it is undergoing reconstruction. There is good fishing in Mosquito Lagoon from the pier here.

HIKE 59   ELDORA HAMMOCK

Finding the trailhead: Starts from parking area Number 9 on A1A.

The hike: A half-mile loop trail through a coastal forest. A portion is on a boardwalk and wheelchair accessible. This sometimes is a good spot for birding early in the morning. Beware of mosquitoes.

MERRITT ISLAND NATIONAL WILDLIFE REFUGE

Created from excess NASA land during the development of the United States space exploration program, the 92,000-acre Merritt Island Refuge is Central Florida's principal wildlife habitat. Essentially, it is a huge expanse of chest-high salt marsh grass (with accompanying mosquitoes) punctuated by small ponds and hammocks, and mosquito control dikes dating from the 1950s.

Thanks to its diverse range of habitats, coastal location, and semi-tropical climate, the refuge is home to nineteen endangered or rare species, more than any other single refuge in the United States. These include bald eagles, manatees, peregrine falcons, gopher tortoises, osprey, and five species of marine turtles.

The impressive bird list identifies 310 species sighted on the refuge over the years. Besides the huge waterfowl migration, spectacular migrations of passerine birds, such as warblers, occur spring and fall. Eight species of herons and egrets are commonly in residence. Nesting populations of bald eagles, brown pelicans, mottled ducks, and wood storks are a special feature at the refuge. If you're seriously interested in birding, be sure to obtain a copy of the bird check-list available at the visitor center. The best birding is always early and late in the day. Binoculars and a powerful telephoto lens enhance the experience tremendously.

Best months for observing the profuse bird life are November to March. Except when walking the nature trails, stay in your car. Waterfowl don't mind an audience, but as soon as a car door opens the birds "drift" well away from the roadside.

During November or December, visitors may be surprised to hear the sounds of shotguns adjacent to the wildlife drives. Duck hunting has been an annual ritual here for generations and is still permitted, but only on a tightly controlled quota basis. The hunting is an important aspect of waterfowl management.

Fishing is allowed on the refuge throughout the year, in the scattered pockets of fresh water found on the property. In addition, wading the shoreline for redfish and trout can be extremely productive in the spring.

Hiking opportunities are quite varied.

A loggerhead turtle prepares a nest in the sand at Merritt Island National Wildlife Refuge.

Loggerhead turtle eggs. The turtles come ashore between May and August to deposit their eggs.

General Description: Hikes of up to five miles through a large waterfowl area, also excellent fresh and salt water fishing.

General Location: Directly east of Titusville.

Maps: None needed.

Difficulty: Easy.

Special Attractions: The best wintering waterfowl habitat on Florida's east coast. Birding tours are offered frequently during the height of the migration. Also plenty of opportunity to see many rare and endangered animal species.

Season: Fall through early spring. Always carry insect repellent.

Camping: None on the refuge. For nearby campgrounds, contact the Titusville Chamber of Commerce, 2000 South Washington Ave., Titusville, FL 32780; (407) 267-3036.

Information: Refuge Manager, Merritt Island National Wildlife Refuge, P.O. Box 6504, Titusville, FL 32782; (407) 861-0667. The visitor center is four miles east of Titusville on State Road 402; Center hours are 8 a.m. to 4:30 p.m. Tuesday to Friday, 9 a.m. to 5 p.m. weekends. Closed Monday.

HIKE 60 BLACK POINT WILDLIFE DRIVE

Finding the trailhead: Stay on State Road 406 from Titusville. A large colorful sign marks the turnoff from 406. This area is closed prior to shuttle launches.

The hike: This six-mile tour is one of Florida's premier birding areas. Most people see it from a car, but hiking along the series of mosquito control dikes which make up the drive is certainly an option. The best time would be early morning, when the birds are still active and traffic is scarce. A detailed guide that explains the habitat on the drive is available at the visitor center. Among the possible stops are bald eagle habitat, mud flats, and shallow water impoundments. You'll probably see alligators by the road in drainage ditches (you should be perfectly safe as long as you don't provoke them), and wading birds such as blue herons, shorebirds, and waterfowl.

HIKE 61 CRUICKSHANK TRAIL

Finding the trailhead: From Titusville, take State Road 406 to the Black Point Wildlife Drive (see above). The Cruickshank trail is about mid-way, stop Number 8, and is clearly marked.

The hike: This five-mile loop path is named after wildlife photographer and naturalist Allan D. Cruickshank who was instrumental in the establishment of the refuge. The walk takes between two and three hours. The hike circles a shallow water marsh that provides excellent birding. An observation platform and a photography blind are located just a short way along the trail.

HIKE 62 PALM HAMMOCK TRAIL

Finding the trailhead: From Titusville take State Road 406 to State Road 402 and go just beyond the visitor center on 402. Palm and Oak Hammock trails both begin from the small parking lot on the left. The trailheads are clearly marked by signs.

The hike: This two-mile loop trail is usually muddy and wet following rains. A sign at the start of the trail indicates whether conditions are "wet" or "dry." Boardwalks span the wettest sections. The trail passes through cabbage palm hammocks, hardwood forest, and open marsh. Don't forget the bug spray.

HIKE 63 OAK HAMMOCK TRAIL

Finding the trailhead: This half-mile loop trail shares a common trailhead (and parking lot) with the Palm Hammock Trail (above).

The hike: This thirty-minute walk winds through a sub-tropical forest. The dense, bright green fern bed at the start of the hike is one of the more colorful parts of the plant community, explained in a series of interpretive signs.

CENTRAL FLORIDA INLAND HIKES

TOSOHATCHEE STATE RESERVE

Pronounced Tos-uh-hatch-ee, the word is actually a simplification of the Indian term Tootoosahatchee, meaning either "chicken creek" or "fowl creek." The Tosohatchee landscape is a showcase of how plant communities are shaped by the alternating cycles of flood and fire that create a patchwork of swamps, marshes, hammocks, and pine flatwoods.

Animals here include numerous wading and shore birds, deer, snakes, armadillos, bobcats, turkeys, gray foxes, hawks, owls, and even endangered species such as the Florida black bear and ospreys. Florida panther sightings have been claimed here, and bald eagles still nest undisturbed in the refuge.

This vast preserve contains a virgin pine flatwoods (one of only a few remaining in the entire United States.) and a huge 900-acre virgin cypress swamp (along Jim Creek). This is perhaps the largest stand of uncut cypress left in the state. Some of the giant slash pines are believed to be as much as 250 years old.

The reason this area remained so well preserved is that from 1930 until the state purchase in 1977, the property was used as a private hunting preserve. The hunters went to great lengths to create and maintain an ideal game habitat. Limited hunts are still conducted on the reserve today.

General Description: A Florida Trail loop through some of Florida's most beautiful wilderness. A public hunting area.

General Location: Along the St. Johns west bank from State Road 50 to the north, through the Bee Line Expressway and State Road 520 to Lake Poinsett.

Maps: Provided at the Reserve.

Difficulty: Easy to moderate depending on rains.

Special Attractions: Virgin stands of pine and cypress trees.

Season: Fall through early spring.

Camping: Two primitive campsites that can be reached only by trekking in. The Tiger Branch camp is about a four-mile walk. Whetrock is about 8.5 miles. Bring water for drinking and cooking. Carry out all trash—don't bury it.

Information: Write the Reserve Manager, Tosohatchee State Reserve, 3365 Taylor Creek Rd., Christmas, FL 32709; (407) 568-5893.

Tosohatchee State Reserve is noted for its bald cypress trees.

HIKE 64 TOSOHATCHEE LOOP TRAIL

Finding the trailhead: Take Taylor Creek Road from State Road 50 at the town of Christmas. After entering the park, take the dirt road on the left leading to the Hoot Owl Hilton.

The hike: The loop trail is blazed in white and begins at an old decrepit hunting cabin known as the "Hoot Owl Hilton." A map and compass are a good idea on this hike, since some of the intersections can be confusing. Also, visitors at the youth camp have been known to rearrange the trail signs.

Parts of the trail definitely feel like an urban hike. It crosses a set of power lines near the beginning and also numerous dirt roads. The walk is mostly over level terrain, an easy stroll through the park. Gradually, the pine forest gives way to a lower swampy area full of the serenades of frogs. Wooden footbridges are provided across some streams, but others must be waded after heavy rains. At one point the trail passes the Beehead Ranch House, an

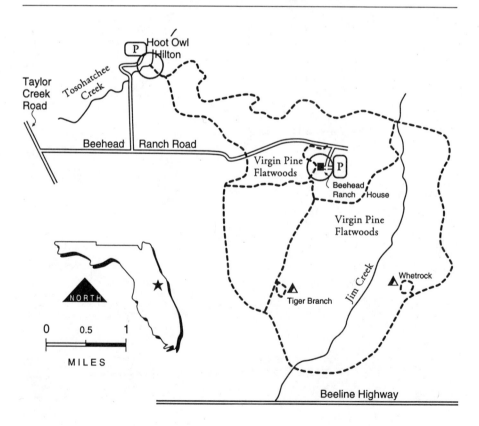

HIKE 64 TOSOHATCHEE LOOP TRAIL

old hunter's house made of cypress and palm logs. One of the finest stands of virgin pine is located near here.

ORLANDO WILDERNESS PARK/ SEMINOLE RANCH

Since its creation in the 1980s, Orlando Wilderness Park area has become a miniature wildlife sanctuary. Found here are more than 140 bird species and many large animals: alligators, deer, otters, and foxes. The habitat is diverse, including a cypress swamp, lake, and forest. This park can become crowded and noisy on summer weekends. If you're seriously interested in wildlife viewing, come early on a weekday.

General Description: A four-mile walk through one of Florida's first large-scale man-made wetlands projects. This segment joins a five-mile leg of the Florida Trail on the Seminole Ranch, which leads to the St. Johns River floodplain.

General Location: Just north of the town of Christmas.

Maps: None needed.

Difficulty: Easy.

Special Attractions: Wonderful birdlife. Guided nature tours are given at Orlando Wilderness park at 8:30 a.m. Saturday and Sunday from May 15 to October 15. No fee.

Season: Anytime.

Camping: Not allowed on property.

Information: City of Orlando, Parks and Recreation Dept., 649 West Livingston Street, Orlando, FL 32801; (407) 246-2288.

HIKE 65 ORLANDO WILDERNESS LOOP

Directions: From Christmas, take State Road 420 from State Road 50 to Wheeler Road, on the right. Follow signs to the park.

The hike: A high-and-dry loop trail, blazed in white, circles four miles of the wetlands open to the public. The park's wetlands are primarily man-made, created from the estimated thirteen million gallons of treated wastewater that is pumped daily into the 1,200-acre wetlands area. Here, aquatic plants remove nutrients from the water, which eventually empties into the Little Econolockhatchee and the St. Johns Rivers. It takes about forty days for wastewater to filter through, from beginning to end.

The Seminole Ranch five-mile loop trail can be combined with the Orlando Wilderness Park for rich wildlife observation in very different habitats. The Seminole Ranch walk leads out onto the edge of the floodplain of the St. Johns River. This is excellent birding territory, particularly for great

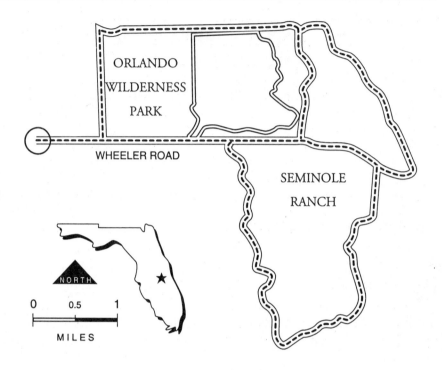

blue heron and migratory snipe. You must sign in at Seminole Ranch before hiking. The trailhead is 0.7 mile west of Orlando Wilderness Park.

WEKIWA SPRINGS STATE PARK

Wekiwa Springs State Park is a 6,400-acre scenic wonder little changed from the days when the Timucuan Indians speared fish in the spring-fed creeks and stalked deer in the uplands. As the metropolitan Orlando area grows ever denser, Wekiwa Springs is turning into a priceless urban preserve of nature. Traffic passing the entrance is so thick it almost demands a stop light in order to drive out. Yet inside Wekiwa, it's back to the Florida of wading birds, otters, raccoons, alligators, and even black bears.

General Description: A wilderness hike with primitive camping in an otherwise heavily developed part of Central Florida.

General Location: Just east of Orlando.

Maps: None needed.

Difficulty: Easy.

Special Attractions: Swimming in a clear spring boil and canoeing the spring run.

Season: Fall through spring.

Camping: To ensure the two primitive sites don't become overcrowded, backpackers must check in at the entrance station just like the regular campers. Then, they register again at a small stand where the trail separates. Also, sixty developed campsites.

Information: Wekiwa Springs State Park, 1800 Wekiwa Circle, Apopka, FL 32712; (407) 884-2009. Please note: streets are known both as Wekiwa (name of the state park) and Wekiva (name of the river running through the park). If that seems confusing to you, the residents don't know what to make of it, either.

HIKE 66 WEKIWA SPRINGS LOOP TRAIL

Finding the trailhead: From Interstate-4 going west toward Daytona take the Longwood exit and turn left under the overpass. Drive to the top of the hill, Wekiva Springs Road, and turn right. Signs mark the way. Park at Sand Lake, a picnic area bordered by sandy hills.

Swimmers enjoy Wekiwa Springs State Park.

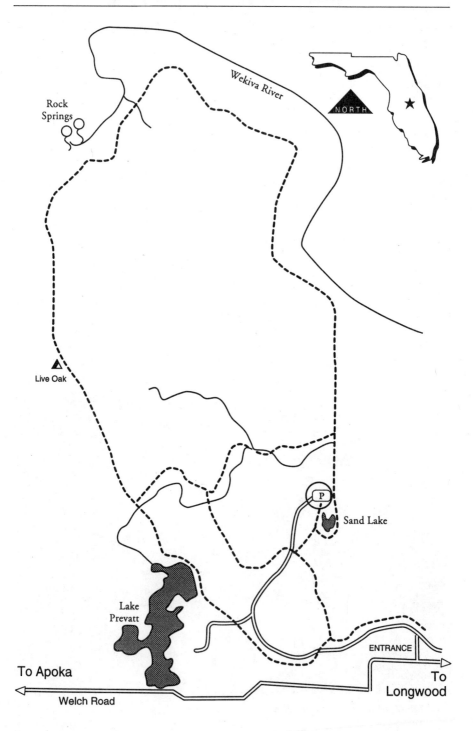

The hike: On weekends, Sand Lake tends to attract a boisterous crowd, but a few hundred yards into the woods, the blaring boom box music will be filtered out. This loop trail soon moves among towering pines, thick palmettos, and a dense ground covering of ferns. If it weren't for the palmettos, it would be easy to mistake this for the pine woods of a more northern state.

Wildlife here is abundant, so don't be surprised to hear bushes moving or dead palm fronds snapping. White-tailed deer and black bear are common in the region, but perhaps nothing more than armadillos will be making all the racket.

The trail comes to a junction after about a mile. Go straight to make the complete 13.5-mile circuit. After rains, the ground becomes swampy, with water standing on both sides. Soon the trail reaches the banks of the spring run, then turns well inland for the rest of the hike.

Following your hike, rent a canoe from the park concession or from the nearby Wekiva Marina. This is one of the most scenic—and crowded—canoe trails in Florida.

TURKEY LAKE PARK

Turkey Lake Park is a 300-acre Orlando city park in a rural setting. The facilities include 125 picnic tables, 77 barbecue grills, 15 large pavilions, 3 playgrounds, 3 miles of bike paths, swimming and an ecology center.

In addition, a Cracker Farm provides a look at ranch life in the 1800s. Children are allowed to pet the animals. The farm is more authentic than most: it includes a hundred year old barn donated by a local church.

The park also has a five senses nature trail for those who cannot see, hear, or walk. Special arrangements allow people to see, smell, taste, or touch many local plants.

The park is designed to accommodate large groups such as company picnics, family reunions, and organized youth groups. It sometimes gets crowded on the weekends.

General Description: Seven miles of hiking trails through an Orlando city park.

General Location: West side of Orlando.

Maps: None needed.

Difficulty: Easy.

Special Attractions: Complete playground and picnic facilities, a 200-foot fishing pier into Turkey Lake, and a Cracker Farm. Playground facilities for physically challenged children; and a five senses walk.

Season: Anytime.

Camping: Thirty-two developed sites and a primitive tent camping area.

Information: Turkey Lake Park, 3401 Hiawassee Road, Orlando, FL 32835; (407) 299-5594. Open all year.

HIKE 67 TURKEY LAKE PARK NATURE TRAILS

Finding the trailhead: Take the East-West Expressway to the Hiawassee Road exit. Go left to 3401 Hiawassee Road.

The hike: Seven miles of nature trails allow hikers to meander the boundaries of the park except for the lake shore, which is best explored by canoe. The nature walks are designed as thru trails, loop trails, and cross trails, so you can tailor the hike to suit your taste and ability.

The most natural pathways go into live oak hammocks and past cattail marshes. Some of the live oaks have massive girths and grow as high as fifty feet.

In the marsh grass growing in the water, look for snail egg masses that may appear between March and September. These white clusters are about the size of BB shot and usually have a hard shell that is surprisingly brittle. The eggs must remain above water or the embryo snails will die. Snails are an important food for some birds species. The limpkin, for instance, lives primarily on apple snails.

An alligator at Withlacoochee State Forest.

WITHLACOOCHEE STATE FOREST

Many of the major battles of the Second Seminole Indian War took place on these 113,431 acres. The state forest is divided into the Citrus, Croom, and Richloam tracts, with extensions of the Florida Trail passing through each. The forest takes its name from the Withlacoochee River, which meanders through all three sections. From March to November, the landscape is often aglow with the brilliant colors of wildflowers.

Each tract of the Withlacoochee State Forest has its own distinct features, as the following descriptions show. The hikes are listed from north to south.

General Description: Overnight hikes of up to forty miles and day-trip loop trails through three different sections of the 123,241-acre state forest. The Citrus and Croom tracts are usually closed to hiking during the muzzleloading season and the first nine days of the modern gun hunting season. The Richloam tract is closed during the first nine days of modern gun humting season; extreme care is advised during the March spring gobbler season.

General Location: Between Inverness and Dade City.

Maps: Available from the Forest Supervisor's Office in Brooksville.

Difficulty: Easy to moderate.

Season: Fall to early spring.

Special Attractions: A rich variety of plant and animal life.

Camping: Available in each of the three tracts (see below).

Information: Forest Supervisor's Office, Withlacoochee State Forest, 15023 Broad Street, Brooksville, FL 33512; (904) 754-6777.

HIKE 68 CITRUS HIKING TRAIL

Finding the trailheads: There are two trailheads popular for day hikes. Both are near the town of Inverness. The Holder Mine Recreation Area is located on forest trail 10, located 2.5 miles south of Inverness on County Road 581; from Holder, go west for two miles.

The Mutual Mine Recreation Area offers a second starting point, five miles south of Inverness on County Road 581. Drinking water is available at both recreation areas.

The hike: The northernmost access to the forty-mile perimeter trail is the Holder Mine Recreation Area. The blazed-in-blue access trail goes past a sawdust pile, then junctions with the "A" loop trail at the end of the first mile. The junction with the "A" and "B" blue-blazed cross trail is at mile 5.2.

Continuing, you'll find the junction with the blue-blazed cross trails for loops "B" and "C" occurs at mile 14.7; for loops "C" and "D" at mile 19.3, and again at mile 31. You'll reach the access trail that comes in from the Mutual Mine Recreation Area at mile thirty-three. From that point, it's only another seven miles back to your starting point at the Holder Mine Recreation Area.

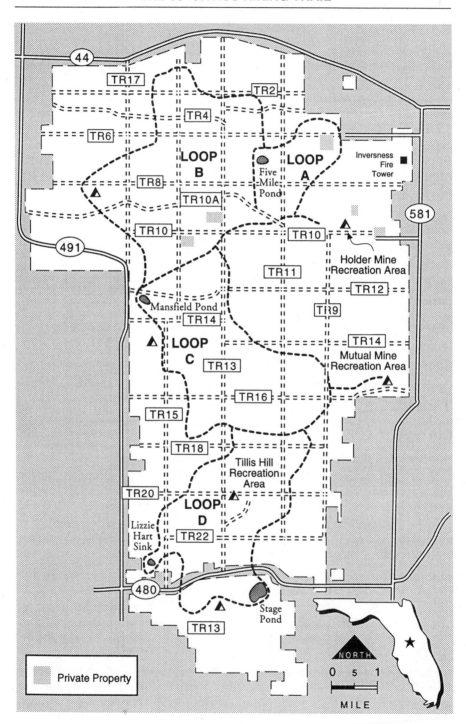

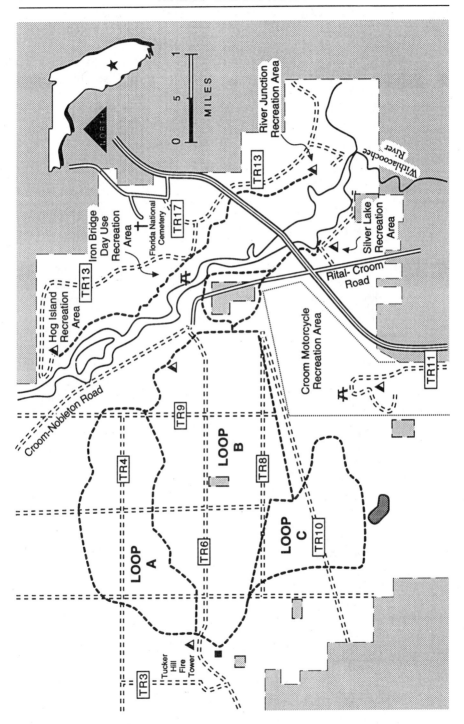

Primitive camping is permitted within designated camping zones marked by white-banded trees. These are situated south of Mansfield Pond; west of Savage Pond; and between forest trails 8 and 10-A. Improved camping facilities are also located at the Holder Mine and Mutual Mine trailheads and the Tillis Hill Recreation Area.

Wildlife on this dry, all-weather trail includes deer, quail, foxes, and fox squirrels. The trail passes through areas of sandhill scrub, oak thickets, and stands of sand pine and longleaf pine. You'll also encounter a number of sinkholes on this alternately hilly and flat terrain.

A trail for horses is marked with blue bands around the trees. You'll want to avoid that and remain on the orange-blazed route which also intersects with blue-blazed side trails.

HIKE 69 CROOM TRACT

Finding the trailhead: Access the Florida Trail from the Silver Lake Recreation Area, four miles north of U.S. Highway 98 on the Rital-Croom Road.

The hike: Located at the center of the forest, the 20,470-acre Croom Tract is also the most popular and most used, particularly the Hog Island section. You have a choice of a twenty-mile perimeter hike or a number of loop trails. The perimeter walk is an all-weather, mostly dry trail that passes cypress ponds and creek bottoms, ravines, prairies, and abandoned rock mines. The wildlife in these longleaf pines, oak thickets, and hardwood hammocks includes white-tailed deer and bobcats.

Look for the Florida Trail sign near the boat ramp at Silver Lake. Follow the blue blazes, which will take you under Interstate-75. Almost immediately you'll come to a junction of the highland and lowland trails. The lowland trail skirts the rivers but may be impassable during flood periods. That's when you want to take the 1.3-mile highlands trail. At about mile three you'll encounter the junction for the main "B" loop trail.

A junction for the "A" and "B" loop 2.9-mile cross trail occurs at mile 5.5 and again at mile 9.5. The 1.3-mile cross trail for loops "B" and "C" is at mile 10.5 and at about mile fifteen. All cross trails are blazed in blue. From mile seventeen until the end you'll be retracing the first three miles of the hike.

The designated camping zones are found north of the Tucker Hill Fire Tower, and northwest of the Croom Road and Croom Nobleton Road intersection. Improved camping is available at the Silver Lake and River Junction Recreation Areas, and Hog Island.

HIKE 70 HOG ISLAND TRAIL

Finding the trailhead: Begin from the northern end at the Hog Island Recreation Area east of Nobleton off County Roads 476 and 635.

The hike: The seven-mile Hog Island Trail is essentially a link between the Hog Island and River Junction campgrounds, both with restrooms and water.

Begin by skirting Sawdust Pond, then passing a river bend. You'll pass beneath I-75 roughly 1.5 miles from the hike's southern end at the River Junction Campground.

HIKE 71   RICHLOAM TRACT

Finding the trailhead: The trail is ten miles north of Dade City, and nineteen miles east of Brooksville on State Road 50. It begins at the Richloam Fire Tower, 0.6 mile southeast of State Road 50 on Clay Sink Road. The fire tower is the only place to find drinking water. For an extended hike, take the trail connector to the eight-mile loop trail in the Green Swamp Management Area.

The hike: On this southernmost tract of 49,200 acres, you have the option of taking a twenty-five-mile overnight hike or abbreviating the walk into five- and ten-mile segments by using the forest roads as hiking shortcuts.

This is the wettest of the Withlacoochee trails system as the dominant type of wildlife shows: alligators, wild hogs, turkey, white-tailed deer, bobcats, and water moccasins. Besides cypress ponds, you'll also pass through pine flatwoods, pine plantations, and hardwood hammocks. The ponds scattered along the route can provide good fishing.

Primitive camping zones are located between Porter Gap Road and Pole Bridge Road; between North Carter Pond Road and Old 50; and south of Lacoochee Grade.

Since you may be encountering gators in the wild, here are a few notes about their life and times. Gators average between eight and ten feet but may grow to nineteen feet long. They have adapted so well to their environment that alligators have not needed to evolve for millions of years.

Females build their nests in the spring. Built of piles of vegetation at the edges of swamps or ponds, the nests hold from thirty to sixty eggs. Heat from the composting vegetation incubates the eggs, which hatch in about two months. Noises made by the eight-inch long babies alert the mother to open the nest and let the youngsters out. At that age they are hardly masters of their domain, and may be eaten by many other animals, including fish, birds, raccoons, snakes, and even other alligators.

Gators themselves dine on fish, insects, turtles, snakes, and crayfish. Gators are notorious for the caves they make in the bottom of swamps and marshes; they stay in these warm "gator holes" in cold weather, and may hide in them and use them as storehouses for their larger kills. During droughts, gator holes become vital watering holes for animals who might otherwise perish.

Be careful about swimming in unknown waters during dry periods or the spring/summer mating season. If you see a gator near the bank, keep your distance. Do not attempt to feed it or do anything else that will lure it to you: they can outrun you in short bursts. Gators often sun themselves on logs or lake banks but it's rare to find them away from water. Alligators are

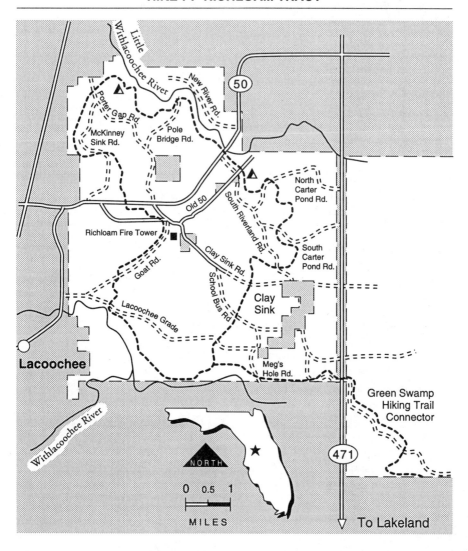

especially fond of dogs, and the animals should always be leashed around lakes.

Starting from the water tower, the trail parallels State Road 50 before crossing it, then passes three ponds in the next 3.5 miles. After going through the Little River primitive camp zone and crossing Pole Bridge Road, the trail again skirts State Road 50 before reaching a second camping zone at mile 13.5. At mile 18.3 you'll encounter the trail connector to the Green Swamp. Camping is also possible at this junction and at mile twenty-two; an alternate highground trail for high-water periods is available just before this final campsite at Big River. The trail then crosses a creek via a log bridge, follows a dirt road, and returns to the Richloam Water Tower.

HIKE 72 WITHLACOOCHEE NATURE TRAILS

Finding the trailhead: Both trails begin near the forest headquarters at 15019 Broad Street, Brooksville, where interpretive trail maps are also available.

The hikes: The 2.5-mile Colonel Robbins Nature Trail is named for an interesting character who made a fortune searching for gold in Alaska's Klondike. He named this tract of land "Chinsegut Hill," an Alaskan Indian word meaning "Spirit of Lost Things." He gave his 2,080 acres of land to the federal government in 1932.

The landscape here is gradually changing from predominantly longleaf pine to hardwood, since fires have not been allowed to burn unchecked since the 1930s. Armadillos (who dig triangular-shaped holes along the trail), possums, raccoons, bobcats, foxes, white-tailed deer, and grey squirrels all live in the reserve. Gopher tortoises and golden silk spiders are also quite common.

HIKE 72 WITHLACOOCHEE NATURE TRAILS

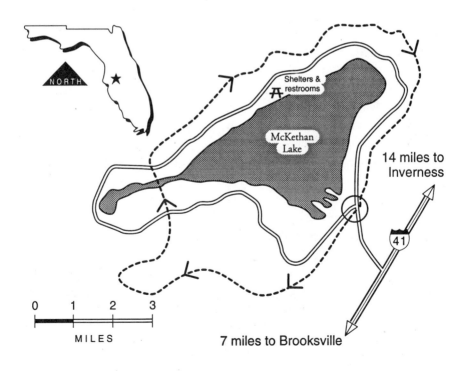

149

The Colonel Robbins trail has twenty-two different interpretive stops, focusing on different plants. Be sure to pick up the trail map and interpretive brochure from the forestry office.

The McKethan Lake Nature Trail is a two-mile nature walk through an unusually diverse forest system. Remarkably, all four species of southern pine (loblolly, sand, slash, and longleaf) grow along the trail. Wildlife is similar to that found on the Colonel Robbins trail and, like it, the McKethan Lake Trail contains an extensive number of interpretive sites. They include stops at the Devil's Walkingstick, a small tree whose trunk is covered with prickly spines; Tree Sparkleberry, an understory plant with leathery oval leaves, the bark of which is suitable for tanning leather; and the Resurrection Fern that alternates from a bright green when moisture is plentiful to a drab brown during drought.

GREEN SWAMP

The name Green Swamp may conjure up swamp monsters or some other sci-fi image, but this 870-square mile area gets its name from its lush vibrant color. Green Swamp contains the headwaters of several important rivers: the Withlacoochee, Hillsborough, Oklawaha, and Peace rivers. It is possible to join the Green Swamp loop from the Richloam Tract of the Withlacoochee State Forest (see Hike 71).

General Description: An eight-mile loop trail through a vital water recharge area.

General Location: Twenty miles north of Lakeland.

Maps: None needed.

Difficulty: Easy to moderate. Some wading may be required during high water periods.

Special Attractions: Wildlife viewing.

Season: Fall to spring.

Camping: Two primitive campsites on the trail.

Information: Southwest Florida Water Management District, (904) 796-7211.

HIKE 73 GREEN SWAMP

Finding the trailhead: From State Road 33, take either Green Pond or Poyner Road, both on the left going north. Both roads lead to Rock Ridge Road and the trailhead, six miles west of State Road 33. Park outside the entrance gate, which is often locked; simply walk around it. The clearly marked trailhead begins just beyond.

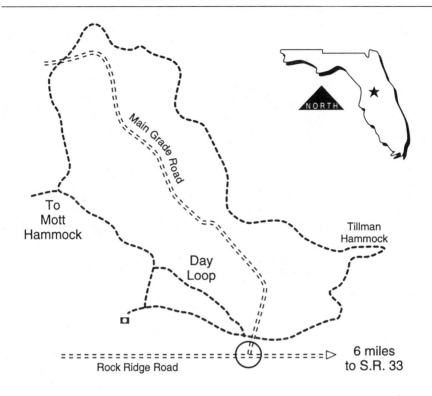

The hike: Going clockwise, the trail first follows an old railroad grade. Less than a mile from the beginning a side trail leads to a scenic overlook. The main trail follows a woods road, passing another side trail to the Mott Hammock campsite. A mile past the campsite is a junction with the fifteen-mile trail that leads into the Richloam Tract.

From here the trail passes through sections of pine flatwoods and a tree farm. The second campsite (Tillman Hammock) is at about mile seven. For the final mile the trail follows a woods road, then crosses a footbridge and returns to the trailhead.

HILLSBOROUGH RIVER STATE PARK

The Hillsborough River flows through this 2,994-acre park and is named for a nobleman with the unusual name of Wills Hills, who lived from 1718 to 1793. Wills Hills, also the Earl of Hillsborough, was instrumental in giving Great Britain control of Florida in general and the Tampa Bay area in particular.

Rapids on the Hillsborough River.

Two small sets of rapids are created by outcrops of Suwannee limestone. The river flows fairly swiftly, and swimming is not permitted; a half-acre, man-made swimming area is available elsewhere in the park.

On weekends and holidays, the Fort Foster Historic Site, located within the park, is manned by personnel in period costumes of territorial Florida.

General Description: A loop extension of the Florida Trail of just over three miles, plus other short nature trails through one of Florida's most scenic state parks.

General Location: Just northeast of Tampa.

Maps: None needed.

Difficulty: Easy.

Special Attractions: Rapids in the Hillsborough River. Not a cause for excitement for most visitors, but the chance to hear rapids while hiking (or boating) is virtually unknown in Florida.

Season: Fall through spring. Often quite crowded in summer.

Camping: 118 campsites.

Information: Hillsborough River State Park, 15402 U.S. 301, Thonotosassa FL 33592; (813) 987-6771.

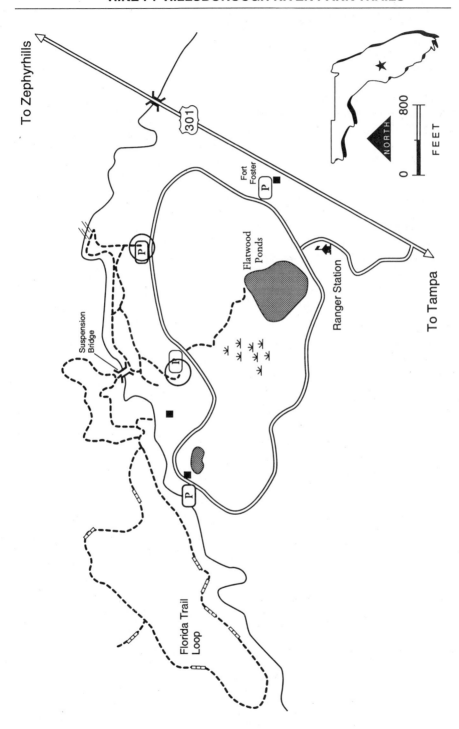

HIKE 74 HILLSBOROUGH RIVER PARK TRAILS

Finding the trailhead: Take U.S. Highway 301 from Interstate-4. The park is on the left, nine miles north of Thonotosassa, six miles south of Zephyrhills. Park at the first parking lot on the right, after Fort Foster.

The hike: The Florida Trail officially extends only 3.2 miles through the park, yet nature trails of almost equal length connect with it to make an enjoyable six-mile walk.

From the trailhead follow the short path that leads to the first set of rapids. Go straight to the rapids, then bear left, bordering the river until you reach the suspension bridge. Cross the river and walk a short ways to the Florida Trail loop. After completing it return to the parking lot on the nature trail loop.

The river and pine flatwoods mixed with oak are home to a considerable number of animals: otters, deer, wild turkeys, pileated woodpeckers, red-shouldered hawks, and barred owls. A walk under the dense old-growth tree canopy here, beside the lively Hillsborough River, can be one of the most memorable of any in Florida.

Beyond the swimming pool, another short trail leads to the edge of a flatwoods pond. This depression was created by rain dissolving the limestone base. Since the water level varies over a large area, there are different rings of vegetation around the pond, according to depth.

HIKE 75 LITTLE MANATEE LOOP

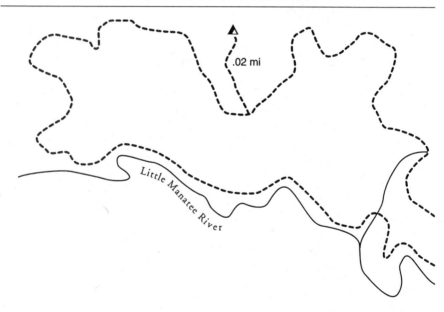

.02 mi

Little Manatee River

LITTLE MANATEE RIVER
STATE RECREATION AREA

This easy walk makes a nice, short stop for those traveling on Florida's west coast. The Little Manatee River divides the park into two sections. The southern part with its developed campground, horse trail, and canoe launch is what most people see. That's because the northern half is open only to controlled foot traffic. Hikers must stop at the ranger station (open at 8 a.m.) to get the lock combination to enter the parking area at the trailhead.

General Description: A leg of the Florida Trail through a natural area of one of Florida's newest state parks.

General Location: Hillsborough County, east of Tampa.

Maps: None needed.

Difficulty: Easy.

Special Attractions: Walking in a scenic area open only to hikers.

Season: Fall to spring.

Camping: A developed campground with thirty campsites, plus the trail has a primitive site.

HIKE 75 LITTLE MANATEE LOOP

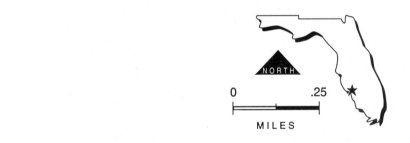

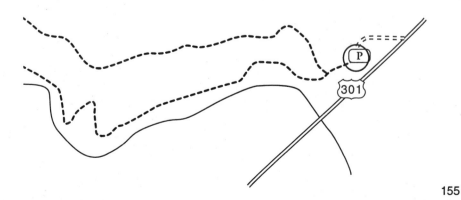

Information: Little Manatee River State Recreation Area, 215 Lightfoot Road, Wimauma, FL 33598; (813) 671-5005.

HIKE 75 LITTLE MANATEE LOOP

Finding the trailhead: Take the Sun City exit from Interstate-75; go east on State Road 674 to U.S. Highway 301 and head south. Look for the entrance signs. The trailhead, on U.S. 301, is three miles north of the park entrance.

The hike: A short access trail leads to the six-mile loop, which is blazed in white. The side trail to the campground (mile four going counterclockwise) is blazed in blue.

The terrain is flat for easy walking, but a lot of effort went into to building this pathway: there are two boardwalks and almost twenty bridges.

About one-third of the walk borders the Little Manatee River. The rest meanders through sand pine, palmetto, and oak hammocks. Wild azaleas along the trail make this a colorful route in February and March. Since human intrusion here is limited, hikers have a good chance of glimpsing the white-tailed deer, turkey, foxes, bobcats, or scrub jays.

LAKE KISSIMMEE STATE PARK

Depending on your interests, trail hiking may become secondary in this 5,030-acre park. Fishermen will enjoy Lake Kissimmee, rated one of the top largemouth bass waters in the entire country. Numerous high-money fishing tournaments have been held on the lake. A boat ramp is available in the park. Best fishing typically is March through May but can be quite productive year-round. A Florida fishing license is required.

Plan on spending at least an hour at the 1876 "Cow Camp," which is staffed by park rangers from 9:30 a.m. to 4:30 p.m. weekends and holidays only. Florida has been one of the top five cattle states for decades. Here, more than 200 acres are reserved for raising a herd of scrub cows and horses, just as Florida "Crackers" did in the 1800s.

The Cow Camp consists of a corral for livestock and a wooden lean-to that a Cracker would have lived in. A ranger explains what life was like and demonstrates some of the skills needed back then, including a little of the whip-cracking that old-time wranglers used to move the herds.

The Cow Camp is not on the main hiking trail. Instead, it has a short pathway of its own from a side road. Signs point the way.

At least fifty animal species considered endangered, threatened, rare, or of special concern, live in this park. Some of the more common animals to watch for are white-tailed deer, sandhill cranes, bobcats, turkeys, and bald eagles.

General Description: Thirteen miles of the Florida Trail system.

General Location: Fourteen miles east of Lake Wales.

Maps: None needed.

Difficulty: Easy.

Special Attractions: An 1876 "Cow Camp" demonstrating living conditions for Florida cowpokes, known as "crackers" because of the whips used to move cattle; open weekends and holidays only.

Season: Fall through early spring.

Camping: Two primitive campsites on the trail; also a public campground with sixty sites.

Information: Lake Kissimmee State Park, 14248 Camp Mack Road, Lake Wales, FL 33853; (813) 696-1112.

HIKE 76 NORTH AND BUSTER ISLAND LOOPS

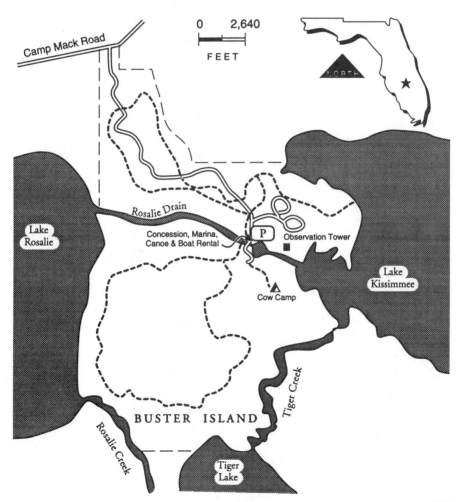

HIKE 76 NORTH AND BUSTER ISLAND LOOPS

Finding the trailhead: From Lake Wales, go east fourteen miles on State Road 60. Signs mark the turnoff to the park. Take the main park road to the parking area located between the two loops. A blue-blazed 0.5-mile access path at the west end of the parking area leads to the loops.

The hikes: The two loop trails, the North Loop and the Buster Island loop, are just under six miles each and traverse floodplains that may be inundated by summer rains.

On the North Loop going clockwise, you'll pass by a turpentine workers' cemetery that dates back to 1912. Also watch for a blue-blazed side trail to Gobbler Ridge, an elevated area said to have been created by high waves off Lake Kissimmee that now contains an abundance of live oak.

The Buster Island Loop tends toward higher ground and features a hardwood hammock.

KISSIMMEE RIVER NATIONAL SCENIC TRAIL

Here is some of the most remote hiking available in Florida. The trail parallels the Kissimmee River, which is natural in some parts and essentially a man-made canal in others. The river is now being restored to its original channel.

Wildlife is relatively abundant in this remote region. Look for sandhill cranes, white-tailed deer, turkeys, wild hogs, hawks, alligators, eagles, and numerous water birds. The trail passes through swampland, oak hammocks, and pine flatlands.

It also traverses the Avon Park Air Force Range, which has been used for bombing practice for many years. Do not stray from the trail here, and certainly do not approach anything that remotely resembles munitions. Hikers cross this area at their own risk. Obviously, if it was all that dangerous, this hike wouldn't be open to the public. Anyone who observes common sense should have no problem.

General Description: A thirty-four mile hike on the west bank of the Kissimmee River; a part of the Florida National Scenic Trail. Also a public hunting area. Trail also crosses an Air Force bombing range.

General Location: East of Lake Wales.

Maps: None needed.

Difficulty: Easy to moderate, depending on rain. Flat terrain.

Special Attractions: Excellent wildlife viewing opportunities.

Season: January through April, the normal dry period.

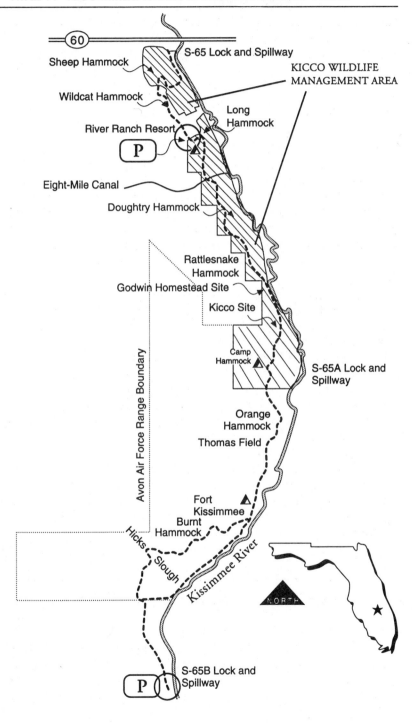

60

S-65 Lock and Spillway

Sheep Hammock

KICCO WILDLIFE
MANAGEMENT AREA

Wildcat Hammock

Long
Hammock

River Ranch Resort

P

Eight-Mile Canal

Doughtry Hammock

Rattlesnake
Hammock

Godwin Homestead Site

Kicco Site

Camp
Hammock

S-65A Lock and
Spillway

Avon Air Force Range Boundary

Orange
Hammock

Thomas Field

Fort
Kissimmee

Burnt
Hammock

Hicks Slough

Kissimmee River

NORTH

S-65B Lock and
Spillway

P

Camping: Several primitive campsites on the trail. Lake Kissimmee State Park is not far from the northern terminus.

Information: No agency offices of any kind on site. For information on the Avon Park Air Force Range call the U.S. Air Force Security Police (813) 452-4195. Or contact the offices of the Florida Trail Association: (904) 378-8823.

HIKE 77 KISSIMMEE RIVER NATIONAL SCENIC TRAIL

Finding the trailhead: From the Florida Turnpike take the Yeehaw Junction exit and follow State Road 60 west for nineteen miles. From Lake Wales stay on State Road 60 to the Kissimmee River bridge.

The hike: Although the hike technically starts at the river bridge on State Road 60, as a practical matter it is best to skip the first five miles of the trail and start from the only available parking lot. Take the road to the River Ranch Resort from State Road 60. Tell security at River Ranch you're there to hike the trail. Then proceed 0.3 mile, turn right, and drive to a fenced area, which is actually the Kicco Wildlife Management Area.

Just a mile in look for the Long Hammock campsite. Afterwards, you'll cross a couple of canals via a bridge and a fence. When you reach the double blaze and the SFWMD fence, you have the option of taking a shell road that follows the channel or following the trail through wetlands; consider the conditions.

At Rattlesnake Hammock the trail passes the home of Owen Godwin, who opened one of Orlando's first tourist attractions long before Walt Disney ever dreamed of coming to Florida. Godwin's Gatorland, located between Orlando and Kissimmee, is still operating today.

Next the trail goes through the abandoned town of Kicco and on to a flood levee, where you can also camp. The blue-blazed side trail here makes a three-mile loop of Tick Island.

Continuing south take the footbridge across the slough, cross a fence and cattle guard, and arrive at old Fort Kissimmee and its cemetery. Water and camping are available here (mile fifteen from the parking lot).

There's another primitive camp about four miles beyond. Then the trail reaches the boundary fence of the Air Force range and follows a dike for the remaining four miles. The southern end is at the S65B Lock Access Road just west of the lock. Arrange a pickup here or you'll have to retrace your steps.

HIGHLANDS HAMMOCK STATE PARK

If you want to feel truly humbled, try standing next to a 1,000-year old oak tree on the Big Oak Trail. One tree's gnarled and twisted girth is an incredible 37.5 feet; you'll never worry about feeling overweight again.

Huge, ancient oaks are only one of the many attractions at this 3,800-acre park. Local citizens, concerned about this hammock turning into farmland, purchased the property in the early 1930s to protect it. Considering the tremendous development close to the park these days, visitors will readily appreciate the foresight of these people.

When Florida's state park system was finally established in 1935, Highlands Hammock was one of the first four original parks.

General Description: Eight hiking trails averaging twenty minutes each through a virgin hardwood forest.

General Location: Just north of the city of Sebring.

Maps: None needed.

Difficulty: Easy

Special Attractions: A boardwalk through a cypress swamp and oak trees as much as 1,000 years old. Many of the trails are wheelchair accessible. Also guided tram rides through the wilderness.

Season: Fall through spring.

Camping: Primitive camping plus 138 developed sites for tents and RVs. Advance camping reservations are highly recommended in winter.

Information: Highlands Hammock State Park, 5931 Hammock Road, Sebring, FL 33872; (813) 385-0011.

HIKE 78 TRAILS OF HIGHLANDS HAMMOCK

Finding the trailhead: Take U.S. Highway 27 to Sebring and turn west onto County Road 634, just north of the city. Follow County Road 634 about three miles to the park entrance. All of the trails begin off the main park road and are clearly signed.

The hikes: The eight trails here are amazingly diverse and specialized. Besides Big Oak Trail, there is the Fern Garden Trail, Young Hammock Trail, and Ancient Hammock Trail, all aptly named and well worth exploring.

Probably the most popular walk of all is the Cypress Swamp Trail, a boardwalk that winds among the moss-draped trees, spanning both sides of Charlie Bowlegs Creek. You may not think a swamp could be beautiful, but this one certainly is. If possible, walk through here late in the afternoon as the sunlight slants through the trees casting spooky shadows on the swamp floor. The swamp boardwalk is an excellent place to view alligators.

Walking through the hardwoods, also watch for the herd of white-tailed deer that live here without any apparent fear of humans. Should they wish to, these deer can dash away at speeds of forty miles per hour and leap over obstacles as much as eight feet high. Though normally silent, they often snort or make a "woof" sound when startled.

The road spanning the park is a level loop trail ideal for bicycling. Park authorities recognize this and have bikes for rent at the ranger station. Bikes are not allowed on the nature trails; park them at the trailhead of each nature walk.

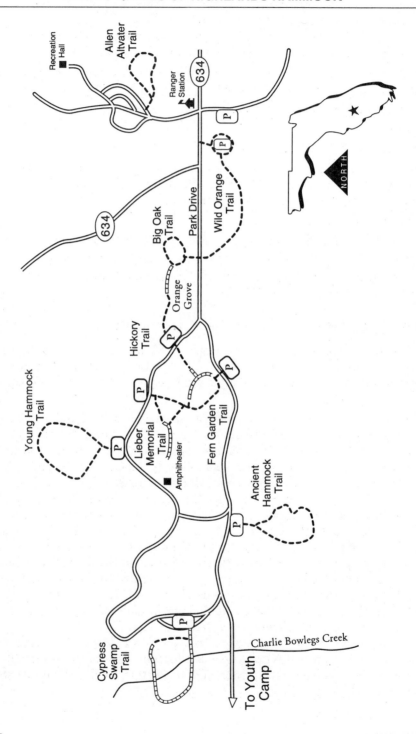

A ranger-led tram tour offers a chance to see wildlife in the park's more remote regions. Animals frequently sighted, besides deer and alligators, are florida scrub jays and otters. Bald eagles are sometimes seen, and even the rare Florida panther has been sighted on occasion. Panther sightings are a once-in-a-lifetime experience in Florida since so few of the animals remain.

A big, 1,000-year-old oak at Highlands Hammock State Park.

BULL CREEK WILDLIFE MANAGEMENT AREA

Bull Creek once had a tram system to haul the cypress from this often wet terrain. The trail follows the old road, and remnants of the tram road are still visible in several places. Turpentine and pitch were also harvested here: some of the slash pines still bear the scars (called "cat faces").

This trail, quite wet at times, passes through pine flatwoods, cypress and hardwood swamps, and scrub oak. In spring and summer, parts of the area are ablaze with wildflowers.

HIKE 79 BULL CREEK WMA

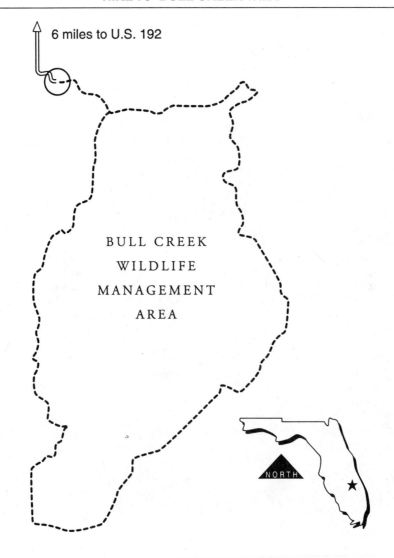

6 miles to U.S. 192

BULL CREEK
WILDLIFE
MANAGEMENT
AREA

NORTH

General Description: An eighteen-mile loop of the Florida Trail through a wide range of habitat. A public hunting area; hiking is open year-round.

General Location: Between St. Cloud and Melbourne in Osceola County.

Maps: None needed.

Difficulty: Easy to moderate depending on rain/mud.

Special Attractions: Hiking an old tram road through rich habitat.

Season: Fall through spring.

Camping: A primitive hunt camp is located near the entrance. Backpack camping permitted year-round but obtain a permit from the Florida Game and Fresh Water Fish Commission (see below).

Information: Florida Game and Fresh Water Fish Commission, Central Region, 1239 S.W. 10th Street, Ocala, FL 32674; (904) 629-8162.

HIKE 79 BULL CREEK WILDLIFE MANAGEMENT AREA

Finding the trailhead: Take U.S. Highway 192 for seventeen miles from St. Cloud or nineteen miles from I-95 at Melbourne. Look for Crabgrass Road and the green wildlife management sign on the south side of the road. Take Crabgrass Road (a dirt road with bumpy, washboard sections) for six miles to the management area entrance. The trailhead is at the hunt camp/check station. Follow Crabgrass Road for almost a mile to Loop Road. Stay on Loop Road for a little over a mile to a junction with the trail.

The hike: Going north to south, the trail first passes through a palm hammock and pine woods, then follows an old railroad grade, which leads to a cypress swamp and Bull Creek. It will probably be wet walking for the next couple of miles.

For much of the remainder of the hike, the trail crosses and follows an old railroad grade and vehicle roads. At mile nine watch for the Little Scrub campsite (no water). In another mile, a foot plank traverses a slough.

At about mile thirteen, there's a junction with a fire break. Follow the fire break, then an abandoned road, and walk the side of a ditch. After crossing the ditch, it's a little over a mile from Loop Road and about two miles to the end of the hike.

THREE LAKES WILDLIFE MANAGEMENT AREA/ PRAIRIE LAKES STATE PRESERVE

A trail of thirty-one miles that also offers added hiking in the Prairie Lakes State Preserve, this is one of longest wooded hikes in the Central Florida region. The path penetrates the heart of a wildlife management area populated with white-tailed deer, bald eagles, and sandhill cranes. Most of the walking is level, but wading may be necessary after heavy rains.

General Description: The twenty-seven-mile Three Lakes Trail passes through a wildlife management area, using sections of the two loop trails of the Prairie Lakes State Preserve.

General Location: West of Melbourne and north of Kenansville.

Maps: None necessary.

Difficulty: Easy to moderate.

Special Attractions: Wildlife viewing, particularly white-tailed deer.

Season: Fall to spring.

Camping: Primitive sites in both areas. Obtain a camping permit in advance for Prairie Lakes (at address below). Camping is restricted in both areas during hunting season; check ahead of time.

Information: Florida Game and Fresh Water Fish Commission, 1239 SW 10th Street, Ocala, FL 32674; (904) 732-1225.

HIKE 80 THREE LAKES TRAIL

Finding the trailhead: Go north of Kenansville on U.S. Highway 441 for 8.3 miles, to the official start of the hike; look for the Florida Trail sign.

The hike: The longer Three Lakes Trail passes not only through hardwood and sabal palm hammocks but also through some fairly open prairie and spiked green palmetto mixed in with the pines. As a practical matter, it is best to park inside the management area, which cuts 2.5 miles from the hike. This is a more secure place to leave your auto than the side of U.S. 441 in the middle of nowhere.

Going south follow an old railroad grade to Williams Road. Turning left follow Williams Road. Soon you'll take an underpass beneath the Florida Turnpike, then move on and off Williams Road via a jeep road. Williams Road eventually takes you to State Road 523, which leads to the Prairie Lakes entrance (mile ten).

The Three Lakes Trail "borrows" about half of each of the two Prairie Lakes loop trails. If you like what you see here (pine forest, hammock, and marsh) it's possible to circuit the loops completely.

Beyond Prairie Lakes, the trail passes Pole Cypress Pond, crosses a bridge, and comes to a campsite with a well and a latrine. At Dry Pond just two miles farther is another campsite with the same facilities.

Next, follow a dike bordering Lake Jackson and tackle a couple of fence crossings: the first by climbing over the fence, the second by using a stile. The trail passes both the north and south edges of Godwin Hammock. After a short jeep road, it crosses a prairie of nothing but spiked green palmettos, good rattlesnake habitat. It's impossible to put blazes on this type vegetation, so the trail is marked by a series of seven posts through this short-cropped green jungle.

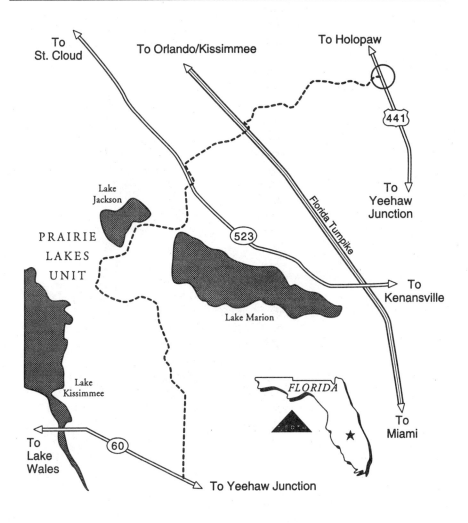

After crossing another fence, the trail follows the fenceline for over mile to the entrance road to Three Lakes off State Road 60. The state road is the hike's official southern boundary.

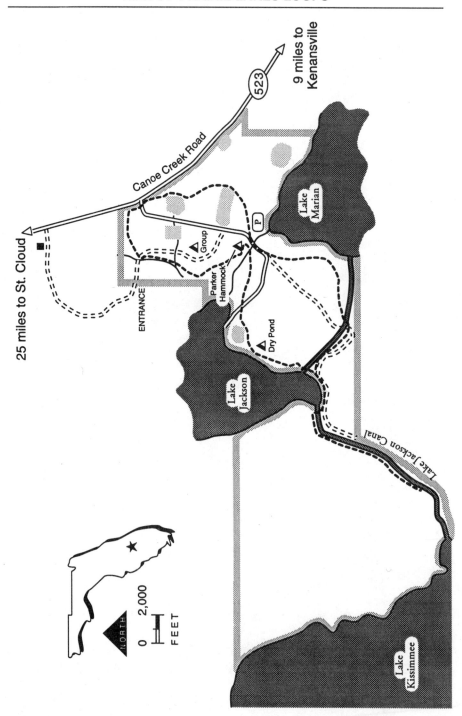

HIKE 81 PRAIRIE LAKES LOOPS

Finding the trailhead: Take State Road 523 (also called Canoe Creek Road) to the preserve. Park where the loops share a common trailhead: at the junction of the north and south loops.

The hikes: The two loop trails of the Prairie Lakes State Preserve are part of the Florida Trail System. Each is just under six miles in length.

Going counterclockwise on the North Loop, the trail skirts the edge of Parker Hammock and enters pine and palmetto. The ranger's office is only a hundred yards off the to the right. Next, you'll pass cypress ponds and pinelands.

Just a few hundred yards from the end of the trail, the Parker Hammock primitive campsite offers a well and latrine.

Go counterclockwise on the South Loop. The trail follows a dirt road for a short distance before skirting Kettle Hammock. The Dry Pond campsite is only 1.5 miles from the trailhead. After crossing a ditch (it may require wading after heavy rain) you'll pass through Thumb Hammock, then reach Parker Hammock about a mile before the trail terminus.

CENTRAL FLORIDA CITY WALKS

TARPON SPRINGS

This is another of those strange, only-in-Florida stories. In 1880, wealthy saw manufacturer Hamilton Disston of Philadelphia purchased four million acres of Florida's west coast from the state's governor for twenty-five cents an acre. This massive land sale is said to have saved the state from bankruptcy.

In 1882, Tarpon Springs was founded by one of Disston's land agents, and it quickly became the most exclusive winter resort on the Gulf Coast. Sponges replaced tourists as the most important product in 1890, when a resident sent out the first boat to "hook" the sponges from the Gulf bottom. Sponges had been found off Key West as early as 1849, but had never been harvested commercially before.

The Key West sponge fleet brought their cargo to sell in Tarpon Springs during the Spanish-American War because of the threat of Spanish warships. This was the beginning of Tarpon Springs' transformation into the world's largest natural sponge market.

Greek divers were brought over in 1905 to harvest sponges on a grander scale. Hundreds of them migrated here, bringing with them their famous "hard hat" dive suits and plans to build boats like those of the Mediterranean sponge fleet. Before long, the sponge industry was earning up to three million dollars annually. A sponge blight in the 1940s and the popularity of synthetic sponges severely damaged the sponge industry. The number of boats dropped from 200 to only a handful.

Today, the sponge industry is enjoying something of a revival. The Gulf sponge beds have returned to health, while at the same time, the Mediterranean has suffered a sponge blight. Natural sponges are popular once again, the demand exceeding the world's supply. Tarpon Springs has regained its title as the world's major source of natural sponges. Still it's doubtful the sponge fleet will again number in the hundreds as it did in its glory days.

General Description: A waterfront walk of several blocks through a genuine Greek sponge fishing community.

General Location: Just north of Tampa.

Maps: None needed.

Difficulty: Easy. Most of this route is also wheelchair accessible.

Special Attractions: Viewing an authentic Greek sponge diving community.

Season: Anytime.

Shrimp boats at Tarpon Springs.

Camping: The Chamber of Commerce has the names of the area's commercial campgrounds.

Information: Greater Tarpon Springs Chamber of Commerce, 210 South Pinellas Avenue, Tarpon Springs, FL 34689; (813) 937-6109.

HIKE 82 TARPON SPRINGS CITY WALK

Directions: Take Alt. 19 to the State Road 582 exit (between Clearwater and New Port Richey) and go west to the town of Tarpon Springs. Follow the signs to the Sponge Docks.

The walk: Although very commercialized, the Sponge Docks on Dodecanes Boulevard is Tarpon Springs' most popular walking area. The sights, sounds, and smells are all important reasons: the colorful sponge boats with their cargoes; the divers conversing in Greek, still the only language of some residents; and the spicy aroma of sizzling lamb emanating from the numerous restaurants.

The Spongeorama is probably the most popular exhibit. This Greek sponger's village depicts the history of sponge diving, including a sponge diving show that includes the thick rubberized suits that revolutionized the sponge industry. With these suits, divers could go deeper and harvest better quality sponges than could be hooked from the shallow waters of the Gulf. Not only were these deep water sponges more valuable, a diver could harvest four times the amount each hour compared to the traditional hook method.

At The Spongeorama you'll learn that we use only the skeleton of the sponge (which is a primitive animal, not a plant). Sponges are able to absorb twenty-five times their own weight in water but can be instantly squeezed almost dry. If you're considering purchasing a sponge, the sheepswool is rated best, the softest and smoothest compared to the grass, wire, and yellow sponges.

On-site sponge diving cruises leave the docks regularly. A fully suited diver goes to the bottom and brings up a handful of live sponges for examination. The diver goes down, taking a webbed string bag, loading it and signaling the life-line tender for another when it is filled.

Many of the sponge boats are decorated with trellises of hanging sponges. Before sponges are stored, they are sorted according to quality and size, then threaded on a cord fifty-eight inches long, which is then tied in a wreath. The number of wreaths on a boat varies from ten to twenty, depending on sponge size. The traditional blessing of the fleet takes place every January 6. Known as the Epiphany, it commemorates the baptism of Jesus Christ in the River Jordan. It is a day of great celebration and feasting, made all the more colorful by the traditional costumes of the Greek men and women.

You can sample the Greek cuisine at any of the numerous restaurants along the Sponge Docks. Some of the more famous dishes are keftedes (Greek meatballs), dolmades (stuffed grape leaves), pastitsio (Greek version of lasagna), calamari (squid), and baklava (a honey-drenched, nut-layered dessert pastry).

After touring the Sponge Docks return to Pinellas Avenue and go one block south to St. Nicholas Church. Built in 1907, it is named after the patron saint and protector of all mariners. The church's icon of St. Nicholas—a painting framed under glass—gained national fame in 1970 when it began "weeping." Beads of water (or tears) formed on the painting inside the air-tight case. Was it a miracle? No final explanation has ever been satisfactorily offered. The icon has not cried in a good many years.

If historic houses interest you continue south until you reach Spring Boulevard. This "golden crescent" contains homes built between 1885 and 1905. Notable homes are at 150, 144, and 184 North Spring Boulevard, and at 22, 110, and 115 Spring Boulevard. A brochure explaining the background of each home is available at the Cultural Center in City Hall, at the corner of Pinellas and Tarpon Avenues, located less than a block south of Spring Boulevard.

TAMPA-YBOR CITY

One of the better-kept secrets of aviation history is that the world's first scheduled airline service began in Tampa, just ten years after the Wright Brothers' flight at Kitty Hawk. In 1914, pioneer aviator Tony Jannus ferried both passengers and cargo between Tampa and St. Petersburg in his "flying boat," yet no one but locals ever seemed to notice.

That seems to have been the pattern for the Tampa area in general. It grew and prospered, but few seemed to notice. But once Tampa hosted its first Super Bowl, people began to realize the city's long history of accomplishments.

Seemingly when almost no one was looking, Tampa had blossomed into Florida's third largest city as well as becoming the industrial and vacation hub of the state's West Coast.

Because so much of its growth came late, Tampa was able to reconcile both its past and present and cling to its cultural diversity. Tampa maintains the rich Spanish heritage from which it sprang and which has played such a vital force in shaping the city over several centuries.

One of the city's most important historic symbols is mirrored in the new downtown highrises: the reflection of the old Tampa Bay Hotel, built in the 1890s and once considered "the world's most elegant hotel." Now a part of the University of Tampa, the former hotel is considered the finest example of Moorish architecture in the Western Hemisphere.

The early Spanish explorers never were able to fully colonize the Tampa Bay area as they did other parts of Florida. Instead, they found the Caloosa Indians "too rough to conquer and too stubborn to convert." Ironically, the first conquistador to visit, Panfilo de Narvaez, landed by accident in 1528 after his ships were blown near the coast by a terrible storm.

Better he had gone elsewhere, for when he came ashore to trade with the Indians, he noticed a gold ornament shining bright in the sand. From this, Narvaez assumed the fabled City of Gold (El Dorado) was close by, and his avarice sparked a ten-year, tragic, harrowing search.

If only Narvaez could have learned the native's language: he would have learned the Indians fashioned the ornament from gold doubloons washed ashore from wrecked Spanish galleons!

The spurious tales of El Dorado were enough to spark the interest of young Hernando de Soto, so he obtained a land grant from Emperor Charles V. In order to secure the Tampa area for his gold quest, he made a peace treaty with the local Indians in 1539. The site of the treaty negotiations is still marked by the giant DeSoto Oak on the University of Tampa campus. De Soto's only notable find—the Mississippi River—turned out to be far from here.

The Tampa area was never truly settled until the establishment of Fort Brooke in 1824, three years after the United States. purchased Florida. Then a controversy broke out over what the area should be called. In honor of the fort, the farming and fishing village that grew up around it also was called Fort Brooke, but long-time locals objected. They preferred the original Caloosa Indian name of "Tanpa," which has the unrelated meanings of "near it" and "split wood for quick fires;" the latter refers to the large amounts of available driftwood. Whatever the original meaning, the settlers preferred the Indian term over Fort Brooke, but map makers corrupted 'Tanpa' to 'Tampa' because it had a more euphonic spelling.

Historians say the Spanish-American War was one of the most important events in Tampa's history, that it in fact made the city. In 1898, many of the better-known seaport cities of New Orleans, Mobile, and Savannah were shocked when the U.S. government decided to use the port of Tampa as its chief embarkation point for U.S. troops being sent to fight in Cuba.

General Description: Walks of about 1.5 hours each through downtown Tampa and the city's Latin Quarter, Ybor City.

General Location: Tampa is located just north of St. Petersburg, inland from the Gulf of Mexico.

Maps: None needed.

Difficulty: Easy. Wheelchair accessible.

Special Attractions: Two very different historic walking tours.

Season: Anytime.

Camping: Hillsborough River State Park or Little Manatee River State Park.

Information: Tampa/Hillsborough Convention & Visitors Bureau, 111 Madison Street, Suite 1010, Tampa, FL 33602; (800) 44-TAMPA.

HIKE 83 TAMPA WALK

Directions: To reach downtown Tampa, take the Florida Avenue exit off Interstate-4.

The walk: As befits a late-blooming city, much of the downtown area is new. Because Tampa lacked Miami's glitter and Orlando's arcade of fun-houses, it developed more with residents in mind than tourists.

For instance, The Franklin Street Mall is a pedestrian mall closed to vehicular traffic. Featuring some of the city's finer restaurants and shops, it is a spacious, pleasant place to be, close to another equally attractive open area, City Hall Plaza.

But for visual appeal, nothing compares to a twilight stroll along the Hillsborough River on the University of Tampa campus or on the river walk behind the Curtis Hixon Convention Center. Both are directly opposite each other. The Moorish minarets of the former Tampa Bay Hotel are silhouetted at dusk.

The riverwalk is not abandoned after sunset. Couples walk hand in hand past elderly residents who stop at a bench to read a book or newspaper in the soft failing light. Their reveries and quiet talk are frequently interrupted by the efforts of the college crew team taking their last practice strokes.

Considering the city's rich history, it's surprising Tampa would go about inventing more of it, but it has. Docked on Bayshore Boulevard near downtown Tampa is the Jose Gasparilla, advertised as the world's only fully rigged pirate ship. It is named after the fierce pirate Jose Gaspar, who supposedly once inhabited these waters and made life miserable for everyone.

As the tale goes, when Gaspar faced certain capture by the U.S. Navy, he committed suicide by wrapping himself in chains and jumping into Tampa Bay. It now appears the entire Gaspar legend is nothing but a public relations dream. That doesn't prevent local businessmen from dressing as pirates each February for the annual Gasparilla Invasion as the pirate ship sails into Tampa.

HIKE 84 YBOR CITY WALK

Directions: To reach Ybor City, take the 22nd Street exit off Interstate-4.

The walk: The year 1886 forever changed the cultural make-up of the Tampa area when Vincent Martinez Ybor brought the Cuban cigar-making industry to Tampa. It was a further migration of the cigar makers, who had fled Cuban during the revolution of the 1860s and moved to Key West.

The cigar manufacturing industry quickly became Tampa's industrial backbone as a hand-rolled cigar brand brought new fame to the area: Hav-a-Tampa? The Cubans created an extensive Latin quarter they called Ybor City, which quickly became known as the world's cigar capital. At one time, two hundred cigar factories operated here.

With its large Spanish-speaking neighborhood, theaters, and restaurants, Ybor City stamped Tampa with a remarkable architecture and an ethnic flair still evident today.

Ybor City played a major role in the Spanish-American War. Cuban patriot Jose Marti in 1893 stood on the steps of present-day Ybor Square to urge the cigar workers to take up arms against Spanish oppression in Cuba.

During its heyday, Ybor City attracted some remarkable people. The Cherokee Club, now the El Pasaje Hotel, was visited by Teddy Roosevelt, Grover Cleveland, artist Frederick Remington, and, of all people, Sir Winston Churchill.

The cultural mix was so diverse that even today Ybor City's weekly newspaper publishes in three languages. "La Gaceta," founded in 1922, runs articles in English, Spanish, and Italian: it is the only tri-lingual newspaper produced in the United States.

Ybor City itself, however, began to lose much of its old vitality due to mechanization and urban renewal. Cigars are still made here (500 million a year), but the need for so much manual labor has passed. The number of residents is about 2,800 people, drastically reduced from 15,000 near the turn-of-the-century. To keep from losing what parts of Ybor City remained, Tampa established a Preservation Park between 9th and 18th Streets, intended to re-create worker's houses, build a new farmer's market, and

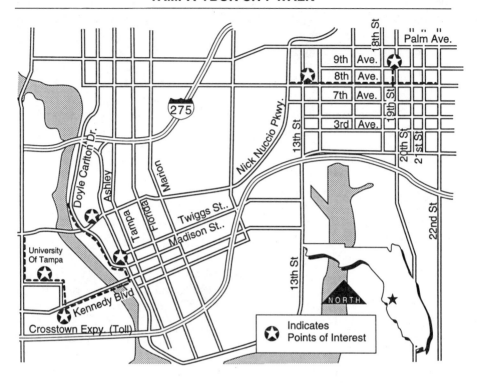

establish a new museum. In 1990, Ybor City became Florida's third National Historic Landmark District, joining St. Augustine and the Pensacola Naval Air Station.

The past is being kept alive at the Ybor State Museum. Housed in an old bakery from the 1800s, it chronicles the political, social, and cultural changes in Tampa's Latin Quarter. The nearby Preservation Park features six renovated cigar workers' homes of the 1890s. One of the homes has also been furnished as a typical cigar worker's cottage.

Today, many new businesses are moving to Ybor City. Ybor Square, the area's central shopping "mall," consists of three huge brick buildings where cigars were once hand-rolled. The original wood interiors, ornate grillwork, and handblown glass windows house a variety of gift and antique shops as well as Spanish, Italian, and American restaurants. The lingering smell of old tobacco is still present in the huge rooms.

Ybor City is home to one of Florida's most famous restaurants, the Columbia. Founded in 1905 and occupying an entire city block, the Columbia is Florida's oldest restaurant and widely renowned for its authentic Spanish cuisine.

Undoubtedly the best way to see Ybor City is with a local tour guide. Free escorted tours are available Tuesday, Thursday, and Saturday at 1:30 p.m.; except from June through September, when they are at 11 a.m. (to miss the afternoon heat/showers).

The tours, which take about an hour and a half, depart from the Ybor Square's Visitor Information Desk on North 13th Street. For information, call (813) 223-1111, ext. 46.

ORLANDO-WINTER PARK

Orlando is a rags-to-riches story that's a press agent's dream. Before October, 1971, Orlando was a city few had heard of, and no wonder.

It was a sleepy agricultural community in the heart of Central Florida with little to attract visitors; where one of the year's social highlights was the Silver Spurs Rodeo in nearby Kissimmee; and where one of the most talked-about dining spots was the buffet in the small regional Herndon airport. Orlando was decades behind its more sophisticated sister cities of Tampa, Jacksonville, and Miami.

Then came Disney World, Sea World, and the rest of the world. Orlando today is the number one tourist destination in all the world, with a tourist flow between one and two million persons a month.

General Description: Circular walk around Lake Eola Park with a side excursion of several blocks to Church Street Station, Orlando's top nighttime entertainment complex.

General Location: The heart of downtown Orlando.

Maps: None needed.

Difficulty: Easy.

Special Attractions: Lake Eola offers a remarkably pleasant urban stroll. Church Street Station is an adult fantasyland.

Season: Anytime. Twilight is the most scenic when the sun sets over the city.

Camping: Numerous commercial campgrounds. Wekiwa Springs is the closest state park.

Information: Orlando/Orange County Convention & Visitors Bureau, 7208 Sand Lake Road, Suite 300, Orlando, FL 32819; (407) 363-5800.

HIKE 85 ORLANDO WALK

Directions: Take Interstate-4 to Robinson Street exit and turn east. Follow Robinson to the far (east) side of Lake Eola Park. Free parking along this side of the lake.

The walk: Lake Eola Park, with its landmark flying-saucer style fountain from the 1950's, has always been downtown Orlando's outdoor hub and the city's most recognized symbol. Three blocks from the heart of downtown,

Lake Eola Park and its surrounding sidewalk are ideal for walking, jogging, or simply relaxing on one of the benches. Ducks and swans, always hungry, circle the shores looking for handouts while white egrets stalk the shallows, intently looking for fish.

Much of Lake Eola Park is shaded with stately oaks. Several sections are planted with colorful flowers that change according to the season. Several times daily, subdued classical music issues from loudspeakers carefully concealed in the park trees. Policeman on foot and on horseback frequently patrol the region, so the park is quite safe even after dark.

This is an eclectic park, and several sections have an Oriental motif. A red pagoda on one shore is placed opposite a great stone monument given to Orlando by an Asian city as a symbol of friendship.

Each spring Shakespearian actors walk the floorboards of the white amphitheater as part of the Shakespeare Festival. The annual program began because an English professor at the University of Central Florida wanted to find a way to bring Shakespeare to more Central Floridians. His plan finally came to fruition at the end of the 1980s when the Lake Eola Amphitheater was rebuilt in a joint effort by the city of Orlando and Walt Disney World.

Just east of Lake Eola is one of the city's main historic districts, on Orange Avenue, the heart of the downtown business sector. Here, in the space of just a few blocks, you'll see twenty different architectural styles. Some of the oldest structures are on Pine and Church Streets, which intersect and branch off Orange Avenue.

The Kress building on South Orange is a good example of art deco with a colored terracotta facade. The Rogers building at the corner of Magnolia and Pine Streets is of the Queen Anne style and features a pressed metal facade. The most visited spot in downtown Orlando is the Church Street Station, the entertainment complex occupying a full block on both sides of Church Street just off I-4. This is one of the few tourist places you're likely to find as many locals as out-of-towners. Church Street is downtown Orlando's favorite night spot.

It is an entertainment complex in the true sense of the word. Although it opens at 11 a.m., things don't get really lively until evening. The music and dancing last until 2 a.m., but the time to really explore Church Street is during the day, well before the crowds arrive.

The oldest and still one of the most popular attractions is Rosie O'Grady's Good Time Emporium, an authentic saloon that recaptures the lively spunk from the Gay 90s to the roaring 20s. The entertainment features Dixieland bands, Can-Can girls who dance on the bar tops, and the torch-singing 'last of the red-hot mamas.'

Apple Annie's Courtyard is a grand Victorian garden decorated with huge, twelve-foot mirrors made in Vienna around 1740. Phineas Phogg's Balloon Works is a high volume disco completely decorated in ballooning memorabilia. The Cheyenne Saloon and Opera House is often packed for the Grand Ole-Opry style stage show is at its peak. Lilie Marlene's Aviator's Pub & Restaurant emphasizes fine dining and genteel imbibing.

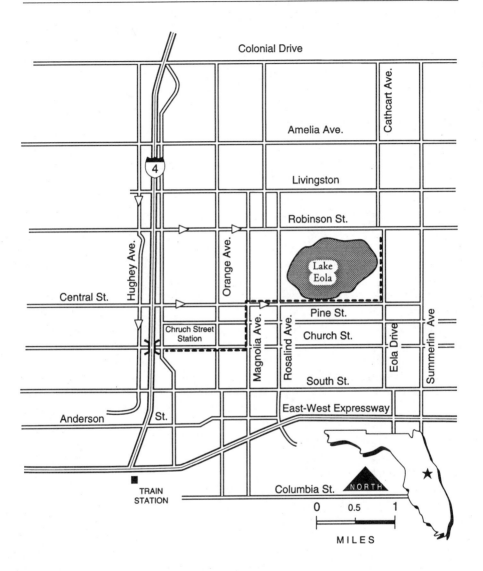

Church Street Station recently opened a huge 87,000-square foot Exchange with 50 different shops. The interior of the Exchange is a mix of the Victorian era and the early 20th century. The walls, floors, and ceiling have the same exhaustive attention to detail that characterize the neighboring Rosie O'Grady's and the Cheyenne Saloon.

The Church Street Market adjacent to the Exchange is technically a separate shopping area. Clowns, jugglers, and other street performers usually appear at dusk.

HIKE 86 WINTER PARK WALK

Directions: Take Interstate-4 to the Fairbanks Road/Rollins College exit (Exit 45) and go east two miles. On reaching Park Avenue, turn left and park on the side of the road or in one of several city parking lots.

The walk: Despite being surrounded by Orlando as well as several small suburbs, Winter Park has managed to remain unique and apart. This almost northern-looking community still retains a distinctive charm and friendly neighborhood atmosphere not found elsewhere in Central Florida.

Perhaps the prettiest section of Winter Park is Olde Winter Park, where the city was founded. With its large oaks draped in Spanish moss and brick streets, Olde Winter Park reminds some visitors of Georgia and the Carolinas more than of Florida.

The area around Rollins College and Lake Virginia contains many homes dating back eighty years or more. The styles are an eclectic mix of old and new, including several Spanish-style homes with red tile roofs.

The Orlando area's best shopping is on Winter Park's eight-block long Park Avenue. One section of the street is known as "Little Europe" because of its wide variety of antique stores, boutiques, French and continental restaurants, and open-air courtyards.

Park Avenue is where you'll find college students promenading hand in hand, matrons shopping for expensive gifts, and suburban professionals going to and from work. Shade-covered benches, several cafes, and many of the area's better restaurants all make pleasant rest stops.

Every March most of Park Avenue is close to traffic for the three-day Winter Park Sidewalk Art Festival that attracts as many as several hundred thousand people. Artists from all over the country enter the prestigious March showing to display sculpture, basketry, artistic jewelry, ceramics, and virtually any other type of art imaginable. The arts festival has also developed into a major social event that includes classical musicians and scores of food and drink vendors.

Far smaller is The Winter Park Autumn Art Festival. It is open only to Florida artists, but the work of the seventy-five exhibitors is normally of a very high quality. Scheduled the first weekend of every October, The Autumn Art Festival is held on the campus of Rollins College, at the southern end of Park Avenue.

SOUTH FLORIDA ATLANTIC COAST HIKES

South Florida hiking is dominated by one of the nation's most unusual and most fragile ecosystems, the great river of grass known as the Everglades. If you have time enough for only one major Florida hike, make it the Everglades. This region probably offers the best overall wildlife viewing in the state.

JONATHAN DICKINSON STATE PARK

This 11,500-acre park is named for Jonathan Dickinson, who in 1696 was shipwrecked about five miles from here. Dickinson was probably one of the first explorers to sample palmetto berries, a staple of the local Jaegas Indian diet. He reported: "They taste like rotten cheese steeped in tobacco juice." Obviously, an acquired taste.

Another local historical character of note was "The Wild Man of the Loxahatchee," a trapper, by name of Nelson, who died in 1968. He had built a popular wildlife zoo near his home that the state took over after his death. It's now the Trapper Nelson Interpretive Site upriver from the state park. Visitors can reach Trapper Nelson's zoo by taking the thirty-passenger "Loxahatchee Queen" from the park.

The trail system here features a series of loop trails. Despite nearby development, more than 500 animal species (including bald eagles, scrub jays, gopher tortoises) live within the park. About twenty percent of the park is covered in coastal sand pine scrub, a habitat so rare it is designated "globally imperiled."

General Description: Fourteen miles of the Florida Trail through sections of habitat designated "globally imperiled."

General Location: Just north of the town of Jupiter.

Maps: None needed.

Difficulty: Easy.

Special Attractions: The shores of the Loxahatchee River, a National Wild and Scenic River.

Season: Fall through early spring.

Camping: Two campgrounds with 135 sites; also vacation rental cabins.

Information: Jonathan Dickinson State Park, 16450 S.E. Federal Highway, Hobe Sound, FL 33455; (407) 546-2771.

HIKE 87 EAST LOOP

Finding the trailhead: Go 3.5 miles north of Jupiter on U.S. Highway 1; the park entrance is on the left.

The hike: This 9.5-mile trail begins at the north end of the parking lot at the entrance station. The path follows a varied path, first going through sand pine scrub, across Old Dixie Highway, and into stands of live oak. The Scrub Jay campsite is about six miles in; use only the fire ring for ground fires and camp within the borders of the trees marked with white rings on their trunks.

The trail then goes south for the next few miles, through pine and palmetto and across a fire road. It also parallels and crosses tracks of the Cross Florida East Coast Railroad before returning to the park gate.

HIKE 88 KITCHING CREEK TRAIL

Finding the trailhead: Go 3.5 miles north of Jupiter on U.S. Highway 1; the park entrance is on the left.

The hike: The four-mile Kitching Creek Trail is an extension of the East Loop. It passes through low pine flatwoods and Kitching Creek, a tributary of the Loxahatchee River. Initially, the trail penetrates thick saw palmetto and south Florida slash pine, once a continuous forest of century-old virgin pines over ninety feet tall and two feet in diameter. Settlers cut most of the trees to make homes from the hard, termite-resistant wood.

Kitching Creek itself is a cypress strand, a long narrow band of trees following a natural water course. The area was logged in the 1940s. The creek is named for the Kitching family, who bought the land from the state of

Snowy egret at Jonathan Dickinson State Park.

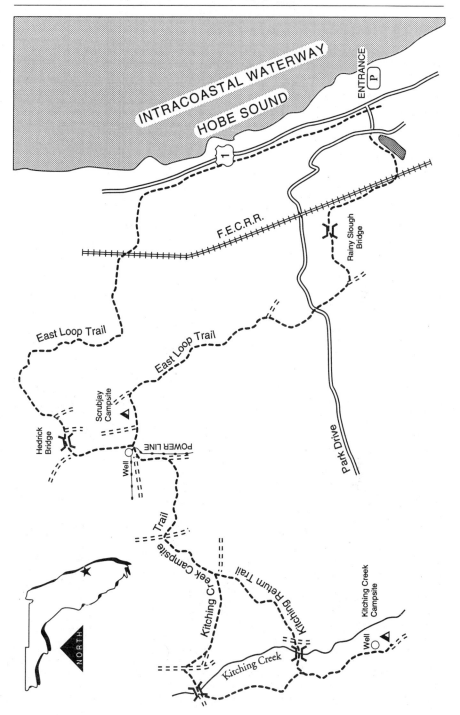

Florida for $1.25 an acre in 1886. The woman who purchased the land lived in England and probably never actually saw the property, or Florida.

Walking here, look for cabbage palm, the official Florida state tree. Similar in appearance to the saw palmetto when young, the cabbage palm is used to make "swamp cabbage" by cutting out the heart of the tree, which kills it. Swamp cabbage is found on many rural menus.

Although Indians ate the berries of the saw palmetto, don't try the black berries of the galberry, a member of the holly family, whose leaves have a few teeth on each side of the leaves. Galberries are poisonous. Like pine trees, saw palmetto is not harmed by fire because its roots are well protected underground. Settlers prized the bushes for making yard brooms.

DUPUIS RESERVE STATE FOREST

Located along the northeastern edge of the Everglades, much of this land was drained for pastureland. The South Florida Water Management District now intends to restore the wetlands.

As a public hunting area, the forest is closed to hikers during scheduled hunts. For current hunt dates, contact the Florida Game and Fresh Water Fish Commission at (407) 683-0748.

General Description: A section of the Florida Trail through a 21,900-acre forest reserve. A public hunting area.

Armadillos are common residents of Dupuis Reserve State Forest.

General Location: In western Palm Beach and Martin counties.

Maps: None needed.

Difficulty: Easy to moderate. May be wet for long stretches.

Special Attractions: Diverse terrain, home to a number of endangered and threatened plants and animals.

Season: Fall through early spring.

Camping: A permit is required to stay overnight at the primitive campsite. Contact the South Florida Water Management District: (800) 847-5067.

HIKE 89 DUPUIS RESERVE

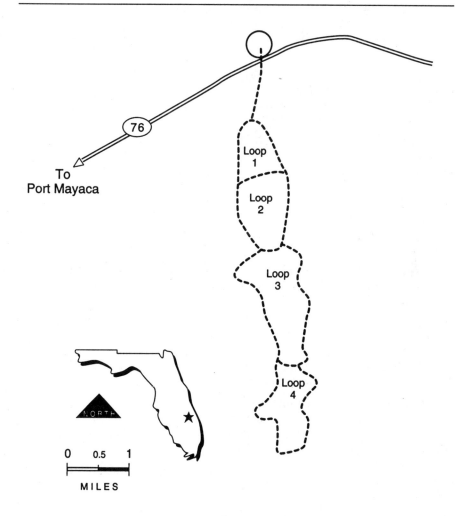

Information: The Florida Game and Fresh Water Fish Commission regulates public access to the land; call (407) 683-0748.

HIKE 89 DUPUIS RESERVE

Finding the trailhead: Take State Road 76 west and go six miles beyond its junction with State Road 710 at Indiantown. The signed trailhead is off State Road 76.

The hike: This fifteen-mile walk meanders through an impressive array of landscapes that include pine flatwoods, ponds, and cypress domes, wet prairies, and cabbage palm hammocks. Hikers have a wide choice of how much or how little of the fifteen-mile length to walk: this is a stacked loop system of four separate loops. Using the first two loops dramatically shortens the walk.

Just under a mile into the walk is the junction for the loops designated "East" and "West." Going eastward, you'll pass several horse trails and a fence before coming to the first east-west link about two miles from the trailhead. The junction for the second crosstrail is just over three miles into the walk after crossing a fence. Another chance to loop from east to west is at about 5.5 miles.

If you follow the trail to mile 9.5, the path makes its final loop to the west for the return trip. Overnighters can continue forward a short distance to the one trail campsite.

Since this is a multi-use area open to trail rides expect to cross a number of horse trails, as well as ditches and fences. They occur as often as one almost every half mile.

As a result, hikers are constantly reminded of people, places, and things; in some other state forests it is possible to go for miles without finding a trace of another person.

CORBETT WILDLIFE MANAGEMENT AREA

Red-cockaded woodpeckers, bald eagles, deer, and wild hogs are just a few of the animals normally found in Corbett Wildlife Management Area. In spring and summer, wildflowers transform the landscape with dramatic color.

Be prepared to wade in low areas after heavy rains and take plenty of water. None of the campsites have water.

General Description: A fourteen-mile section of the Florida Trail through classic pine flatwoods and saw palmetto. A public hunting area. Hikers must have a wildlife management permit, available at sporting goods stores and county tax offices.

General Location: West of Palm Beach and adjacent to the DuPuis Reserve State Forest.

The brown pelican is a common resident of Central Florida.

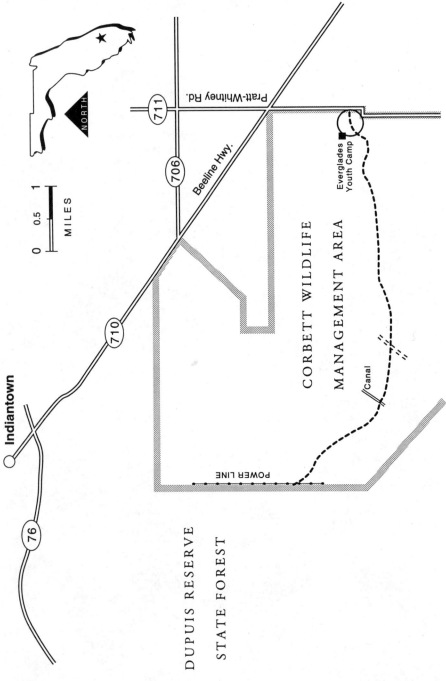

Maps: None needed.

Difficulty: Easy to moderate.

Special Attractions: The variety of bird and animal life.

Season: Fall through early spring.

Camping: Two primitive campsites on the trail.

Information: The Florida Game and Fresh Water Fish Commission is responsible for public access: (800) 432-2046; (407) 683-0748.

HIKE 90 CORBETT WILDLIFE MANAGEMENT AREA

Finding the trailhead: Go about seven miles northwest of the Old Military Trail and State Road 710 intersection in West Palm Beach. The trailhead is at the Everglades Youth Camp on Stumper's Grade Road, almost four miles south of the entrance to the wildlife management area.

The hike: The trail crosses wet prairie (prime wildflower territory) almost immediately. After crossing both improved and unimproved roads look for a side trail to the first campsite about five miles in.

The second campsite is at eleven miles in, shortly after crossing an unimproved road. Near the end of the hike the trail passes an electrical transmission line loaded with a half-million volts. The trail ends fourteen miles in at the western boundary of Corbett Wildlife Management Area. At this point you must retrace your steps, since there is no access for a vehicle to pick you up.

SOUTH FLORIDA GULF COAST HIKES

SANIBEL-CAPTIVA ISLANDS

The barrier islands of Sanibel and Captiva are two of the most popular vacation spots on the entire Gulf coast. A four-lane causeway moves literally hundreds of thousands of people back and forth to the mainland annually. The beaches are superb and the fishing for snook, trout, and redfish is excellent.

In the 1880s, all of Sanibel was a wildlife refuge. Today, much of the island is developed with restaurants, resorts, and condominiums. The natural places are growing increasingly scarce.

Sanibel is world famous for its excellent shelling, which is at its best following fall and winter storms when waves push thousands of shells onto the beach. It's possible to find many varieties of shells, but probably the most sought-after is the Florida horse conch, a huge orange shell large enough for Neptune himself to use as a horn.

Although most of the half-million people who annually visit the J.N. "Ding" Darling National Wildlife Refuge do so by car, biking and walking offer a slower pace in which to enjoy this area and to view wildlife. Bike paths extend for more than twenty miles on Sanibel, winding beside the main thoroughfare from the southern to northern tip. Also, it's quite easy to walk the five-mile roadway atop a mosquito control dike that passes through mangrove forests and tidal pools. Waterfowl are particularly plentiful, but also look for herons, egrets, plovers, and ibis stalking the mud flats in search of shrimp, marine worms, aquatic insects, and other tidbits. Alligators, too, of course. Far less known are the following trails, located at the Sanibel-Captiva Conservation Assoc. on Sanibel Island.

General Description: Three different nature trails totaling 4.5 miles on one of Florida's most beautiful barrier islands.

General Location: Sanibel Island, west of Fort Myers.

Maps: None needed.

Difficultly: Easy.

Special Attractions: Guided trail and nature walks; also a nursery growing native plants.

Season: Anytime.

Camping: Not available on the islands.

The Sanibel-Captiva Islands offer some of the best sea shell hunting.

Information: Sanibel-Captiva Conservation Association, P.O. Box 839, Sanibel, FL 33957; (813) 472-2329. Trails, exhibit and education center open 9 a.m. to 4 p.m. Monday through Saturday. Native plant nursery open 9 a.m. to 5 p.m. Monday through Friday and 9:30 a.m. to 2:30 p.m. on Saturday.

HIKE 91 SANIBEL-CAPTIVA NATURE TRAIL

Finding the trailhead: Take the causeway to Sanibel Island. Go one mile west of Tarpon Bay Road. The Sanibel-Captiva Conservation Foundation will be on your left.

The hikes: The nature walks criss-cross a thousand acres of sensitive habitat leave from the education center of the Sanibel-Captiva Conservation Foundation. All are quite short: the East River Loop is 1.1 miles; the Upper Ridge Trail is 0.47 of a mile; the Booth Courtenay Trail is 0.36 of a mile; and the West River Trail is 0.22 of a mile. One of the most popular walks is to Alligator Hole, a roundtrip of 1.27 miles.

Stay on the pathways since poison ivy abounds everywhere, and come dressed to get your feet wet. It's not uncommon for hikers to see alligators on the trails: never approach or feed them.

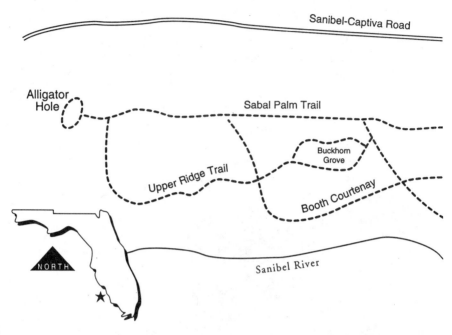

The alligator is considered the region's most popular animal attraction, and the foundation spends a good deal of time educating visitors about the importance of the gators. For instance, of the twenty-six different kinds of crocodillians around the world today, the American alligator typically is the least aggressive.

In the early 1900s, alligators were plentiful throughout the southern United States, found in freshwater systems from the Rio Grande of Texas into southern Oklahoma, and from North Carolina to the Keys.

MYAKKA RIVER STATE PARK

This 29,000-acre state park has long been noted for its wildlife: bald eagles, sandhill cranes, deer, turkey, ospreys, bobcats, otters, wild hogs, alligators, and waterfowl. In a sense, Myakka is a microcosm of the animal life found in many other South Florida refuges, though Myakka is comparatively farther north than most.

The landscape, too, is incredibly diverse. The trail will take you into live oak and cabbage palm flatwoods, open expanses of palmetto, and past small marshes.

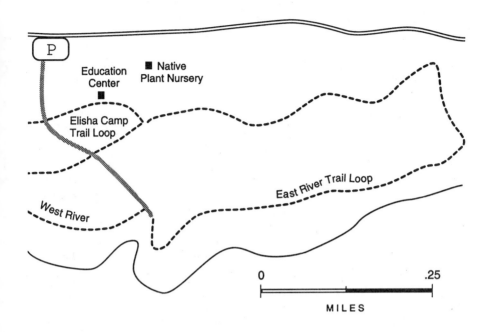

P

Education Center
■

■ Native Plant Nursery

Elisha Camp Trail Loop

West River

East River Trail Loop

0   .25

MILES

The park's crowning glory is the 7,500-acre wilderness preserve at the southern end, virtually untouched for hundreds of years. Access here is strictly limited to hikers and canoeists.

General Description: A stacked loop trail of thirty-three miles; this section of the Florida Trail goes through Florida's largest state park.

General Location: Fifteen miles east of Sarasota.

Maps: None needed.

Difficulty: Easy to moderate.

Special Attractions: This is mostly flat, dry terrain with abundant wildlife that includes a 7,500-acre wilderness preserve.

Season: Fall to early spring.

Camping: Five different campsites on the trail, the first a little more than four miles in. Also seventy-six developed sites.

Information: Myakka River State Park, Route 1, Box 72, Sarasota, FL 33577; (813) 361-6511.

HIKE 92 MYAKKA RIVER

Finding the trailhead: From Sarasota, go seventeen miles east on State Road 72 to the park. Hikers must register at the park office to obtain the lock combination for the trailhead gate. To locate the trailhead, go 0.3 mile beyond Bird Lake and pass through two chain fences. Park at the second. Follow the access trail several hundred yards to the main trail.

The hike: This stacked loop trail provides three points where you can turn the walk into a short day hike. If you intend to do all thirty-three miles, plan to camp overnight.

The loops are Bee Island, Honore, Deer Prairie, and East Loop. The crosstrails come at mile four, where the blue-blazed crosstrail extends for two miles; at just over eleven miles where the crosstrail known as Bobcat is just under a full mile; and at mile sixteen with a 1.5-mile crosstrail.

Carry binoculars to take advantage of the prolific animal life: spindly-legged sandhill cranes, the barred owls that appear near sunset, and possums, raccoons, and ibis. Despite the great amount of wildlife residing here, what you see depends on luck as much as anything else. Even if you don't see anything, keep your ears open. What you hear (the chorus of frogs and crickets or the bellow of a distant alligator) is often as entertaining as what you see: sometimes better, since your imagination can conjure up sights stranger than you (or anyone else) could ever encounter.

The trail's primitive campsites are located near a well and an old cattle dip vat, but the water is not drinkable. Either treat the well water or bring plenty of your own. Going counterclockwise, the campsites are: Bee Island, mile 4.2; Honore, mile 8.5; Panther Point, mile thirteen; Prairie, mile twenty-one; and Oak Grove, mile twenty-four. Only twelve campers are permitted at each site.

Ferns cover much of the ground in Myakka River State Park.

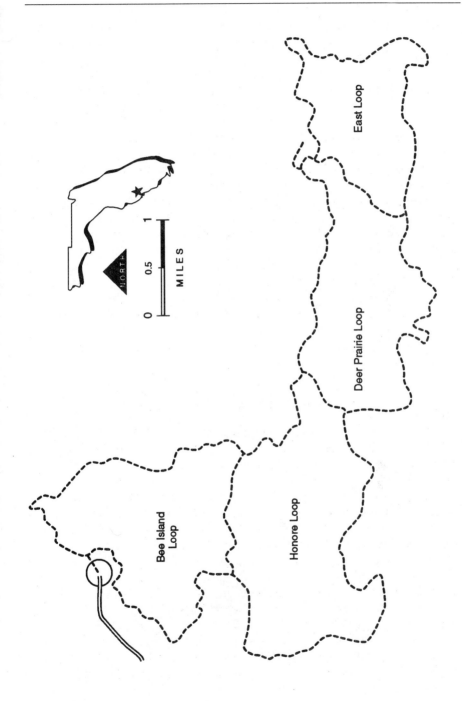

THE EVERGLADES REGION–EAST

The Everglades are the largest remaining subtropical wilderness in the continental United States. Thanks to the popularity of Everglades National Park, many people believe the park is THE Everglades. Unfortunately, it is not. Everglades National Park (1.5 million acres) and the adjoining Big Cypress National Preserve (716,000 acres) protect only about twenty percent of the huge area the Indians called "Pahayokee," or "grassy waters."

Over a million people a year visit Everglades National Park to see the profusion of bird and animal life that is America's equivalent of an African big game safari. Many animals are so accustomed to seeing three-eyed humans (that third eye being a camera lens) you'll be able to approach them quite closely.

Part of the Everglades was in the direct path of 1992's Hurricane Andrew, the costliest storm in the nation's history. Although the 165-mile-per-hour winds snapped pine trees in half and uprooted some larger trees, animal life fared remarkably well. For instance, all thirty-two of the park's radio-collared deer survived the storm and the entire deer herd seemed little affected. Ibis and egret populations also escaped serious damage. It was the coastal mangrove rookeries that appeared the most disrupted.

Ironically, Andrew's greatest impact may not be what it removed from the Everglades but what it added. Scientists are concerned that new non-native vegetation may now take root in the park to compete with native plants.

WHAT MAKES THE EVERGLADES UNIQUE?

The terrain of the Everglades is extremely low and flat, with the highest point only about eight feet above water. Obviously, the terrain hasn't risen very far since it was part of the sea bottom as recently as 6,000 to 8,000 years ago.

The bedrock beneath the Glades is unusual. Known as oolite or "egg stone," oolite granules resemble a cluster of fish eggs. This is the result of South Florida repeatedly sinking into the sea and then re-emerging from it, which has occurred at least four times in recent geologic history. Each time the land disappeared, millions of plants and animals perished, decomposed, and deposited calcium carbonate on the sea floor. In turn, the calcium carbonate hardened around grains of sand to create the oolite.

A visit to the Everglades is almost like a visit to the Caribbean: Everglades plants are more akin to those of the Caribbean than North America. The gumbo limbo with its reddish bark and twisting branches is one of the best-known examples. Although tree hammocks are found throughout the park, the Everglades primarily are a shallow plain of sawgrass growing in water only six inches deep.

This blanket of water has been likened to a tropical, primordial soup of algae and bacteria. Unappetizing as that may sound, it nourishes snakes, turtles, fish, and insects, which in turn feed the incredibly rich population of birds.

Traditionally the Glades' most important water source has been Lake Okeechobee, located sixty miles north of the park. Each summer, Okeechobee (second-largest fresh water lake in the continental United States) would overflow and send a sheet of water fifty miles wide that moved over the landscape. The water advanced about 100 feet a day, thoroughly watering and flushing the sawgrass, eventually reaching the mangrove estuaries on the Gulf of Mexico.

This annual flood was always followed by a six-month dry season. Birds and animals adapted and patterned their lives based on this alternating cycle.

THE HUMAN IMPACT

Archaeologists say that at least three different Indian tribes lived in the Everglades before Europeans arrived. Indians living in the western-most region were called Calusa; those around Lake Okeechobee in the central section were the Mayaimi; the Indians living near the east coast were the Tequesta. The names of the two latter tribes are memorialized in the names of two South Florida cities.

Most of the Native Americans you see in the Everglades today are descendants of the Seminoles who moved into the area in the 1800s. They remained free here only because the land was considered so inhospitable that no one else wanted it.

However, the soil was found to be rich and fertile, so beginning in the twentieth century, massive attempts were made to regulate the water flow for the benefit of farmers and cattlemen. From 1905 to 1925, the state and federal governments opened several thousand acres for farming, but a hurricane in 1928 caused considerable destruction and killed 1,800 people. That prompted the federal government to dam and dike Lake Okeechobee to prevent another such disaster.

A disaster occurred anyway. This time, it was the wildlife that suffered. Though the Everglades may receive sixty or more inches of rain in a year, almost four-fifths of it is lost to evaporation and runoff. Consequently, Lake Okeechobee's floodwaters have always been essential to maintain the proper, delicate balance. By altering Okeechobee's annual overflow, life in the Glades was severely disrupted.

The statistics are almost sickening. Since the 1930s, water birds have declined an astounding ninety-three percent. Today, about 18,500 water birds inhabit in the park, dramatically fewer than the estimated 265,000 residing here in the 1930s.

The thriving alligator population also plummeted. Gators, like the water birds, suffered not because there was too little water—instead, there was often far too much of it. Gators build their nests at the normal high-water level, and if floodgates release more water and the level goes higher, the gator nests are flooded and destroyed.

Another species virtually decimated was the snail kite. The entire North American population declined to only about two dozen birds by the 1960s. Snail kites feed predominantly on apple snails, which lay their eggs above the high water line. Add too much water, and there go the snails. Wood storks, considered one of the key barometers of the Everglades' health, are still in considerable trouble. Since the 1960s they have dwindled from 6,000 to 500 individuals.

In addition, Everglades water quality has seriously deteriorated, due to massive runoffs of farm nutrients that kill beneficial algae and promote the growth of harmful marsh vegetation. The dairy industry was one of the most unlikely culprits: a single dairy cow daily produces as much raw waste as twenty people, and there are a lot of dairy cattle in the water basin that supports the Everglades.

High levels of mercury, evidently fallout from power plants and other sources, have also infected the food chain. In fact, fishermen today are advised to limit their consumption of fresh water fish from the Everglades to about one a week.

On top of all this, people are in the process of drinking Florida dry. Florida has the fourth-largest population in the United States and it is still growing. An estimated 1,000 persons move into the Sunshine State each and every day, a group which gulps down or flushes another 200,000 gallons of water daily. Another forty million visitors drink and flush water on their vacations.

Paving over the land to build roads, homes, schools, and shopping centers has reduced the amount of rainwater reaching the underground aquifers that supply the water in the first place.

If the water table continues to drop, saltwater incursion into the fresh water aquifer could have dire consequences. It would impact soil quality and the ability of plants to grow, and eliminate the potable water. People will have to rely on desalinization plants, quite a costly process.

As you will discover on a score of hiking trails, the Everglades is an irreplaceable land that can provide many unforgettable experiences. Shouldn't your descendants enjoy them, too? Anytime you hear Congress or anyone else discussing the fate and future of the Everglades, let your elected representatives know how important this region is to you.

We all need to be vigilant about keeping the Everglades a memorable place—and not let it fade into a memory.

The following sites are all in the Everglades region, though not necessarily in Everglades National Park itself. They are listed from north to south and from east to west, a route most Florida visitors take.

This Everglades resident is called a limpkin.

LOXAHATCHEE NATIONAL WILDLIFE REFUGE

Loxahatchee offers excellent wildlife viewing. It is one of the best places to encounter alligators in the numbers most visitors expect to find in Florida. In fact, there's usually a gator in the slough right in front of the visitor center.

Loxahatchee Refuge provides vital habitat that protects endangered and threatened creatures such as the wood stork, snail kite, alligator, and others. It is also an important wintering ground for waterfowl and other migratory birds.

About half of the 220-square mile refuge is closed to the public. Hunting and fishing are permitted in several sections, but all the hiking is conveniently located near the visitor center off U.S. Highway 441.

General Description: A northeastern section of the Everglades outside the National Park, featuring a short boardwalk through a dense cypress swamp and paths along marsh-filled water compartments.

General Location: West of Palm Beach and Lake Worth.

Maps: None needed.

Difficulty: Easy. The boardwalk is wheelchair accessible.

Special Attractions: An excellent opportunity to see alligators up close. Also many types of water birds.

Camping: None on property.

Information: Refuge Manager, Route 1 Box 278, Delray Beach, FL 33444; (407) 734-8303. Once in the Palm Beach area, tune your radio to 530 AM for the latest Loxahatchee information. The refuge is open daily from sunrise to sunset.

HIKE 93 CYPRESS SWAMP AND MARSH TRAILS

Finding the trailhead: From the Florida Turnpike or Interstate-95, take U.S. Highway 98 west to U.S. Highway 441. Go south about ten miles on U.S. 441. The main refuge entrance is on the right off U.S. 441 between State Road 804 and State Road 806. The visitor center and its boardwalk are just inside the park, on the right.

The hikes: The boardwalk behind the visitor center penetrates a dense cypress swamp that is truly eerie in its stillness and closeness. One of the more remarkable sights here is the tremendous number of air plants rooted to the trees. They are attached to the skinny cypress trunks and branches one after another, like decorations on a Christmas tree.

The air plants, or epiphytes, are among the most interesting plants in the Everglades. They are nonparasitic and use their roots only as anchors. Because of the alternating cycle of drought and high humidity, many of them have tough skins to reduce moisture loss while others have thick stems in which to store it. Many are shaped to collect water at their bases.

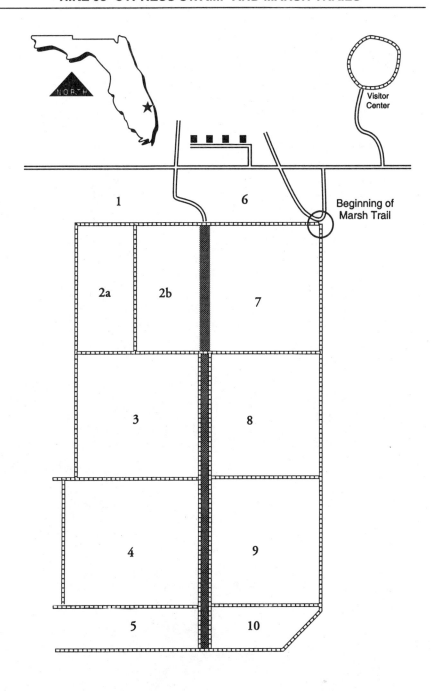

The boardwalk takes between twenty and thirty minutes, at most. Afterwards, walk or drive just a few hundred yards farther into the refuge and turn left at the Marsh Trail. Here you can walk along the levees (dikes) that border a series of water impoundments. As the map shows, this is a rectangular arrangement where almost a dozen sections are bordered by a pathway, allowing fairly close access to the birds. A canal splits the area almost down the middle, but a walkway allows you to crossover.

If you're truly fortunate, you may be able to spot the emblematic bird of the Everglades—the roseate spoonbill. It is quite distinctive with bright pink plumage on its body and the sides of its wings. When feeding, it shakes its spoon-shaped bill back and forth in the water to trap food. Unfortunately, like some other wading birds, roseate spoonbills are not so common anymore.

To many, the representative Everglades animal is the alligator. Although they may seem to do little else but bask in the sun and play dead, they can move incredibly fast. This is one reason they enjoy such a diverse diet of turtles, garfish, wading birds, and anything else that comes too close to the water's edge at dinner time. Incidentally, one of the gator's favorite delicacies is dog (as in family pet). Alligators have frequently created great commotion by sneaking into the backyards of homes built along canals to dine on the dogs that lived there. If you are traveling with a dog, never leave it alone near gator-inhabited water anywhere in South Florida.

A roseate spoonbill.

LAKE OKEECHOBEE

Okeechobee, the Seminole Indian word for "big water," is located only forty miles northwest of Palm Beach. At 448,000 acres, Lake Okeechobee is the second-largest freshwater lake in the continental United States with a shoreline of 135 miles.

It is also the all-important water supply for the megalopolis of Miami, and for the Everglades.

Long regarded one of Florida's best fishing lakes, Okeechobee is relatively shallow: the average depth is about seven feet, the maximum about fifteen. Since 1881, attempts have been made to control the lake's annual overflow during the rainy season. This finally was accomplished by an eighty-five mile levee constructed on the southern shore and at other low stretches.

This levee, or dike system, also constitutes the official Florida Trail surrounding the lake. Don't worry about wading during heavy rains: the dike averages thirty-four feet, or about twenty feet above the lake level. As a result, hikers enjoy striking views of the lake and the surrounding area. Where canals intersect with the lake, trails leave the dike and cross the waterway by bridge, then return to the dike.

Although the hike is divided into four sections, the trails are contiguous, and avid hikers could loop the entire lake atop the dikes.

General Description: Four sections of the Florida Trail varying from twenty to forty miles, atop the dike system bordering the nation's second-largest freshwater lake.

General Location: Highlands, Okeechobee, Martin, Palm Beach, Glades, and Hendry Counties.

Maps: Since most of the trail borders Lake Okeechobee, maps are not required.

Difficulty: Easy to moderate. The dikes lack shade, so sun protection is essential. Some sections are quite remote.

Special Attractions: A first-hand look at the extensive engineering required to keep the Miami area supplied with water, often to the detriment of the Everglades.

Season: Fall through early spring.

Camping: Allowed on the dike at specified sites. Also available at the different recreation areas and several of the fish camps.

Information: Call the Army Corps of Engineers at (813) 983-8101. They have jurisdiction over this area and can inform you of any changes and where camping is permitted.

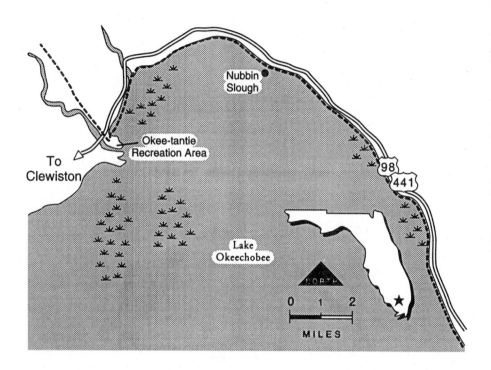

HIKE 94 OKEECHOBEE EAST

Finding the trailhead: Okeechobee East begins at the Okee-tantie Recreation Area on State Road 78 about six miles southwest of the town of Okeechobee; that's the north shore of Lake Okeechobee, where the Kissimmee River drains into the lake.

The hike: This 36.2-mile leg begins on Taylor Creek Lodge Road and crosses Taylor Creek before the trail actually stays on the dike for any period. Even then hikers must detour to cross Nubbin Slough on U.S. Highway 441 (at about mile nine) and the bridge at Henry Creek (about mile twelve). Afterwards, the dike runs continuously for about six miles until the bridge at Chancy Bay, also site of the J&S Fish Camp.

At Port Mayaca (about mile twenty-seven) take the bridge over the St. Lucie Canal and cross several small inlets to reach the official end at Canal Point Recreation Area.

HIKE 95 OKEECHOBEE SOUTHEAST

Finding the trailhead: From the town of Okeechobee go approx. 33 miles along U.S. Highway 98/441 (which borders the lake) to Canal Point. The trail is off to the right, on an unpaved access road through the gate to the dike. Look for the Florida Trail sign.

The hike: This 29.2-mile leg runs from Canal Point to Clewiston. You'll reach the northern boundary of Pahokee State Park at about mile 3.5, the park's southern boundary a little over a half-mile later; you can camp in the park. Then you'll pass through several gates before crossing the State Road 717 bridge and reaching Slim's Fish Camp at about mile fourteen.

It's necessary to call ahead to Slim's—(407) 996-8750—to arrange boat passage past the hurricane gates. Following that crossing, you'll have several access roads to U.S. 27 if you need them.

The trail ends at the Clewiston floodgate at the U.S. 27 bridge inside the Clewiston city line.

HIKE 95 OKEECHOBEE SOUTHEAST

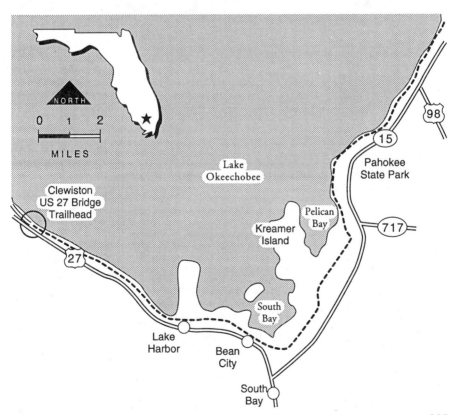

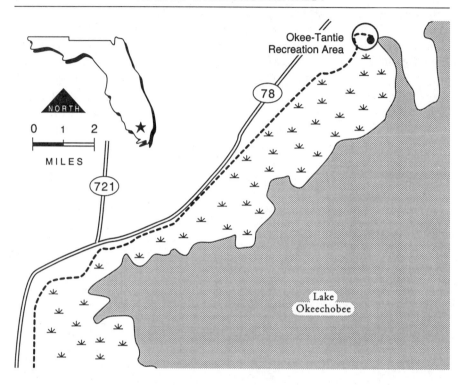

HIKE 96 OKEECHOBEE WEST

Finding the trailhead: The northern trailhead for Okeechobee West begins at the Okee-tantie Recreation Area on State Road 78, about six miles southwest of the town of Okeechobee.

The hike: You won't have very good views of the lake on this 21.9-mile leg: runaway exotic plants—melaleuca and Australian pine—tend to obliterate the view. What makes the walk worth doing is so you can later say you've walked around the entire lake.

Going west, cross the Kissimmee River and the Indian Prairie Canal via the State Road 78 bridge. This leg isn't as subdivided with canals as the other Okeechobee trails. The walk ends after crossing the Curry Island slough and canal (near Sportsman Village), also on State Road 78.

HIKE 97 OKEECHOBEE SOUTHWEST

Finding the trailhead: The dike trail starts at State Road 78 before the Moore Haven Recreation Area.

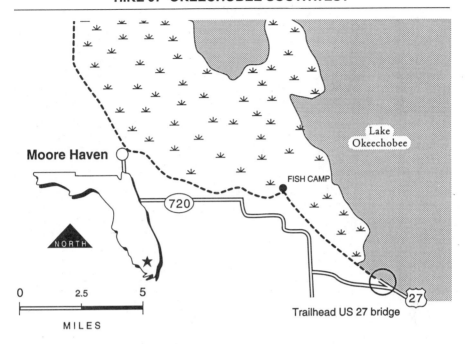

The hike: This 20.5-mile leg also parallels State Road 78, then leaves it to pass the Moore Haven Recreation Area, and crosses the Caloosahatchee River via U.S. Highway 27 to reach the Moore Haven flood gate (at about mile nine). Remaining atop the dike much of the way, you'll pass Liberty Point and Anglers Marina. For about the last 0.5-mile, the route follows U.S. 27 to dead-end at the U.S. 27 bridge in Clewiston, also the terminus for the east shore hikes.

EVERGLADES NATIONAL PARK

It's possible to walk the forty-mile length from the visitor center at the main park entrance to Flamingo at the southern tip, but do it only in cooler weather. Most people prefer to drive the paved road, stopping periodically at the series of hiking trails located along the route. Park admission is slightly less for walk-ins.

Take time to collect all available material at the visitor center and to inspect the selection of books for sale. This is an excellent place to collect a library on the flora and fauna of Florida.

Rangers like to keep the park in as much of a natural state as possible, and that means leaving undisturbed both the bad and the good. Since mosquitoes are a natural part of the Everglades environment—more so than

Gumbo limbo trees in the Everglades.

man—they are allowed to bite whom they want whenever they want; no spraying is conducted.

At twilight be in your tent, your car, or your Flamingo hotel room unless you want to undergo a truly hellish experience. I personally have never encountered mosquitoes as thick and hungry anywhere else in the world, and that includes all seven continents. Trailheads in Everglades National Park are found in three distinct areas: along the main park road from Homestead to Flamingo; from the Flamingo visitor center and campground; and at Shark Valley off of U.S. Highway 41.

General Description: Florida's premier wildlife preserve, Everglades is the second-largest national park in the contiguous United States (after Yellowstone).

General Location: The main park entrance is about an hour south of Miami.

Maps: None needed to actually find your way, but pick up a copy of the free park brochure at the main visitor center, which gives the general location of the trails within the park.

Difficulty: Easy. Many places are wheelchair accessible. A tram ride is available for the fifteen-mile Shark Valley loop road.

Special Attractions: 2,000 species of plants, 51 types of reptiles, 17 of amphibians, 40 different mammals, and 347 assorted birds.

Season: Winter. There are more birds and fewer mosquitoes.

Camping: Camping is normally available in several locations throughout the park, but Hurricane Andrew affected some facilities. Call ahead.

Information: Everglades National Park, P.O. Box 279, Homestead, FL 33030; (305) 247-6211. Be sure to obtain a copy of the booklet "Everglades Wildlife" at the visitor center. Also obtain the latest schedule of ranger-led activities; it is possible to spend an entire day attending one program after another in both the Royal Palm and Flamingo areas.

ALONG THE PARK ROAD

HIKE 98 ANHINGA AND GUMBO LIMBO TRAILS

Finding the trailhead: Take State Road 9336 from Homestead to the park entrance. Drive two miles and turn left to the Royal Palm visitor center. Both trails begin from the visitor center.

The hikes: The half-mile Anhinga Trail—the park's most popular—is named for one of Florida's most distinctive birds. The anhinga is also called the water turkey and snake bird: it swims almost totally submerged, with only its snaky-looking long neck and head above water. It captures food by diving

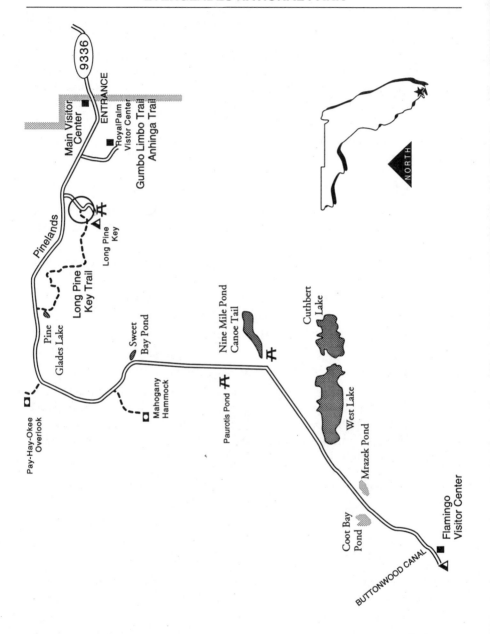

underwater and spearing fish with its beak, then surfaces and tosses the fish into the air, catches it, and swallows it head first.

Definitely a neat trick, but that's not what makes the anhinga so distinctive. The anhinga is the bird seen sitting on branches with its wings extended like it is in a state of alarm. Actually, the anhinga is drying its feathers because it lacks the oil glands most other water birds have to keep their plumage dry. If the anhinga didn't dry itself regularly, it could get so water-logged it would sink.

Anhingas are alluring but alligators are arresting. Look for gators in the pond behind the Royal Palm visitor center. You may find a big one nearly close enough to touch, with just a waist-high stone wall separating you from the reptile. Great pictures!

The Anhinga Trail boardwalk penetrates a sawgrass prairie and also offers superb views of Taylor Slough, one of the best places for wildlife in the park. Polarized sunglasses will help in sighting the prehistoric-looking garfish with their narrow streamlined bodies and long snouts. Compared to a garfish, a gator looks positively pleasant.

The Gumbo Limbo Trail is right next to the Anhinga Trail. Also a short, half-mile walk, this totally land-based loop winds through a hardwood hammock that is truly jungle-like. The trail is named for the tropical tree with the distinctive red bark; some park rangers call it the "tourist tree" in honor of sunburned visitors.

The trail wanders among ferns, orchids, air plants, and long trailing woody vines (you can't help but look for Tarzan), all the classic characteristics of a lush Caribbean forest. In places, a thick canopy high overhead dims the sunlight and seems to trap the humidity; bring bug spray.

The effects of Hurricane Andrew on some of the gumbo limbo trees will be demonstrated here for years to come. The winds toppled a number of the trees but did not destroy them. Native to a part of the world where hurricanes frequently occur, gumbo limbo trees survive—even if toppled sideways—by sending out a new root system. The gumbo limbo is a true survivor, and the hurricane's destructive effects graphically demonstrate this.

HIKE 99 PINELANDS TRAIL

Finding the trailhead: This trail begins just six miles from the visitor center on the road to Flamingo.

The hike: This half-mile trail loops through a forest of slash pines (also called Caribbean or Dade County pine). These slash pines are the only pine species that grow in the Glades.

These trees are able to grow here by setting their roots on a key, a Florida term for both hammocks and pinelands where the limestone rock rises above the surrounding wetlands. The pinelands have some of the highest and driest elevation in the park: three to seven feet above sea level.

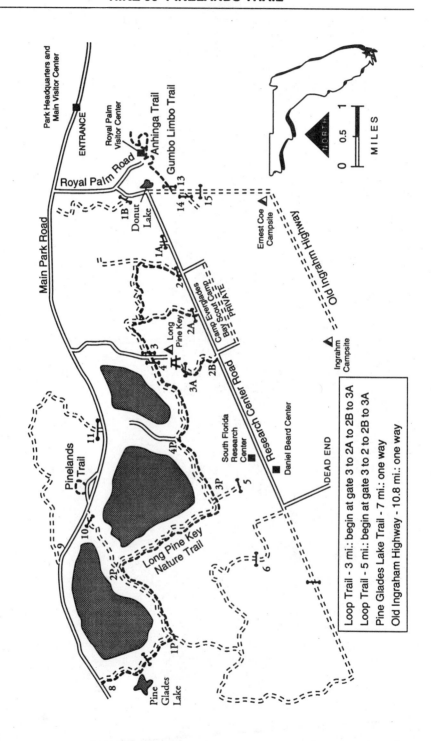

Park Headquarters and Main Visitor Center

ENTRANCE

Royal Palm Visitor Center

Anhinga Trail

Gumbo Limbo Trail

Royal Palm Road

Royal Palm Road

Main Park Road

1B

Donut Lake

14

13

15

1A

2

Ernest Coe Campsite

Old Ingrahm Highway

Long Pine Key

3

2A

Camp Everglades Bay Scout Camp PRIVATE

4

3A

2B

Ingrahm Campsite

Research Center Road

Pinelands Trail

11P

South Florida Research Center

4P

Daniel Beard Center

5

3P

DEAD END

Long Pine Key Nature Trail

10P

2P

6

9

1P

8

Pine Glades Lake

Loop Trail - 3 mi.: begin at gate 3 to 2A to 2B to 3A
Loop Trail - 5 mi.: begin at gate 3 to 2 to 2B to 3A
Pine Glades Lake Trail - 7 mi.: one way
Old Ingraham Highway - 10.8 mi.: one way

NORTH

0   0.5   1

MILES

Slash pines also require very little soil. In many places, the pines are rooted in the potholes that pock the limestone bedrock. Not much space for most trees, but these hollows also hold a rich combination of peat and marl.

Pinelands gradually evolve into a hardwood hammock if the area is not periodically burned. Young pine seedlings require plenty of sun to grow, and an unchecked understory of hardwoods will shade them out. Controlled burning, which culls the young hardwoods, leaves the pines sooty but undamaged. The Park Service has used fire since the 1950s to sustain the pinelands.

The Indians practiced the first fire management. They burned the pinelands to ensure that hardwoods did not replace the saw palmetto, which was important in their diet. Its starchy roots provided their source of flour.

From Homestead, you've been seeing the impact of Hurricane Andrew on the slash pines bordering the road. This area, too, sustained damage. It is a strange pattern of destruction: some trees still grow tall and straight, while others next to them are snapped in two.

HIKE 100 PA-HAY-OKEE OVERLOOK TRAIL

Finding the trailhead: Just over twelve miles from the visitor center on the road to Flamingo.

The hike: The Pa-hay-okee Overlook Trail is a short elevated boardwalk leading to an observation tower. This spot has always been a landmark for viewing the immense sawgrass prairie and its scattered, island-like hammocks.

The boardwalk extends for just under a quarter mile into the sawgrass, one of the oldest plant species in the world. Sawgrass richly deserves its name, but it's better to learn that by sight than by touch. Its tiny sharp teeth both discourage animals from grazing on it and help trap water during the dry season. On foggy nights the dew will condense on the plant's teeth and roll down the V-shaped midrib to the roots.

Classified as a sedge (*Cladium jamaicense*), the sawgrass extends as a river one hundred miles north and south from Lake Okeechobee to the Gulf Mexico, and fifty to seventy miles from east to west. Even during the wettest periods, the average water depth is only six inches.

You may see an alligator here but more likely it will be the birdlife that attracts your attention: red-shouldered hawks, red-winged blackbirds, and that most essential scavenger, the vulture. In Florida, vultures are protected by law.

HIKE 101 MAHOGANY HAMMOCK TRAIL

Finding the trailhead: Go about 19.5 miles from the visitor center on the road to Flamingo.

An anhinga drying its wings in the sun.

The hike: This half-mile trail is noted for having the nation's largest mahogany tree, with a girth of twelve feet and a height of ninety feet. Although winds were strong here, the tree survived Hurricane Andrew.

Andrew did reshape Mahogany Hammock by uprooting other trees. Eventually, ferns, moss, and lichens will colonize these newly fallen trees, repeating the cycle of regrowth.

Mahogany hammocks like this one are rare today in Florida. In the 16th and 17th centuries, the Spanish cut down most of the mahogany in the nearby Keys. Hard and durable, mahogany has long been highly prized for making furniture and boats.

HIKE 102 WEST LAKE TRAIL

Finding the trailhead: Located 30.5 miles into the park on the Flamingo Road.

The hike: The half-mile West Lake Trail is a good introduction to the mangrove forests that grow in brackish lakes like this one and on the coast. All four types of mangroves are found at West Lake. This lake is also a rare opportunity to see the almost extinct American crocodile.

Mosquitoes and mangroves go hand in hand, so take repellent.

Mangroves are a vital part of the Everglades ecosystem. They are nurseries for shrimp, crabs, lobsters, and small fish: the tight mangrove roots make wonderful hiding places to protect the tiny marine life from predators.

Mangroves also serve as important bird rookeries, secure from most land predators. Raccoons, in search of oysters growing on the prop roots, will sometimes dine on birds' eggs instead.

In trying to spot a crocodile here, remember that crocs vary in color from greenish to grayish, while alligators are blackish. The most pronounced difference between the two is the head: crocs have a narrow snout, gators have a broad, blunt one. You'll be fortunate to spot a crocodile, truly a vanishing species: only a few hundred remain in South Florida, compared to the state's estimated one million alligators.

HIKE 103 LONG PINE KEY

Finding the trailhead: On the road to Flamingo, just north of the town.

The hike: Long Pine Key boasts a seven-mile network of connecting trails through a forest of slash pines. Residents include opossums, raccoons, white-tailed deer, and even the endangered Florida panther.

A subspecies of cougar that adopted to Florida's tropical environment, the Florida panther has several distinctive characteristics: a cowlick in the middle of the back and a crook at the end of the tail. It also is lighter in weight, darker in color, and has smaller feet and longer legs than other cougar subspecies.

The panther is probably Florida's most endangered animal: only an estimated fifty of them remain. These cats survive only in remote and undeveloped areas; such habitat is increasingly scarce.

Like all cougars, the Florida panther is basically tawny in color along the back with a lighter color on the in the lower chest, belly, and inner legs. This color pattern closely mimics that of the white-tailed deer, the panther's primary prey.

Florida panthers make a surprising variety of noises, including chirps, whistles, moans, peeps, and growls; young kittens communicate with their mothers with chirps.

Don't look for panthers only in the woods. They are good swimmers and have been sighted swimming rivers as much as a mile wide. There is no recorded case of a panther attack on a person, ever. They shy away from humans.

Although panther sightings come in from all over the state, most are discounted. Panthers have definitely been seen in the Eastern Everglades, the Big Cypress Preserve, and the Fakahatchee Strand.

Because the Florida population is so low, panthers in captivity may be bred with cougars from other parts of the country, then the offspring released into the wild.

Unfortunately, not even the Everglades is a safe haven for the big cats. A dead panther was found to contain levels of mercury so high they would have been fatal for a human. How mercury is entering the South Florida environment is still not totally understood.

The elusive Florida panther.

THE FLAMINGO AREA

Once upon a time, this formerly quiet fishing village could only be reached by boats coming across Florida Bay and later through the Homestead-Flamingo Canal. Today, you can drive right up to Flamingo's visitor center, restaurant, lodge, and marina at the Everglades' southernmost tip.

Will you see flamingoes at Flamingo? Probably not, although they are being sighted again in Everglades backcountry for the first time in years.

However, on the Flamingo trails you may see unusually bold bobcats who, instead of running away, are usually little bothered by human presence. It's possible to watch a bobcat fairly closely and for a surprising length of time, even in daylight. Everglades bobcats are just as likely to be found in water as on land, as they search for marsh rabbits, rodents, and birds to feed on.

Flamingo is the gateway to Florida Bay and the coastal prairie. Florida Bay, a huge expanse larger than some states, extends from Flamingo to the Keys. It is incredibly shallow: parts of it are high and dry at low tide. Nine feet is the maximum recorded depth.

This is ideal habitat for the scores of birds that feed on the mudflats and in the shallows. Look for sandpipers, ospreys, egrets, pelicans, and others.

The magnificent snowy egret once thrived here in such large numbers that in the late 1800s Flamingo became an important center for the trade in bird plumage. Thousands of egrets, roseate spoonbills, and others were killed to supply plumage for women's clothing.

The collecting methods were particularly brutal. Plumage hunters normally waited until the birds were nesting, when the plumage was at its finest and the birds easiest to kill. Hunters would kill all the adult birds in a nest and leave the young to die. The National Audubon Society ended this wholesale slaughter by having the sale of plumage outlawed in New York, headquarters of the fashion industry.

Walking the coastal prairie bordering Florida Bay, you'll see such salt tolerant plants as mangroves and grasses. You'll notice hardwood hammocks, too, which survive here thanks to the Indian shell mounds that keep their root system high and dry. But you'll find these trees stunted because of the salty, harsh environment.

Flamingo offers eight separate hikes through the coastland. Most walks are less than five miles, but a thirteen-mile coastal trek will take most of a day and you may want to overnight on this trail.

HIKE 104 SNAKE BIGHT TRAIL

Finding the trailhead: On the park's main road to Flamingo, north of Mrazek Pond, on the left.

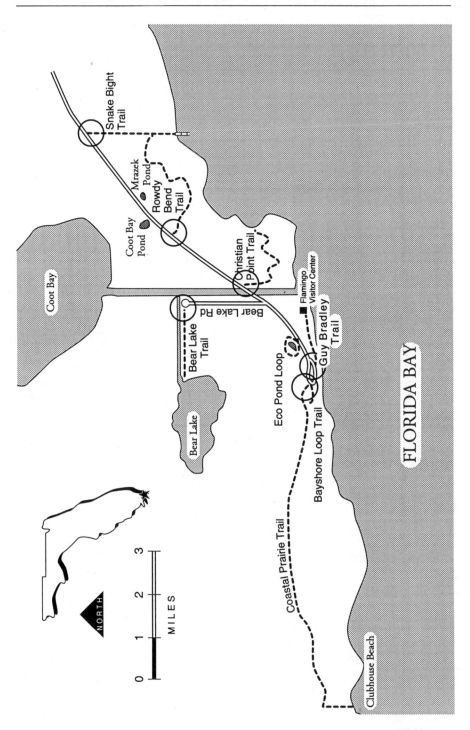

The hike: Snake Bight Trail is just 1.6 miles each way. Besides passing through a tropical hardwood hammock, it offers good bird watching on a boardwalk at the end of the trail.

HIKE 105 ROWDY BEND TRAIL

Finding the trailhead: This trail begins on the main park road just south of Coot Bay Pond and joins Snake Bight Trail.

The hike: Rowdy Bend Trail is 2.6 miles each way. It follows an old road bed shaded by buttonwoods, then meanders through open coastal prairie.

HIKE 106 CHRISTIAN POINT TRAIL

Finding the trailhead: On the road to Flamingo, on the left, just before the Buttonwood Canal leading to Coot Bay.

The hike: Christian Point Trail is 1.8 miles each way. It begins by following a path shaded by buttonwoods, then opens on the coastal prairie along Snake Bight. This is a good place to look for birds of prey.

HIKE 107 BEAR LAKE TRAIL

Finding the trailhead: Follow Bear Lake Road, which begins on the right near the Flamingo visitor center.

The hike: Bear Lake Trail is 1.6 miles each way. It is rich in both bird and plant life. First, the trail passes through a dense hardwood hammock mixed with mangroves containing more than thirty different tree species. This is an excellent spot for woodland birds. The trail ends at Bear Lake.

HIKE 108 ECO POND TRAIL

Finding the trailhead: Off the main road just past the Flamingo visitor center.

The hike: This is just a 0.5-mile loop but it can be loaded with birds and animals. At this fresh water pond you'll normally see wading birds, songbirds, alligators, and other wildlife. The best bird watching is early and late, from the ramped viewing platform.

HIKE 109 GUY BRADLEY TRAIL

Finding the trailhead: Starts at the Flamingo visitor center.

The hike: This is a one-mile shortcut between the Flamingo visitor center and campground amphitheater. Birds and butterflies are the main sights here, along the shore of Florida Bay. Guy Bradley was a warden killed by bird poachers here before the trade in plumage ended.

HIKE 110 BAYSHORE LOOP

Finding the trailhead: The walk begins in the Flamingo Campground at the Coastal Prairie Trailhead at the back of Loop C; go left at the trail junction to the Bay.

The hike: Bayshore Loop is a two-mile walk along Florida Bay that leads to the remains of a small fishing village.

HIKE 111 COASTAL PRAIRIE TRAIL

Finding the trailhead: The walk begins in the Flamingo Campground at the back of Loop C.

The hike: At 7.5 miles each way, the Coastal Prairie Trail is Flamingo's longest. The path follows an old road once trod by fishermen and cotton pickers. You'll pass through shaded sections of buttonwoods and open coast. To camp overnight first obtain a permit from the visitor center.

SHARK VALLEY

Shark Valley is in the northernmost sector of Everglades National Park. It cannot be reached from the Homestead to Flamingo Road. Instead, follow the Florida Turnpike to the U.S. Highway 41 exit, then head west. This park entrance is thirty miles west of Miami, on the left, adjacent to the Miccosukee Indian Village.

Although Shark Valley is not as well-known as other regions in the park, its fifteen-mile long, hard-surfaced trail penetrating directly into the wilderness is a prime wildlife viewing area. However, be prepared to share it with lots of other people unless you arrive when the Shark Valley gates open at 8 a.m.

Beginning on the hour, from 9 a.m. almost until closing, the park operates a two-hour tram ride along the road for less mobile visitors to see the birds, gators, deer, turtles, and other animals. At the end of the road is a fifty-foot high observation tower with a panoramic view deep into the Glades. The tram returns by a different road that parallels the first, so the scenery is totally different on the route back. Bikes also can be rented here, so hikers are bound to see quite a few other people. Most of Shark Valley's visitors ride instead of walk, so don't feel badly if you decide to join them. Reservations are recommended for the tram ride December through March; call (305) 221-8455.

Off the road, two short hiking trails lead through vegetation common to Everglades bayheads and hardwood hammocks. Phone number for the Shark Valley park office is (305) 221-8776.

HIKE 112 BOBCAT HAMMOCK BOARDWALK

Finding the trailhead: The trailhead is about a hundred yards from the visitor center following the tram road.

The hike: This boardwalk is only about 500 yards long and goes through a sawgrass prairie that also has extensive cattails. It then enters a lowland hammock of willows and other tree species which can survive wet conditions. Interpretive signs identify various plants and ecosystems.

HIKE 113 OTTER CAVE TRAIL

Finding the trailhead: On the tram road leading into the Everglades located 0.5 mile from the visitor facility.

The hike: The Otter Cave Trail is a loop trail only about 200 yards long. It penetrates a hardwood hammock of Caribbean and Bahamian type trees including gumbo limbo and stranger fig (a huge strangler is marked by a sign). Following Hurricane Andrew, this area is more open which is allowing new growth to emerge. As a loop road, this trail returns to the same tram road: if you do not pay close attention to the signs/markers here it is easy to become disoriented and mistakenly walk toward the distant observation tower instead of returning to the visitor center.

EVERGLADES REGION—WEST

BIG CYPRESS PRESERVE

Because of plans in the 1970s to turn part of the Big Cypress Swamp into a giant airport, Congress in 1974 established the 900 square mile Big Cypress National Preserve, a vital source of water for the Everglades.

Big Cypress is not really a swamp since the terrain is mostly areas of slash pine, hardwood hammocks, marshes, mangroves, and prairies both wet and dry. About a third of the preserve is covered with dwarf pond cypress.

Also found here are bald cypress as much as 700 years old, their girths larger than four people can span with joined hands. Look for lots of air plants and orchids growing on many of these trees.

This is also a land rich in bird and animal life. Herons and ibises, once counted according to the number of acres they covered at a single sighting, are still plentiful. This is also home to the wood stork, bald eagle, red-cockaded woodpecker, and wild turkey. Alligators are common, and the watchful hiker may find a panther track or traces of the black bears that still roam here.

This land once was so bountiful that it provided all the Indians needed to live. This is why you will still find many small Indian villages along the

Tamiami Trail. The alligator is still an important source of the Indians' livelihood, only today they hunt the alligator by airboat to show to tourists.

These Indians are mostly Miccosukees or "Trail Indians," who are a different tribe from the Muskogees or "Cow Creek Seminoles"; the two tribes do not share a common language. Many still live in dwellings similar to their ancestors: open-sided, thatch roofed dwellings (called "chickees") on stilts.

General Description: This thirty-one mile-walk marks the southern boundary of the Florida Trail.

General Location: On the Tamiami Trail between Miami and Naples.

Maps: Available at the Oasis Ranger Station.

Difficulty: Moderate, due to length and possible wading during the rainy season.

Special Attractions: The longest hike available in one of Florida's most pristine wilderness areas.

Season: December through March.

Camping: Two primitive campsites on the trail offer drinking water. The preserve also has a campground, and additional space is available at several commercial sites close by.

Information: Big Cypress National Preserve, Star Route Box 110, Ochopee, FL 33943; (813) 695-2000 (park headquarters) or (813) 695-4111 (Oasis Ranger Station).

A turtle stretches in the sun.

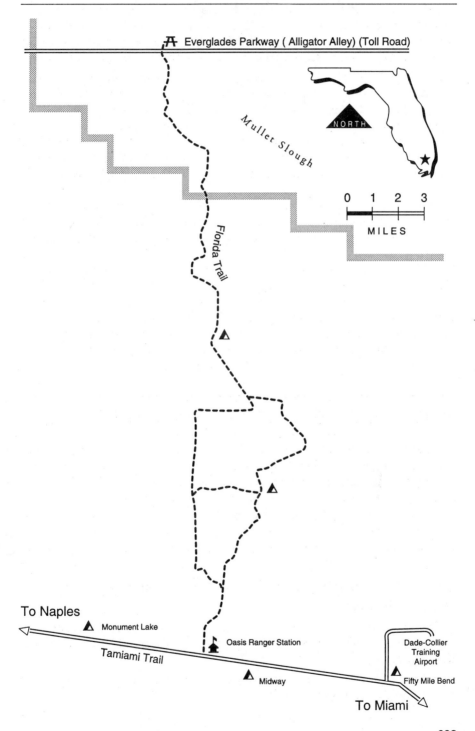

Everglades Parkway (Alligator Alley) (Toll Road)

Mullet Slough

NORTH

0   1   2   3

MILES

Florida Trail

To Naples

Monument Lake

Oasis Ranger Station

Tamiami Trail

Midway

Dade-Collier
Training
Airport

Fifty Mile Bend

To Miami

HIKE 114 BIG CYPRESS PRESERVE

Finding the trailhead: From Miami drive fifty miles west on U.S. Highway 41 to the Oasis Ranger Station visitor center. Officially, the trailhead is another eight miles south of the ranger station, beginning at Loop Road or State Road 94. As a practical matter, most hikers begin at the ranger station.

The hike: First, check at the ranger station about trail and camping conditions. Be prepared to wade certain areas almost any time of year, though January to April is normally driest. The trail passes through all the types of terrain, including prairies, hammocks, and cypress swamps.

As the map shows, this trail is not a single path but diverges about three miles beyond the ranger station. This gives you a choice of two loop trails and avoids the necessity of arranging a pickup on the Everglades Parkway (U.S. 75).

From this junction three miles in, the shorter loop encompasses a distance of about eleven miles, the longer one about 22.5 miles. Camping is available at several spots, so you can overnight regardless of which leg you take.

The main trail bears to the east to reach Seven Mile Camp, also the distance from the ranger station. This camp is noted for its after-dark entertainment of bobcat screams, and the more tranquil sounds of the chuck-will's-widow. A second camp is about seventeen miles into the hike.

The walk ends at the northernmost boundary of the Big Cypress Preserve. Florida Trail members can continue north but non-members must stop here since the trail now moves onto private land.

FAKAHATCHEE STRAND STATE PRESERVE

The Fakahatchee Strand, about twenty miles long and three to five miles wide, is the major drainage slough of the southwestern Big Cypress Swamp. It holds the largest stand of native royal palms and the largest concentration and variety of orchids in North America. Overall, Fakahatchee Strand is considered to have greater natural significance than anywhere of comparable size in Florida.

General Description: A 2,000-foot boardwalk through virgin cypress swamp.

General Location: On U.S. Highway 41 between Miami and Naples.

Maps: None needed.

Difficulty: Easy. For several hundred yards you must follow a dirt path that borders the Indian village; most of the time this should be wheelchair accessible.

Special Attractions: The forest is unique, consisting of bald cypress, royal palms and thousands of air plants.

Season: December through March.

Camping: Closest is at Collier-Seminole State Park (see below).

Information: Fakahatchee Strand State Preserve, Box 548, Copeland, FL 33926; (813) 695-4593.

HIKE 115 FAKAHATCHEE BOARDWALK

Finding the trailhead: Go west on U.S. 41. The boardwalk is on the right at Big Cypress Bend, seven miles beyond the junction with State Road 29. It is marked both by a state sign and a small Indian village.

The hike: As important as this area is, development for public use has been quite limited. Unlike other state parks and preserves, there is no need to visit the strand's ranger station near Copeland. Instead, go right to the boardwalk at Big Cypress Bend. This is a lengthy walk so plan to take an hour or more to truly appreciate this unique landscape.

This portion of the Big Cypress Swamp is a smooth, sloping limestone plain. During the rainy season of June through September, water flows over this plain to the mangroves lining the Gulf of Mexico. Channels cut into the limestone by the rainfall are referred to as drainage sloughs. These drainage sloughs are essentially elongated swamp forests that are a marked contrast to the open areas that border them. "Strand" is the local name for such elongated swamps.

The Tamiami Trail in the 1920s first made the Big Cypress Swamp accessible. You'll see plenty of alligators in the canals beside this roadway: imagine how wild this land was before any of it was developed. The Tamiami Trail took thirteen years to build, cost $13 million, and required three million pounds of dynamite. A considerable number of lives were lost along the way.

Fortunately, despite the intense logging efforts in the Big Cypress Swamp after the Trail opened, Fakahatchee Strand endured. Wood stork, black bear, mangrove fox squirrel, and the Everglades mink have all been sighted here, so look sharp.

COLLIER-SEMINOLE STATE PARK

This 6,423-acre park is named for Barron Collier, a developer who had planned to turn the land into a park, and for the Seminole Indians who made the area their home. The park is located where the Everglades and Big Cypress Swamp overlap. This accounts for unusually diverse wildlife habitats: tropical hammocks and pine flatwoods, salt and freshwater marshes, and mangrove and cypress swamps.

Rare Florida royal palms occur naturally here. One particular tropical hammock contains trees more characteristic of Mexico's Yucatan and the West Indies. A 6.5-mile segment of the Florida Trail is located outside the main park area.

General Description: A six-mile loop of the Florida Trail, perhaps the most tropical trail in the country.

General Location: Seventeen miles southeast of Naples.

Maps: None needed.

Difficulty: Easy to moderate, depending on water level.

Special Attractions: A walk through true Everglades environment where majestic royal palms line parts of the trail. Also a 13.6-mile long canoe trail with a primitive campsite.

Season: December through March.

Camping: The park has 111 sites with facilities and another 19 in a wooded area for tent camping. Trail campers must register first at the ranger station.

Information: Collier-Seminole State Park, 20200 Tamiami Trail, Naples, FL 33961; (813) 394-3397.

A spider web in early morning sun.

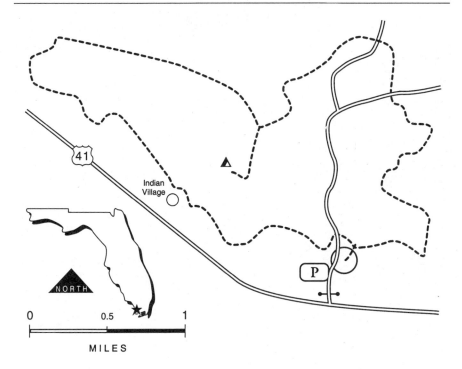

HIKE 116 COLLIER-SEMINOLE

Finding the trailhead: Off U.S. Highway 41, a quarter-mile beyond the intersection with State Road 92. Blazed in white, the trail begins on the north side of U.S. 41 on a park service road.

The hike: Starting out, look for the blue-blazed access trail close to the parking area. Going clockwise, you'll find a blue-blazed trail to a campsite in a tropical hammock about 2.5 miles into the hike. An Indian village is located close to the trail at about mile five, but do not approach it. The trail passes through primarily tropical hammock but some sections to the west are often wet.

If you use the trail campsite, you'll encounter an animal problem found almost nowhere else in Florida: bears. Black bears do frequent the park, so hang your food above ground so they can't reach it (or be inclined to crawl in your tent with it and you). Florida panther and bald eagles have also been sighted in Collier-Seminole Park.

So have an incredible number of vicious mosquitoes; repellent is essential.

An air plant growing in the Corkscrew Swamp Sanctuary

CORKSCREW SWAMP SANCTUARY

The 11,000-acre Corkscrew Swamp, owned and operated by the National Audubon Society, protects the world's largest remaining sub-tropical old-growth bald cypress forest. This northern tip of the Big Cypress Swamp contains towering bald cypress more than 130 feet high and as much as 700 years old; these are the oldest trees in eastern North America.

The dry winter period is best for wildlife viewing, when wading birds and other animals are forced to concentrate at the feeding pools near the boardwalk.

The Audubon Society began protecting the swamp's great egrets and wood storks from plumage hunters back in 1912. But it wasn't until 1954 that Society members began purchasing land to create the preserve.

Their actions were timely. Although this was a very isolated region back then, development encircles Corkscrew Swamp today. Yet it is still, as someone once said, "a million years from Miami." Or Orlando, or any other urban area. This is the genuine Florida that existed for thousands of years before man invented plastic pink flamingoes and plaster brown pelicans.

General Description: A two-mile boardwalk through a world-renowned old-growth forest.

General Location: Northeast of Naples.

Maps: None needed.

Difficulty: Easy and barrier free.

Special Attractions: Excellent wildlife viewing: birds, alligators, deer, bobcats, and wood storks.

Season: January to May, the normal dry season. Open 7 a.m. Dec. 1—May 1 and 8 a.m. the rest of the year.

Camping: Not available.

Information: Corkscrew Swamp Sanctuary, National Audubon Society, Route 6, Box 1875-A, Naples, FL 33964; (813) 657-3771. Trail walks are not allowed after 5 p.m. Admission fee charged.

HIKE 117 CORKSCREW SWAMP BOARDWALK

Finding the trailhead: Take Exit 17 from Interstate-75 and go east on State Road 846 for about sixteen miles. A sign leading to the swamp is on the left.

The hike: The entire two-mile boardwalk is barrier free. It leads through a tremendous variety of landscapes, and you're welcome at any time to stop for extended periods to photograph, relax, or just sit and contemplate.

The area here was roadless until the 1950s, and Indians, cattlemen, and hunters all had to use canoes, horses, or swamp buggies to travel this extremely wet area. Any high elevation of pines and cabbage palms were

You'll also pass through sections of wet prairie land that is not wet enough for cypress or dry enough for pines. Grasses and sedges are the dominant vegetation, but in spring and summer the wet prairie is a showcase of wildflowers.

The swamp water is not stagnant but constantly flowing slowly toward the Gulf of Mexico. During dry periods you may see pools that are scummy due to drought, but they will be flushed and refilled with clean water once the rainy season begins.

Look for the mosquito fish that are so numerous in the swamp water—and thank heaven for them! Mosquito fish feed primarily on mosquito larvae, and that helps keep the mosquito population bearable along the trail.

Ferns are a common and colorful sight throughout the swamp. The swamp fern, which grows to considerable size in the shade, is the most abundant.

Bald cypress receive their name from their pattern of wintertime leaf-shedding that makes them look lifeless. Although bald cypress often looks a dingy gray in the bright sunlight, its dark wood is highly valued, which accounts for why virtually all the large cypress stands throughout the country have been cut. The first sections of this boardwalk were made of cypress until it became too scarce. "Lighterwood" pine—highly impregnated with resin and almost rot-proof—was used thereafter.

Almost 200 bird species have been recorded in Corkscrew Swamp. You'll probably encounter the largest of Florida's common woodpeckers—the pileated—with its red crest and black and white pattern. The size of a crow, the pileated woodpecker feeds on beetles and carpenter ants that live inside dead cypress. The bird's loud calls and drumming noises are sounds heard frequently throughout the walk.

SOUTH FLORIDA CITY WALKS

FORT LAUDERDALE

Fort Lauderdale's 165 miles of navigable waterways have earned it the title "Venice of America." It has ten times the number of canals as Italy's Venice, so a boat is as important as a car to the Lauderdale lifestyle. There are more than 40,000 registered boaters, one of the heaviest concentrations in the United States.

The huge canal system with its system of bridges and causeways partly resulted from the creation of numerous man-made islands for residential acreage in the 1920s.

The city is named after Major William Lauderdale, who built a stockade here during the Second Seminole Indian War in 1837.

It's not necessary to have a boat to sight-see on Fort Lauderdale's waterways. Paddlewheel boats provide a closeup view of some of the finest canal homes, many with lawns so carefully manicured that residents actually practice golf putts on them. A water taxi also makes frequent rounds to the commercial areas. Seven miles of public beach are famous for hosting the annual college spring break, but in the 1980s the celebrants were urged to go elsewhere to leave the city in peace.

Because of the traditional emphasis on Fort Lauderdale's beaches, it may come as a surprise to discover the city has an interesting walking tour. Most of the walk is beside the New River, which is almost as good as being at the beach.

General Description: A 2.5-mile walking tour through the city's downtown shopping and historic districts.

General Location: Downtown Fort Lauderdale, a few blocks west of the famous beach.

Maps: None needed.

Difficulty: Easy.

Special Attractions: A great variety of city sights: shops, museums, historic homes, and waterways.

Season: Anytime.

Camping: Check with the Convention & Visitors Bureau.

Information: Greater Fort Lauderdale Convention & Visitors Bureau, 200 East Las Olas Boulevard, Fort Lauderdale, FL 33301; (305) 765-4466 or (800) 22-SUNNY.

Riverwalk at Fort Lauderdale.

HIKE 118 FORT LAUDERDALE WALKING TOUR

Directions: From Interstate-95, take the Las Olas Boulevard exit and park to the north of Las Olas Shops, east of S.E. Ninth Avenue.

The walk: This three-hour walking tour starts at the Las Olas Boulevard Shopping District. A ten-block area filled with boutiques, restaurants, and galleries, it could test your resolve to window shop only.

From Las Olas go west to S.E Sixth Avenue, then south to the New River. The legend of New River is a bizarre and doubtful one since South Florida is not earthquake prone. But, supposedly, hundreds of years ago a powerful storm battered the area. The Indians fled to the Everglades to sit it out. When they returned to their homes, they found a river where one had never been before. Everyone began shouting "Himmarshee—a new river!"

What is definitely new here is Riverwalk, a brick walkway that follows the waterway and guides most of the walking tour. Notice the names of people on hundreds of bricks; these are local residents who purchased their own brick to help fund the Riverwalk project.

The first riverside stop is the city's oldest remaining structure, the Stranahan House, built in 1902. It was saved from decay by the local historical society and today is a popular social center and museum.

Turn back to Las Olas and go west (left) to S.E. Fifth Avenue, then south (left) to the New River. This block spans the New River Tunnel—the only tunnel anywhere in the state of Florida.

You're now at Riverwalk and the Museum of Art, which houses a large collection of American Indian, Pre-Columbian, West African, and Oceanic paintings and sculptures. The museums special CoBRA Collection (Copenhagen, Brussels, and Amsterdam) is one of the world's largest.

Continuing along Riverwalk, stroll pass the Broward County Library to reach Stranahan Park, named for the settler who built the Stranahan House. Now go south on Andrews Avenue to S.W. Second Street, which leads into Himmarshee Village, Fort Lauderdale's original downtown area. Most of the homes here date from the early 1900s.

The Fort Lauderdale Historical Museum at 219 S.W. Second Avenue contains photos, furniture, and clothing related to the city's history. Adjacent are the historic Philomen Bryan Homes, King-Cromartie House, The New River Inn, and the old schoolhouse.

The King-Cromartie house is of special note. It was built in 1907 by Edwin King, the contractor who popularized the use of concrete blocks in Florida construction. His home also had the city's first indoor plumbing.

The grounds of the Performing Arts Center are a popular weekend gathering place for festivals and concerts. The nearby Museum of Discovery, opened in 1992, features an IMAX theater with an eighty-by-sixty-foot screen.

From this point, retrace your steps.

FORT LAUDERDALE WALKING TOUR

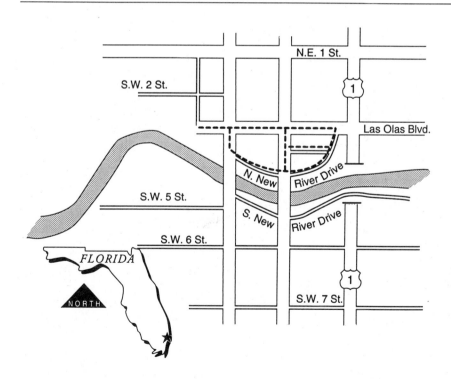

MIAMI BEACH

Before the existence of Orlando's mouse whose roar was heard round the world, Miami Beach was Florida's best-known symbol. Collins Avenue and its legendary resorts were a frequent winter homes for northern vacationers and international celebrities.

Miami Beach went into eclipse in the 1970s, but it is now returning with renewed energy. Perhaps the best example of that is the dramatic age shift of its 92,000 residents. The average age is now 44.5 years, down from 67 in 1980. As the country grows older, Miami Beach gets younger.

General Description: Collection of Art Deco-style buildings on the National Register of Historic Places.

General Location: South end of Miami Beach.

Maps: From the Art Deco Welcome Center at 1244 Ocean Drive.

Difficulty: Easy; flat terrain.

Special Attractions: More than 800 buildings in the Art Deco, Streamline Moderne, and Spanish Mediterranean Revival styles.

Season: Anytime; walking tours are offered Saturday mornings.

Information: Visitor Services Department, Greater Miami Convention & Visitors Bureau, 701 Brickell Avenue, Suite 2700, Miami, FL 33131; (800) 283-2707 or (305) 539-3063.

HIKE 119 MIAMI BEACH ART DECO DISTRICT

Directions: Take the MacArthur Causeway from downtown Miami to South Beach. The Art Deco district is located just north of South Pointe Park.

The walk: South Beach's one-square mile area of cotton-candy colored buildings were added to the National Register of Historic Places in 1979, thanks to the efforts of the Miami Design Preservation League. The Art Deco District is the youngest district on the National Register.

The district's 800 buildings cover eighty square blocks, from 6th to 23rd Streets, and from the Atlantic Ocean to Lennox Court. In addition to becoming a popular dining and entertainment area, this section is also a frequent location for fashion and film industry shoots.

No wonder, the way the delicate pastel colors are applied to the ornamental curves and crevices which are Deco design signatures. So are the iron stairways, and ziggurat rooflines which look like terraced pyramids, each higher story smaller than the lower ones. The style actually originated thousands of years ago with the Assyrians and Babylonians.

Ocean Drive, which hugs the water before turning onto Collins Avenue, contains many of the premiere Art Deco hotels, most lined with sidewalk cafes.

Your first stop should be the Art Deco Welcome Center in the Leslie Hotel, 1244 Ocean Drive. Operated by the Miami Design Preservation League, it provides excellent introductory material to the district. Walking tours depart the center every Saturday morning at 10:30; bike tours depart at 10:30 Sunday mornings. Call for reservations at (305) 672-2014. The center is open from 11 a.m. to 6 p.m. daily.

FLORIDA KEYS

The forty-two islands that make up the Florida Keys curve 150 miles out into the Gulf of Mexico, arranged like carefully placed stepping stones dotting the water. The term "Keys" comes from the Spanish word *cayos*, meaning "little islands."

Originally a haven for pirates, the Keys became the wrecking ground for Spanish treasure ships, and home to British loyalists after the American Revolution.

Today, they are America's version of the Caribbean, and this is more than just exaggerated advertising. The plants of the Keys owe their origins to the Caribbean, their seeds carried to the Keys by wind or waves.

The road connecting the island chain is known as both the Overseas Highway and U.S. 1. A completely toll-free road with bridges as short as forty feet and as long as seven miles, it moves through lowlands surrounded on all sides by sea and sky. The route is lined with mile markers all the way, measuring the distance to Mile Marker 1 in Key West. Mile marker numbers are the landmarks everyone in the Keys uses for giving directions.

Throughout the Keys you'll find some of America's finest seascapes: the blue waters of the Atlantic to the east and south, the green seas of the Gulf of Mexico on the north and west. Because of all the emphasis on water sports, hiking is not normally associated with the Florida Keys. However, the state has provided a handful of unspoiled oases that provide a close-up look at this unusual landscape.

One of the biggest surprises—and disappointments—for first time Keys visitors is the lack of beaches. Unlike the Panhandle with its beach walks that go for miles, sand beaches in the Keys are a rarity. Those that do exist are either protected as state parks or tend to be man-made. Instead of soft sand, hard coral rock forms the majority of the shoreline.

Where there is sand, it's often swathed in seaweed.

Accumulated seaweed helps prevent the erosion of the existing sand, and the tangled mats filter out and trap sand stirred up by wave action, adding sand to the beach. And finally, it provides fertilizer for plants that colonize and stabilize the shoreline.

The Upper Keys extend from Key Largo to Lower Matecumbe. After Key West, Key Largo is probably the most famous destination in the Keys, thanks in part to the film "Key Largo" in which Humphrey Bogart and Lauren Bacall survived both Edward G. Robinson and a hurricane.

The tourist information bureau for the Upper Keys is on the right in a small shopping center just as you enter Key Largo.

JOHN PENNEKAMP CORAL REEF STATE PARK

Twenty-one nautical miles long and eighteen nautical miles wide, Pennekamp is the most popular place for snorkeling and scuba diving in the entire United States. Most of the park is not on land, but offshore. Pennekamp is a permanent haven for 650 species of colorful reef fish (such as neon-colored queen angels, grunts, snapper and grouper), and more than twenty-five kinds of coral.

General Description: Two short hikes of less than a mile each: one along a nature trail, the other through a mangrove forest.

General Location: Key Largo in the Upper Keys.

Maps: None needed.

Difficulty: Easy. Some facilities are wheelchair accessible.

Special Attractions: Exhibits of the offshore marine life for which this park, the first underwater state park in the nation, is world-famous.

Season: Anytime. Summer weather is more consistent for snorkeling or scuba diving offshore.

Camping: Forty-seven campsites.

Information: John Pennekamp Coral Reef State Park, P.O. Box 487, Key Largo, FL 33037; (305) 451-1202.

HIKE 120 PENNEKAMP NATURE TRAILS

Finding the trailhead: Look for the big brown and white Pennekamp Park sign that looms over the roadway almost as soon as you arrive in Key Largo; you can't miss it.

The hikes: Frankly, few people visit Pennekamp to hike, but two trails of several hundred yards each are available. One is a trail through a mangrove forest, the other a self-guiding nature trail.The mangrove zone here is dominated by the red mangrove.

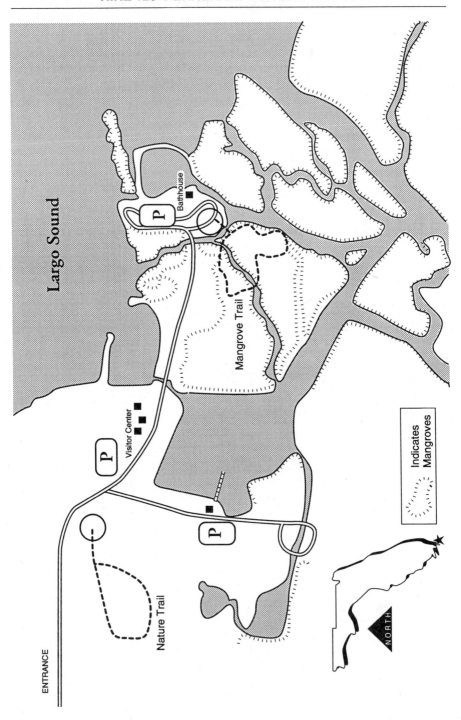

Largo Sound

Bathhouse

Mangrove Trail

Visitor Center

Nature Trail

ENTRANCE

Indicates
Mangroves

NORTH

LIGNUMVITAE KEY STATE BOTANICAL SITE

At 16.5 feet above sea level, Lignumvitae Key enjoys one of the highest elevations in the Keys. It contains one of the last virgin tropical hammocks of typical West Indian trees, including the endangered lignumvitae, which can live a thousand years. Lignumvitae is an incredibly durable wood said to outlast steel or bronze, thanks to its rich resins.

Some very fanciful myths surround the tree. In the Fifteenth Century it was cataloged as a tree found in the Garden of Eden and said to be the wood used to make the Holy Grail (though other sources say the grail was of metal). In the Bahamas, lignumvitae is still known as holywood and is said to cure impotence.

General Description: A 280-acre offshore key in the Gulf of Mexico boasting a virgin tropical forest not found anywhere else in the Keys.

General Location: A mile offshore, northwest of Upper Matecumbe Key.

Maps: None needed.

Difficulty: Easy; however, most facilities are not barrier free.

Season: Anytime. The trees bloom the first two weeks of April.

Camping: At Long Key State Park (see below).

Information: Lignumvitae Key State Botanical Site, P.O. Box 1052, Islamorada, FL 30336; (305) 664-4815.

HIKE 121 LIGNUMVITAE KEY

Finding the trailhead: Tour boats leave the landing at the southern tip of Upper Matecumbe. Boats operate Thursday through Monday at specified times between 8:30 a.m. and 2:30 p.m. Check ahead for the specific seasonal schedule and fee. If the tour boat is not running, rentals are available at Robbie's Marina at Mile Marker 77.5.

The hike: The tour boat docks at the Matheson House, belonging to the family who owned the island between 1919 and 1953. The limestone house, windmill, and cistern still stand, surrounded by such West Indian trees as mastic, sapodilla, and banyan.

The thick forest hammock contains an estimated 133 different tree species: gumbo-limbo, poisonwood, and strangler fig, all true natives of the Caribbean. It's believed they arrived here as seeds from other tropical islands, carried by waves, wind, or in the digestive tracts of migratory birds. The seeds sprouted and began the endless cycle of birth, death, and decay that transformed this once-barren coral island to a miniature jungle.

Many islands of the Upper Keys once contained similar growth, but unfortunately it was deliberately destroyed for one of the most bizarre reasons imaginable: to increase the value of the snails collected from the different hammocks.

The hardwood hammocks housed tree snails whose colorful shells were once highly prized by collectors around the world. Because the snails from different hammocks had different color patterns on their shells, collectors would take a sampling from a particular location, then set fire to the hammock to increase the rarity/price of that snail variety. The tree snails of Lignumvitae carry bands of red and green on their cream-colored shells.

HIKE 122 INDIAN KEY

If you want to do more island-hopping by boat, it's also possible to visit Indian Key Historic Site, which sits a short distance from Upper Matecumbe on the Atlantic side. Indian Key is a considerably smaller island that began as a wrecking station, then became the Dade County Seat in 1836.

Ruins of an old town are still evident. The vegetation here is markedly different from Lignumvitae Key, since agave and other desert-dwelling plants were introduced on Indian Key in the 1800s and allowed to replace many of the native plants. You'll find a self-guided tour to lead you around the island; formal tours are not provided at Indian Key.

LONG KEY STATE RECREATION AREA

The Spanish called Long Key *Cayo Vivora*, meaning "Rattlesnake Key." Fortunately, this description applied more to the shape of the island—a rattlesnake with its jaws open—than the resident fauna.

Camping platforms at Long Key State Recreation Area.

Long Key was home to one of the greatest fishing camps of all time, the Long Key Fishing Club founded by railroad builder Henry Flagler. Perhaps the best-known angler was dentist-turned-western-novelist Zane Grey, who visited here frequently to stalk and battle bonefish.

General Description: Two short trails of forty and fifteen minutes through some of the most beautiful natural scenery in the Keys.

General Location: Near the town of Layton, just south of the Matecumbe Keys.

Maps: None needed.

Difficulty: Easy.

Special Attractions: The most pleasant oceanside camping in the Keys.

Season: Fall through early spring.

Camping: Sixty campsites. This is one of the most popular camping spots in the Keys. Advance reservations are essential.

HIKES 123, 124 GOLDEN ORB AND LAYTON TRAILS

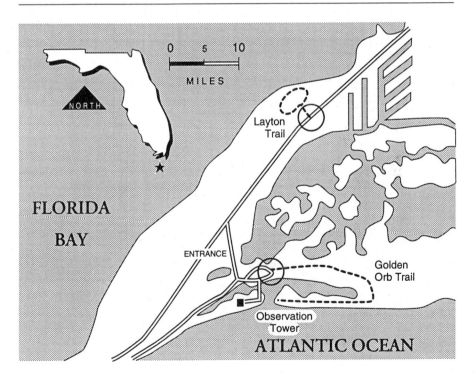

Information: Long Key State Recreation Area, P.O. Box 776, Long Key, FL 33001; (305) 664-4815. This is also where you make arrangements for the boat tour to Lignumvitae Key.

HIKE 123 GOLDEN ORB TRAIL

Finding the trailhead: Follow U.S. Highway 1 south to Mile Marker 67.5. The park entrance is on the left. Take the turnoff on the left to the Golden Orb Trail/Boardwalk. If you arrive at the water without making the turn, you've gone too far.

The hike: Long Key is a narrow ribbon of park on 965 acres. Long Key could also be called Narrow Key: in some places the oceanfront boundary is only a hundred yards from U.S. 1 and traffic is clearly visible from the beach.

The Golden Orb Trail, longer of the park's two nature walks, takes about forty minutes to complete. It is accessed by a boardwalk that penetrates a dense mangrove forest. An observation platform about midway offers an excellent overview of the region, though you'll probably see mostly mangrove tops and a few birds in flight.

Follow the boardwalk to the end and you will arrive at a section where you can camp as the Seminoles did. On both sides of the boardwalk, quite close to one another, are a handful of thatch-covered platforms with open sides. These are essentially the Seminole Indians' "chickees."

The only way to sleep comfortably on these wooden platforms is with a thick air mattress. If the wind dies, expect mosquitoes to swarm out of the mangroves and attempt to transfuse all your blood—into themselves. A far better choice for camping here would be the regular sandy campsites shaded by a canopy of Australian pines that are guaranteed to lull you to sleep as they rustle in the breeze.

Retrace your steps on the boardwalk a few yards and The Golden Orb trailhead is on the ground to the right. The trail is named for the large, golden orb weaver spider commonly seen on this walk. The path leads through different types of Keys' plant communities. After crossing a mangrove creek, it follows a sandy berm above the narrow beach. From this vantage, it's easy to see the transition from salt-tolerant plants on the low ground to the tropical hammock on the higher ground.

HIKE 124 LAYTON TRAIL

Finding the trail: The Layton Trail is located off the main highway on the Gulf side, south of the park entrance.

Where the Golden Orb Trail skirts the Atlantic side, the Layton Trail meets the huge expanse of Florida Bay which extends from the Keys to the Everglades. More birds are typically seen on the Gulf side, particularly flocks of pelicans. This walk takes about fifteen minutes.

SPECIAL NOTE—THE BAT TOWER: Leaving Long Key and continuing south to Key West, look for the tiny sign pointing to the famed bat tower. It's on the right, just past Sugarloaf Lodge on Sugarloaf Key near Mile Marker 17. The bat tower was one of the most ingenious failures in Keys' history. In 1929, an aspiring land developer who wanted to build a resort and casino here found his plans hampered by the huge mosquito population. He learned he might able to reduce the mosquito population if he could attract bats who would dine on the ferocious insects. He built an elaborate shingled tower about thirty-five feet tall for the bats to roost in and acquired an exclusive bat bait as an attractant. But the bats never came—not one, ever. All the developer's plans folded but the virginal bat tower still stands, a proud reminder of the days when Keys' life was a little more zany.

KEY WEST

Key West is a unique combination of Southern, Bahamian, Cuban, and Yankee influences that are visible in the architecture, savored in the cuisine, and felt in the relaxed, individualistic atmosphere. Traditionally, fishermen, artists, and writers were the ones most drawn to this tranquil slip of sand and sea.

Key West.

These days, Key West receives about one million tourists a year, who come to experience the once-rugged, free-wheeling Key West lifestyle.

True Key Westers may be a dying breed, but they have left monuments and memories everywhere. Probably the most famous resident was writer Ernest Hemingway, who lived here during his most productive period, writing *To Have and Have Not*, *For Whom the Bell Tolls*, among other novels, and one of his greatest short stories, "The Snows of Kilimanjaro." His Spanish Colonial-style house is Key West's most popular attraction, with many original furnishings and memorabilia on display.

Other notables attracted to Key West were Harry Truman (who established a Little White House here); John James Audubon, who painted Keys' birds in 1832; Tennessee Williams; Robert Frost; and John Dos Passos.

The homes and haunts of these immortals are mixed with such popular tourist attractions as a marine aquarium, a lighthouse museum with a Japanese submarine captured at Pearl Harbor; Mel Fisher's Treasure Museum, featuring gold, emeralds, and other priceless riches from the wreck of the *Atocha,* the richest Spanish galleon ever found; and innumerable clothing stores.

Key West residents often proudly refer to themselves as "conchs," the nickname originally given loyalists who fled to the Bahamas during the Revolutionary War. Many loyalists later ended up in Key West, proudly continuing to call themselves conchs (pronounced konks). Indeed, the conch was such a popular and cherished symbol that when the British moved the Spanish out of Key West, they marked the victory with a conch shell mounted at the end of a flagstaff. The conch name is from the pink, hard-shelled marine animals you see sold in huge piles in front of many stores; conch meat is served in delicious fritters, salads, and chowders.

The entire Keys are known as the Conch Republic, but what has happened to the conch itself is indicative of just how much these islands have been developed. The conch animals have been so over-fished that the state now bans their harvest by fishermen and divers, in an attempt to resurrect the meager mollusk population.

General Description: A walk through the southernmost city of the United States, an area long known for colorful characters and sunsets.

General Location: Take the Overseas Highway across 43 different bridges, including the famous 7-Mile Bridge. The distance is carefully marked the entire route. Mile Marker 1 is in Key West.

Maps: None needed.

Difficulty: Easy. Tram and trolley city tours are also available.

Special Attractions: Homes of many famous people including Ernest Hemingway; also the chance to engage in the nightly street show known as "sunset."

Season: Afternoon showers are frequent in summer when the heat/humidity can also be overwhelming.

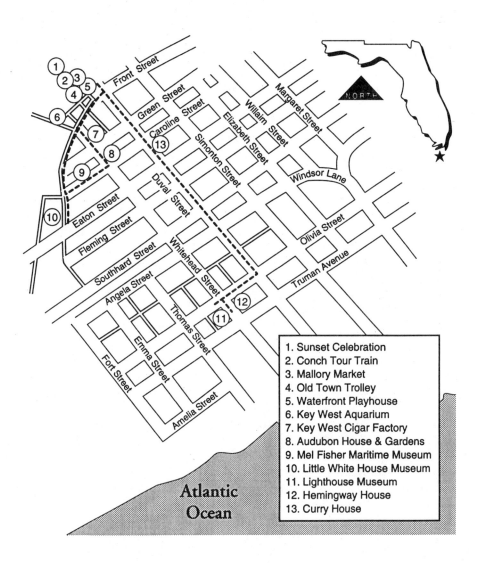

1. Sunset Celebration
2. Conch Tour Train
3. Mallory Market
4. Old Town Trolley
5. Waterfront Playhouse
6. Key West Aquarium
7. Key West Cigar Factory
8. Audubon House & Gardens
9. Mel Fisher Maritime Museum
10. Little White House Museum
11. Lighthouse Museum
12. Hemingway House
13. Curry House

Camping: For RVs only in the city itself.

Information: Call toll free, (800) LAST KEY.

HIKE 125 KEY WEST CITY WALK

Directions:

The walk: This is a long walk of three to four hours. It is possible to climb aboard the Conch Train at Mallory Square for a 1-1/2 hour narrated tour of the city. However, the Conch Train usually zips past all the city's attractions; to stop and explore, you really need to hoof it.

The following descriptions highlight only several of the major points around Key West. It would take another entire guidebook (you'll find several) to do the city justice. Expect to pass by plenty of interesting spots not mentioned here: that's what discovery is all about.

Start your walk from the same place you want to be at the end of the day, Mallory Dock, scene of Key West's most spectacular display: sunset. Sunset is an elaborate ritual that includes jugglers, amateur magicians, musicians, and politicians, all of whom turn out to entertain you during the daylight's final hour. But it's the spectacular sunsets everyone really comes to see, and they often draw a standing ovation from the crowd.

Taking Front Street, you'll pass the small local aquarium, Key West's oldest attraction. A Sea World this is not, but what the attraction lacks in size, it more than makes up for in allowing you to get close to the marine animals. Like most of the city's attractions, there is a fee.

The Truman Annex is the location of The Little White House, a wooden building from the 1890s. Actually the Naval Commandant's Quarters, it gained its popular name after Harry Truman began using it in 1946 as a vacation retreat during his presidency. He stayed here almost a dozen times during his single term, demonstrating that this Midwesterner definitely appreciated all the sun, salt, and sand of the Keys.

After the Annex, you'll pass by the Mel Fisher Museum with its "Atocha" treasure. The admission price is steep and, considering how much treasure was salvaged, the museum does not have a great deal on display.

At the corner of Whitehead and Greene is the famous Audubon House, apparently never used by painter John James Audubon when he was in Key West briefly in 1832. In fact the house probably didn't even exist when Audubon visited. The house is connected with Audubon because Audubon may have used a twig from the tree in the front yard to paint his portrait of a white-crowned pigeon. There is almost nothing displayed inside the house directly connected with Audubon. Most tourists don't realize this until they've paid their admission.

From the Audubon House proceed to Caroline Street. This is the site of the Airways Building, used in the 1920s by Aero-Marine Airways, which flew people and mail to Cuba. This being a somewhat precarious adventure, each flight carried a passenger pigeon to be dispatched in case of trouble.

Aero-Marine went out of business in 1924, replaced by Pan American Airways, which the U.S. Post Office says was the first true international carrier.

At 511 Caroline Street is the Milton Curry Mansion, a lavish cottage built in 1905 as a wedding present to himself and his bride. It is now open to the public.

From here move onto Duval Street, the city's main thoroughfare. Numerous shops and restaurants border this stretch, as does the Keys' most famous bar, Sloppy Joe's (corner of Duval and Greene). Sloppy Joe's is supposed to have been Hemingway's favorite watering hole, though Capt. Tony's Saloon (on Caroline Street) also claims the same distinction and is generally recognized as the appropriate spot.

Key West's Oldest House is at 322 Duval Street. You'll note it sits on three-foot tall pilings, a safeguard from the days when storm tides would flow down Duval Street. Now a public museum, the house also boasts the city's only remaining outside cookhouse. Cookhouses often were not attached to the main building in case of fire, not an uncommon problem with wood burning stoves.

If the Audubon House is a bit of an imposter, the Hemingway House on Whitehead Street is not. Novelist Ernest Hemingway purchased the house in 1931 and wrote *The Green Hills of Africa,* "The Snows of Kilimanjaro," and other classics while in residence. You may view but not enter the top room of the carriage house where Hemingway did his writing. He left Key West in 1940.

The Lighthouse Military Museum across from Hemingway's is an old lighthouse keeper's cottage. You can climb to the top of the seventy-eight-foot tall lighthouse tower (eighty-eight steps each way) whose light stopped operating in 1969.

Continue southeast along Whitehead Street to the Southernmost Point in the continental United States, marked by a brightly painted, heavy marker that looks like a nun buoy. This giant marker replaces a continually futile attempt to designate the spot with signs, which people kept stealing. However, sellers have set up tables loaded with conch shells and other souvenirs available for take-away, at a price.

On your return take South Street back to Duval Street to see the Southernmost House. You can't miss the pink and green structure built in the 1800s. It was a night club for a time. Once more a private home, it is not open to the public.

FORT JEFFERSON, DRY TORTUGAS

Key West is not the southernmost place you can walk in Florida. That honor belongs to Fort Jefferson in the remote Dry Tortugas, another seventy miles south. Fort Jefferson, called the Gibraltar of the Gulf and built in the mid-1800s, has walls eight feet thick and fifty feet high, with tiers designed for 450 guns. It is named after Thomas Jefferson who intended the fort to dominate the entrance to the Gulf of Mexico.

General Description: A walking tour of America's largest coastal fort.

General Location: The daily seaplane service from Key West will take you another seventy miles south to the fort. Planes leave in the morning, return late afternoon.

Maps: Obtain one at the fort.

Difficulty: Easy; some stair climbing is required.

Special Attractions: This was the prison of Dr. Samuel Mudd, who set the leg of John Wilkes Booth, accused assassin of President Abraham Lincoln.

Season: Cooler weather is best; afternoon rain showers can be a problem in summer.

Camping: Permitted overnight on the fort grounds.

Information: Call toll free (800) LAST KEY.

HIKE 126 FORT JEFFERSON

Finding the trailhead: The seaplane from Key West takes you to the fort entrance.

The walk: The largest of America's coastal citadels, Fort Jefferson never fired a shot. It wasn't built on very firm foundation, either, as the builders discovered after laying sixteen million bricks on the sand of the tiny sixteen-acre key. The firm limestone base that was supposed to be at the surface turned out to be eighty feet down, so the fort began slowly sinking.

A prison after the Civil War, Fort Jefferson was the Alcatraz of its time, the place no one wanted to be sent. Guards supposedly disciplined prisoners by hanging them by their thumbs or having them carry around cannonballs all day.

The most famous inmate was Dr. Samuel Mudd, the Maryland physician who unwittingly set the broken leg of Lincoln's assassin, John Wilkes Booth. Mudd was sentenced to Fort Jefferson for life, but he was pardoned because of his diligent work during a devastating yellow fever epidemic that killed almost forty people. Mudd was freed in 1869.

There are no formal camping facilities on the island. You can pitch a tent outside the fort walls, but plan precisely, because you must bring all your own supplies, especially water and bug spray. In summer, camping here may be a hellish experience.

RAILS-TO-TRAILS

Florida's rails-to-trails program is perhaps the fastest growing aspect of hiking in the state. Similar to programs around the country, the rails-to-trails program involves state acquisition of abandoned railway beds and converting them into trails that can be used by walkers, cyclists, and horseback riders.

Purists might consider these corridors mini-highways through the wilderness, but it is possible to spot wildlife and undergo something of a wilderness experience on two of the trails in particular, the Gainesville-Hawthorne and the Van Fleet trails.

As of mid-1993, Florida had 150 miles of rails-to-trails already open to the public. The goal is to create a backbone of trails in Central Florida with connectors that will criss-cross the entire state. Although only five trails currently exist, rights are being acquired to create more than twenty links in the system.

A portion of the Tallahassee-St. Marks Historic Railroad State Trail.

For the latest information, contact the Florida Rails-to-Trails chapter in Tallahassee at (904) 942-2379; or Collier Clark, Manager, Trails and Advisory Services Section, Department of Natural Resources in Tallahassee, (904) 488-7896.

Generally, all trails are open daily from 8 a.m. to sunset.

HIKE 127 TALLAHASSEE-ST. MARKS HISTORIC RAILROAD STATE TRAIL

Location: Between Tallahassee and the town of St. Marks.

Length: 15.8 miles.

Access: The town of St. Marks.

Opened in 1988 as Florida's first rails-to-trails site, the eight-foot wide path has an asphalt surface and an equestrian trail in the swale on the west side. It is more used by cyclists than hikers.

It runs from just south of Tallahassee to the costal town of St. Marks. Trail walkers have the opportunity to visit such close-by sites as Fort San Marcos de Apalache State Historic Site, Natural Bridge Battlefield State Historic Site,

HIKE 128 GAINESVILLE-HAWTHORNE RAIL TRAIL

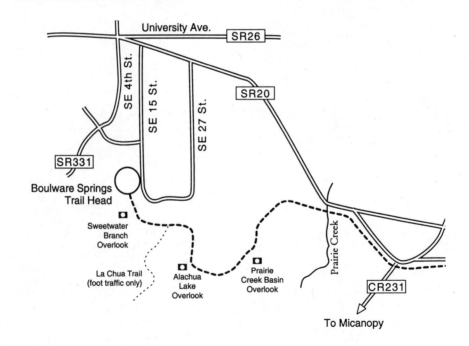

Wakulla Springs State Park, St. Marks National Wildlife Refuge, and the Munson Hills Fat Tire Bicycle Trail in the Apalachicola National Forest.

This railway corridor of the old Tallahassee-St. Marks railroad was in use as recently as 1984. It was in service continually since 1837, making it the longest operated railroad in Florida. The railway was built to transport cotton to the port at St. Marks.

The southern terminus is easily accessible in the town of St. Marks near the St. Marks River and next to Posey's Restaurant, renowned for its seafood.

HIKE 128 GAINESVILLE-HAWTHORNE RAIL TRAIL

Location: Alachua County.

Length: 17.2 miles with another extension planned.

Access: The city of Gainesville at Boulware Springs Park Road.

This trail is covered with crushed limestone and ballast and is available for hiking, fat tire bicycling, and horseback riding. It begins in the southeast side of Gainesville and continues east to County Road 24 one mile west of

---

HIKE 128 GAINESVILLE-HAWTHORNE RAIL TRAIL

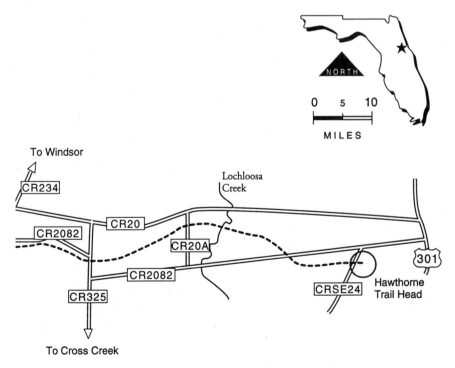

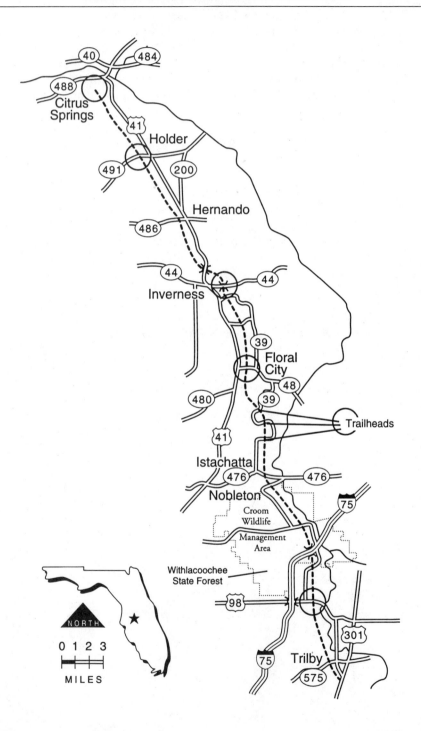

the town of Hawthorne. Private property borders the route in many areas, so stay on the trail.

Running parallel to State Road 20 much of the way, this trail passes through areas of outstanding natural importance including Paynes Prairie State Preserve, Prairie Creek, and the Lochloosa Wildlife Management Area. Extensions are planned into downtown Gainesville and Hawthorne.

This corridor is part of the route that once ran from the town of Ferdandina northeast of Jacksonville to the town of Cedar Key on the Gulf Coast. Built in the 1850s, this land route eliminated the often dangerous passage for ships through the Keys.

HIKE 129 WITHLACOOCHEE STATE TRAIL

Location: Citrus, Pasco, and Hernando Counties between Tampa and Lakeland.

Length: 47 miles.

Access: State Road 41 and U.S. Highway 301 intersect the trailheads. Access is also available at intermediate points at County Road 491, County Road 486, State Road 44, County Road 48, County Road 39, County Road 476, State Road 50, and County Road 575.

The longest continuous rails-to-trails pathway, this trail links together Fort Cooper State Park, the Croom and Citrus units of the Withlacoochee State Forest, Croom Wildlife Management Area, Withlacoochee River State Canoe Trail, the Florida Trail, and several towns. It parallels U.S. Highway 41 for seventeen miles, and state, county, and forest roads for 8.5 miles.

Gopher tortoise nesting areas are along the pathway, and this is also habitat for the hairstreak butterfly, a species of concern.

This trail eventually will connect with trail systems in the Ocala National Forest.

HIKE 130 VAN FLEET STATE TRAIL

Location: Sumter, Lake and Polk Counties.

Length: 27.5 miles.

Access: The trailheads are accessible from State Road 50 and Interstate-4 via State Road 33 or County Road 559.

For two-thirds of its length, this trail passes through the Green Swamp, providing a semi-wilderness experience. In most places, natural vegetation buffers the trail from any residential development.

The Van Fleet trail links Green Swamp with the Richloam Unit of the Withlacoochee State Forest.

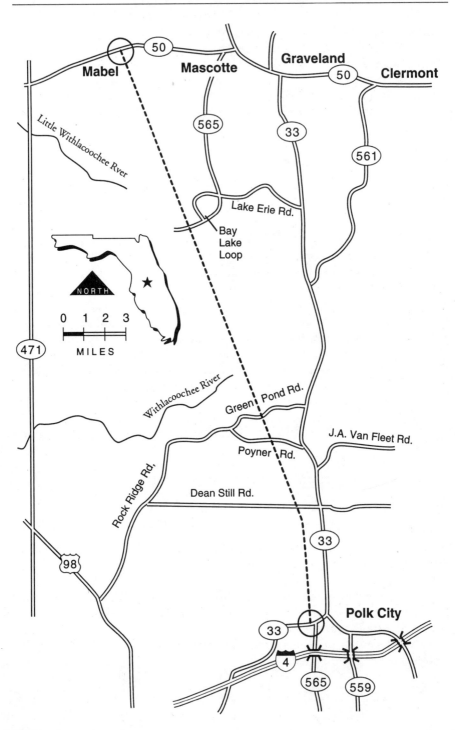

HIKE 131 PINELLAS TRAIL

Location: Pinellas County between St. Petersburg and Tarpon Springs.

Length: 35 miles.

Access: St. Petersburg or Tarpon Springs.

Called the longest and narrowest county park in Florida if not the nation, the Pinellas Trail is maintained by Pinellas County. Eventually the trail will extend for at least forty-seven miles, penetrating one of the more densely populated areas of the state.

HIKE 132 JACKSONVILLE-BALDWIN TRAIL

Location: Duval County.

Length: 14.8 miles.

Access: West side of the town of Baldwin at State Road 121.

After passing under U.S. Highway 301, the trail goes east through timber and agricultural areas to the east side of Jacksonville near Interstate-295. Much of the trail has a natural tree canopy and vegetative buffer.

THE HIKER'S CHECKLIST

To realize the importance of a good checklist is be on a wilderness trail about fifteen miles from the trailhead and discover that you have forgotten an important item. The thing you forgot may be only an inconvenience or it may be serious. A good checklist will help prevent this.

This is only a suggested list. Base your list on the nature of the hike and your own personal needs. Items will vary depending on whether you are camping near your vehicle or backpacking to more remote campsites and staying out one or more nights. Remember, if you are carrying it on your back select items judiciously. Weight is an important factor.

Check each item as you pack.

Clothing
___ dependable rain parka
___ windbreaker
___ thermal underwear
___ shorts
___ long pants
___ cap or hat
___ wool shirt or sweater
___ warm jacket
___ extra socks
___ underwear
___ lightweight shirts
___ T-shirts
___ gloves
___ belt

Footwear
___ comfortable hiking boots
___ lightweight camp shoes

Bedding
___ sleeping bag
___ foam pad or air mattress
___ pillow (deflating)
___ ground cloth (plastic or nylon)
___ dependable tent

Cooking
___ one-quart plastic water container
___ one-gallon collapsible water con
      tainer for camp use
___ backpack stove w/ extra fuel
___ funnel
___ aluminum foil
___ cooking pot
___ bowl or plate
___ spoon, fork, knife, spatula
___ matches in waterproof container

Food and Drink
___ cereal
___ bread and/or crackers
___ trail mix
___ margarine
___ powdered soups
___ salt/pepper
___ main course meals
___ snacks
___ coffee, tea
___ hot chocolate
___ powdered milk
___ drink mixes

Photography
___ camera and film
___ accessories
___ large zip-lock bag
___ camera bag

Miscellaneous
___ maps and compass
___ toilet paper
___ tooth brush
___ water filter or chemical purifier
___ first-aid kit
___ survival kit /including duct tape
___ pocketknife
___ insect repellent
___ flashlight, spare batteries and bulb
___ candles
___ small trowel or shovel
___ extra plastic bags to pack out trash
___ biodegradable soap
___ towel/washcloth
___ waterproof covering for pack
___ binoculars
___ watch
___ sewing kit
___ fishing gear and license

CLIMB IT
HIKE IT
FLOAT IT
BIKE IT

A FALCON GUIDE

Whatever you do outside, helps you find a better place to do it. Maps, photos, safety tips, and charts accompany detailed descriptions of state-by-state rock climbing sites, hiking trails, river routes, and mountain biking trails. Falcon also publishes information about many more outdoor activities and nature gift ideas.

For a free catalog of books, maps, recreational guidebooks, and nature gift ideas, please return this card with the following information.

Name _____

Address _____

City _____

State _____ Zip _____

☐ **YES!** I'd like to send a catalog to a friend.

Name _____

Address _____

City _____

State _____ Zip _____

Or call for a **FREE** catalog.

1-800-582-2665

FALCON®
P.O. BOX 1718
HELENA,
MONTANA
59624

FALCON™

BUSINESS REPLY MAIL
FIRST-CLASS MAIL PERMIT NO 80 HELENA MT

POSTAGE WILL BE PAID BY ADDRESSEE

FALCON PRESS PUBLISHING CO
PO BOX 1718
HELENA MT 59624-9948

ABOUT THE AUTHOR

M. Timothy O'Keefe

Tim O'Keefe, a past president of the Florida Outdoor Writers Association and a member of the Florida Trail Association, has lived in the Orlando area since 1968. For more than two decades, his articles and photographs have appeared in numerous publications, including eight National Geographic Society books, Time-Life Books, Travel & Leisure, Florida Sportsman, Sports Afield, Outside, Newsweek, New York Times, and Chicago Tribune.

Tim received a Ph.D. from the University of North Carolina at Chapel Hill and is a professor in the School of Communication at the University of Central Florida, where he established the journalism program.

His other books include: *Caribbean Afoot!, A Hiking & Walking Guide to 29 Islands; AAA Photo Journey to Central Florida; Manatees, Florida's Vanishing Mermaids; Fish and Dive the Caribbean* and *Fish and Dive Florida & The Keys* (both with Larry Larsen); *Diving to Adventure;* and *101 Uses for a Dead Cockroach* (with Michele Simos).

A member of the Outdoor Writers Association of America and the Society of American Travel Writers, Tim's work has won more than forty regional and national awards. He has published almost 4,000 photographs worldwide.

Out here—there's no one to ask directions

...except your **FALCON**GUIDE.

FALCONGUIDES is a series of recreation guidebooks designed to help you safely enjoy the great outdoors. Each title features up-to-date maps, photos, and detailed information on access, hazards, side trips, special attractions, and more. The 6 x 9" softcover format makes every book an ideal companion as you discover the scenic wonders around you.
    FALCONGUIDES...lead the way!

HIKING NOTES

HIKING NOTES